Philosophy and Love

Philosophy and Love

From Plato to Popular Culture

Linnell Secomb

Indiana University Press
Bloomington and Indianapolis

This book is a publication of

Indiana University Press
601 North Morton Street
Bloomington, Indiana 47404-3797 USA

http://iupress.indiana.edu

Telephone orders   800-842-6796
Fax orders   812-855-7931
Orders by e-mail   iuporder@indiana.edu

Originally published by Edinburgh University Press Ltd, 22 George Square, Edinburgh

Cataloging information is available from the Library of Congress.

ISBN 978-0-253-34979-8 (cl.); 978-0-253-21947-3 (pbk.)

1 2 3 4 5 12 11 10 09 08 07

Contents

Acknowledgements

Thanks first to the students in my course on 'Love and Friendship' at the University of Sydney in 2004, 2005 and 2006 whose enthusiasm and desire for more materials and references suggested the need for this book. I am also most grateful for the friendship, encouragement and intellectual community offered by Cathryn Vasseleu, Jodi Brooks, Gail Mason, Sara Knox, Katrina Schlunke, Nikki Sullivan, Fiona Probyn-Rapsey, Celia Roberts, Adrian MacKenzie, Catherine Driscoll, Anna Gibbs, Ruth Barcan, Cristyn Davies, Joanne Finkelstein, Leela Gandhi, Nicole Anderson, Wendy Brady, Penny Rossiter, Jane Hobson and Caroline Williams. Penelope Deutscher's generous support and wise counsel, especially with early chapters, was invaluable. Moira Gatens, Robyn Ferrell and Rosalyn Diprose all read and provided useful suggestions on an earlier version of the last chapter. Various other friends and colleagues have provided specific information or engaged in inspiring conversations: Melissa Hardie, Kate Lilley and Viki Dunn on Sappho; Kath Albury on websites and pop culture; Annie Noack, Kathy Sport, Annie Heath, Susan Brock, Kellie Greene, Brenda Bartlett, Chris King, and Sue Aujard on same-sex marriage, dating and romance.

My colleagues in the department of Gender and Cultural Studies at the University of Sydney facilitated this project in various ways and the Research Institute for Humanities and Social Sciences at the University of Sydney provided funding to support its completion, which is most gratefully acknowledged. Early drafts of various chapters have been reworked following the generous and astute responses offered at a number of conferences and seminars including: The Political Futures of Jacques Derrida Conference, Macquarie University, January 2005; Images of Community Workshop, Australian National University, April 2005; the Institute for Women's Studies departmental seminar, Lancaster University, January 2006. The final chapter is loosely based on a paper published as 'Amorous Politics: Between Derrida and Nancy' in *Social Semiotics*, 16:3, 2006. At Edinburgh University Press, my thanks to Jackie Jones and Carol Macdonald for their helpful guidance and encouragement.

Special thanks to my immediate and extended family for their various and endless love, support, acceptance and understanding. Finally, for 1,001 stories about friendship and love and for reading and dissecting every word, this book is dedicated to Diana Caine.

Grateful acknowledgement is made to the following sources for permission to reprint material:

If Not, Winter – Fragments of Sappho by Anne Carson, copyright © 2002 by Anne Carson. Used by permission of Alfred A. Knopf, a division of Random House, Inc; and also by permission of Little, Brown Book Group Limited.

Introduction

֍

A montage of disparate excerpts from commercial and independent films, Tracey Moffatt and Gary Hillberg's video collaboration, *Love*, tells the iconic story of love gone wrong. From its initial enraptured obsession, depicted through recurring scenes of passionate embrace and tender caress, love quickly degenerates into argument, accusation, hatred and finally into violence. Editing together similar scenes from diverse films, the video represents men berating their partners, shouting degrading and insulting abuse. The women then retaliate with ineffectual slaps, slamming doors, throwing objects, and pounding the chests of their impassive lovers before falling, broken, at their feet. In the following sequence of filmic pastiche this cycle of violence escalates causing, now, not just psychological pain but also physical injury as the men punch, throw, cut and beat the women. This violence can only conclude in death – the women set aside futile protestations, resorting to more effective means, using guns to slay their male companions.

The irony of the title now becomes evident. The video, which is intended for screening on a continuous loop – ends with an embracing couple and their final exchange. She asks 'is this the end' and he responds 'it's only the beginning' signalling the return to the first scenes of love as the video loops back to the start. The video depicts the cycle of interpersonal violence in which love is used to justify and explain the violence itself as well as the repentance and forgiveness that are all too often a precursor to the renewal of violence.

Yet, if this suggests an unremittingly bleak portrayal of love this belies the complexity of Moffatt and Hillberg's video. The video opens with a voice-over conversation as the black screen merges into the opening title and then the first embracing couple. He says: 'You take my breath away . . . When I'm close to you like this there's a sound in the air like the beating of wings. You know what it is? . . . My heart – beating like a schoolboy's.' She responds: 'Is it? I thought it was mine.' This filmic collage flashes from one film clip to another but each replicates the corny, clichéd, feel of this first scene. Nevertheless, these scenes of love also evoke the obsession, the enchantment, and the longing of passionate love. She says: 'You make me feel . . . oh I don't know . . . warm . . .' He finishes: 'Wanted, beautiful'. 'Yes,' she confirms. The video succeeds in depicting not only the violence and madness that love may precipitate but also the intoxication and rapture, the fascination and felicity that love inaugurates.

The *Love* video starts with an analogy between the beating heart and the sound of beating wings, evoking an image of the heart having wings that emerges first in antiquity. Sappho, the Greek poet for whom Sapphic love is named, describes how the sight of her beloved 'puts the heart in my chest on wings' (Sappho 2002: fragment 31) beginning the association between love and soaring flight. Plato, commonly associated with non-sexual Platonic love though he writes also of erotic experience, soon expands this image. He explains that seeing the beloved causes a 'shivering fit' and a 'high fever' (Plato 2002: S251a) that unfurls the wings of the soul creating a pulsating pleasure as the wings 'throb like pulsing veins' (Plato 2002: S251d). Plato points out that Eros is a winged god suggesting perhaps the origin of this recurring equation of love and the heart with wings and flight. The repetition of this metaphor from Sappho and Plato to the video on *Love* suggests that the stories of love are recalled, reiterated and remodelled, perpetuating and transforming our images of love.

Just as the *Love* video creates a pastiche of stories, Roland Barthes' *A Lover's Discourse* also compiles an ocean of stories of love. Contesting the repudiation of love as sentimental, and self-indulgent, Barthes brings together diverse philosophic, literary and psychoanalytic reflections on love. A collector of stories, Barthes also describes the transformation of experience into narrative. For Barthes, love is a story we invent and retrospectively impose onto our experience, transforming it into narrative:

> I believe (along with everyone else) that the amorous phenomenon is an 'episode' endowed with a beginning (love at first sight) and an end (suicide, abandonment, disaffection, withdrawal, monastery, travel, etc.). Yet the initial scene during which I was ravished is merely reconstituted: it is after the fact. I reconstruct a traumatic image which I experience in the present but which I conjugate (which I speak) in the past. (Barthes 1984: 193)

If for Barthes love is a retrospective fabulation, for Umberto Eco each expression of love is already a self-conscious quotation of earlier romances. While each new love feels like the first and only, original and authentic experience in postmodernity this ecstatic illusion is shadowed by an awareness of the repetition and banality of love. Eco explains:

> I think of the postmodern attitude as that of a man who loves a very culti-
> vated woman and knows that he cannot say to her, 'I love you madly,' because
> he knows that she knows (and that she knows that he knows) that these words
> have already been written by Barbara Cartland. Still, there is a solution. He
> says, 'As Barbara Cartland would put it, I love you madly' . . . both will
> accept the challenge of the past, of the already said, which cannot be elimin-
> ated: both will consciously and with pleasure play the game of irony . . . Both
> will have succeeded, once again, in speaking of love. (Eco 1995: 32–3)

This self-conscious, ironic quotation that expresses while duplicating
love stories also structures Moffatt and Hillberg's video. The video compiles and iterates endless scenes of love (and its destruction) indicating
the significance of romance narratives in forming our experiences and
perceptions of love. But love is not just a narrative because it mimics past
romances but also because, as Julia Kristeva argues, the experience of
love is allusive, defying direct description and relying on metaphorical
allusions – the beating heart as beating wings for example. All postmodern representation replicates, while also refiguring the past but, in addition, love is also turned into literature as we attempt to communication
the intoxication it generates: 'The language of love is impossible, inadequate, immediately allusive when one would like it to be most straightforward; it is a flight of metaphors – it is literature' (Kristeva 1987: 1).

Love stories are not just told through literature and other cultural productions but are also elaborated in philosophy (among other discourses).
In this book I continue the reiteration and reformulation of love stories
by bringing together philosophy, cultural analysis and gender theory supplementing the proliferation of tales of love. The stories here range from
the banal to the scandalous: from hackneyed boy-meets-girl narratives to
controversial accounts of same-sex marriage, from myths about bifur-
cated souls seeking their lost mates to modern tales of internet dating,
from horror stories of friendless monsters searching for love and reveng-
ing their failed quest to celebrations of the ethical and political potentialities of benevolent love. Love scripts, it will become evident, are
endlessly circulated and in that process reformulated as each performance, enactment and depiction of love supplements and disseminates
love's possibilities.

While love as story is one theme traced throughout this book, images
of troubled love also recur. The *Love* video already gestures to love's
paradoxes and dangers suggesting that the Hollywood fantasy of romantic love – the happy-ever-after embrace that fades out into the final credits
– disguises and perhaps also justifies the violence unleashed within
unequal gender relations. But inequality in the gender relation is not all

that unsettles love: controversies about same-sex desire, cross-cultural romance, and the fragility of love in the postmodern age also disturb halcyon visions of ideal love. These difficulties might suggest that love is not simply and only felicity but that it also contains a sting – love is also suffering. Love is, for Nietzsche, inherently paradoxical: it is longing and this longing involves both a search for fulfilment and also a painful lack. Paradoxically, it creates both suffering and intoxication (Nietzsche 2003; Düttmann 1993). The troubles and the paradoxes of love, then, are also elaborated throughout the following chapters revealing a complexity that is often disguised in love's idealization.

The paradoxes of love do not, however, simply suggest that it harbours violent and damaging potentialities but also hints at the obverse – that love also founds human sociality through the connection and recognition, the caring and giving, it offers. Recalling the stories of love reveals not just its passions and its difficulties but also its ethical and political potentialities. While Moffatt and Hillberg's *Love* video portrays only the potential violence and madness of love I will trace also the care and generosity and the passionate engagements facilitated by love that form the basis for political and ethical life. The third recurring theme that structures the love stories told here, then, is this: that ethics and politics are not simply founded on duty or on rational agreement but that human sociality requires the generosity and the sharing offered through love.

These three themes – love as narrative, love's troubles and paradoxes, and an ethics and politics of erotics – are elaborated through a conversation between philosophy, cultural analysis, and gender theory. Leaving aside biological stories about pheromones and psychoanalytic narratives of Oedipal identifications, I focus on cultural formations, gender constructions, and philosophical ruminations. Limiting the discussion (mostly) to the recent European philosophical accounts narrows the focus further. The long history of philosophic accounts of love, that is thereby overlooked, is already well documented elsewhere (Nussbaum 2001; Rougement 1983; Singer 1984; Solomon and Higgins 1991).

Bringing together philosophical, gender and cultural theory with portrayals of love in literature and film is not without its complications. Philosophy has often used the cultural example as a pedagogical tool illustrating its abstract conceptions. This strategy risks destroying the affects, resonances and sentiments communicated by the structure, style and technique of the cultural work. Utilising only the content or idea of the work, philosophic appropriations eliminate the sensations, the nuances and the ambiguities of the work. By focusing on the sense, philosophy overlooks the sensibility of the artwork or cultural object.

Cultural studies, resenting this anaemic appropriation and even more the imposition of philosophic theories onto cultural objects, has, at times, rejected philosophic formulations branding them as 'subservience to theory'. Yet this should not, I suggest, negate the possibility of engagement and conversation between these disciplines.

Throughout this book I entwine philosophic, gender and cultural theory texts with cultural texts (poetry, novels, films, TV series, websites and ceremonies and rituals) hoping that this interdisciplinary conversation about love augments and enriches the perceptions and interpretations of erotics and relationship. Creating an encounter between these various discourses, I hope to reveal rather then obliterate the passions and troubles, the turmoil and yearning, the rapture, intoxication and seduction of romantic experiences and representations. I attempt to create this encounter, not as combat and contestation, but as an impassioned exchange that allows philosophy, cultural analysis and gender theory to touch and affect, to reflect and respond to cultural works while also maintaining the differences and specificities of these various discourses and productions. I do not attempt either an amalgam of discourses nor a combat between antagonistic discourses but an exchange across the boundaries of these arts and disciplines. Instead of assimilation on the one hand and segregation on the other, I hope to create a hospitality between discourses that may blur the boundaries and transform identities but that nonetheless preserves the differences of each party.

Derrida speaks of 'an attempt to blur the borders between literature and philosophy . . . in the name of hospitality – that is what hospitality does, blur the borders – . . . which put[s] in question the limits of what one calls philosophy, science, literature' (Derrida 1999: 73). Following this lead, I attempt in this book to create a hospitable welcome between the cultural productions and the cultural analyses offered by philosophic, cultural and gender theories. This requires a strategy of close reading – of both the theoretical texts and the cultural objects. In order to overcome the 'subservience to theory' the cultural object needs to be able to speak in its own name – and not merely via the theoretical frame imposed upon it. Similarly, theoretical and philosophical accounts of love also require detailed analysis. My aim is to allow each to express, through their differing rhetorics and techniques, their varying representations and conceptions of love. Wishing to keep the diverse images of love alive – rather than dilute their seductive passions – I engage with the specificity of each text or object. I also create conversations between objects and theories so as to identify the parallels, divergences, and ambiguities in the varying reflections and depictions of love. Discussing a similar strategy Mieke Bal writes:

> Making sweeping statements about objects, or citing them as examples, renders them dumb . . . Even though, obviously, objects cannot speak, they can be treated with enough respect for their irreducible complexity and unyielding muteness – but not mystery – to allow them to check the thrust of an interpretation, and to divert and complicate it . . . Thus, the objects we analyse enrich both interpretation and theory. This is how theory can change from a rigid master discourse into a live cultural object in its own right. (Bal 2002: 45)

Adopting techniques of close reading and interdisciplinary hospitable welcome, I attempt in this book to create respectful engagements that enrich the interpretations of both cultural productions and theoretical reflections bringing each to life.

This book starts with Plato and Sappho, the philosopher and the poet, who each reflects on love and bequeaths enduring phenomenological accounts of love. While Sappho's erotic poetry appears at first opposed to the concept of non-erotic Platonic friendship and to philosophic love of beauty and the good that Socrates espouses, their formulations, I will suggest, display surprising similarities. Socrates' story locates the origin of philosophical contemplation in erotic desire and the final tale in the series that unfolds in Plato's *Symposium* returns to a particular embodied erotic love – that of Alcibiades for Socrates. Sappho's poetry contemplates love between women as well as love between the sexes; the Platonic stories more often reflect on love between men. The image of the beating heart as beating wings originates with Sappho and returns in Plato's *Phaedrus*, homoerotics is central in each case, and while Plato is often read as advocating a higher form of non-erotic love of the good this clearly originates in erotic intimacy.

In this first chapter the focus on love as narrative already becomes evident with Plato's *Symposium* structured as a series of stories of love exchanged between friends at a drinking party. Sappho's poetry, though fragmentary, also constructs mini-narratives of love through word pictures that evoke the longing and the exhilaration of erotic desire. This chapter attempts from the start to enact a hospitable blurring of boundaries between philosophic accounts of love and poetic images of love. Pointing to Plato's reference to Sappho, this chapter traces her influence on his work but also identifies the specificities of their particular formulations of love.

Leaping over the next two and a half millenia of philosophical and cultural stories of love, Chapter 2 brings together Mary Shelley's *Frankenstein* with Friedrich Nietzsche's fragmentary speculations on love and friendship. While there may seem little in common between Shelley and Nietzsche there are surprising resonances in their articulations of love. They each, though in differing forms, reveal the complexities and paradoxes inherent in love. In Shelley, the monstrosity of love is not, as we may expect, revealed only in the creature's revenge but more subtly in the anodyne depiction of familial relations. In Nietzsche, the paradox takes a different form – love though egoistic and possessive facilitates a yearning for more, not just for more love but also for a life beyond the restrictions of conventional sociality.

In Chapter 3 Simone de Beauvoir's reflections on love are read alongside the USA TV series *Desperate Housewives*. Nietzsche accuses women of becoming slaves and tyrants within love relations. Beauvoir elaborating this proposition, suggests that it is gender inequality that provokes these reactions. *Desperate Housewives* represents this subordination while also revealing the performative mimicry involved in the scripted re-enactments of love. If the philosophy of Beauvoir and the TV soap seem opposed genres, I deliberately bring them together to suggest that it is not only high theory that elucidates the love experience but that 'trash' culture also reveals much, and sometimes more, about the experience and the structures and mechanisms that enable it.

Emmanuel Levinas' ethics of love is outlined in Chapter 4 along with a reading of Marguerite Duras's film script *Hiroshima, mon amour*. Levinas distinguishes between the egoism of erotic pleasure and the self-less love of ethical responsibility, demarcating Eros from Agape in his account of ethics and politics. Nevertheless, love is central to these ethical and political relations modifying even the reasoned judgements of justice. For Levinas ethics is the relation to the Other and within this relation we are required to take responsibility for the Other, prioritising her needs over our own. Politics introduces other Others, the broader community, and also the need to judge between the competing needs of these many Others requiring justice rather than responsibility. Yet ethics and politics are not distinct, as all ethical relations already recognise the broader community beyond the particular Other encountered in the ethical relation. Duras's story of tragic love cut short by war also entwines the ethical and the political. However, unlike Levinas, for her the erotic may also be an expression of ethical relating.

Frantz Fanon's reflections on the risks of interracial love in colonial contexts of racial inequality are elaborated in Chapter 5. The black woman or man may desire the white other who represents an escape from the economic, social and psychological 'inferiority' complex the black person experiences in colonialism. Yet this escape may itself be a trap that perpetuates racial inequality and destroys the identity and culture of the subordinated race. Looking at colonial love from another perspective Tracey Moffatt's experimental short video *Night Cries* explores the complexities of assimilation and the ambiguity of hybridity. An Australian Aboriginal daughter cares for her dying white mother, obligated by love and duty to remain despite her wish for another life. This video story indicates that, in colonial contexts, white humanist love for the subordinate culture may disguise and justify forced assimilation undermining the subordinate culture and leaving assimilated people ('adopted' children for example) caught between cultures.

Perceiving the troubles that beset love, Luce Irigaray attempts to formulate another model for expressing love, through indirection. Chapter 6 examines this new articulation of love. For Irigaray the declaration 'I love you' demands not only a reciprocal affection but also imposes an obligation, a debt, or a duty on the beloved. The direct expression gives love but this gift requires a return of gratitude and devotion for the lover. In order to avoid this expectation of return or exchange of love, Irigaray proposes that love be expressed indirectly so as to make of love a pure gift that avoids reducing it to an exchange relation. 'I love to you' expresses this indirection. Irigaray's reformulation is read alongside Sally Potter's film *Orlando* enabling an exploration of the differing representations of sexual difference in Irigaray and Potter and also enabling a comparison of Orlando and Shelmerdine's love relation with Irigaray's love as indirection.

Chapter 7 turns to the work of Roland Barthes, summarising his theories of textual interpretation – his theories of myth and code – as a basis for understanding his reflections on lover's discourses. Despite the antipathy to the sentimentality of love, Barthes creates a pastiche of fragments from the representations and analyses of love with Goethe's *The Sorrows of Young Werther* a constant refrain but many others – Sartre, Plato, Freud, Nietzsche, Sade, Sappho – also contributing to these recollections and reflections. Creating an unlikely pairing, Barthes' text is read in combination with Nora Ephron's *You've Got Mail* – a film that replicates the sentimental clichés of conventional happy-ever-after love. Yet this pop romance – a remake of the earlier *The Shop Around the Corner* – also illuminates the continual reproduction of the stories and images of love preserving these conventional images even while engaging with the new courting and dating rituals introduced through internet romance.

A book on love must surely include a reflection on marriage – that institution that legally recognises and validates romantic love. In Chapter 8 same-sex marriage is examined and the public and political implications of marriage elaborated through the work of Judith Butler. Michel Foucault's comments on gay friendship and love are also introduced. For Foucault, it is not sex between men that unsettles society but love between men, and while he doesn't endorse conventional institutions such as marriage and family his recognition of the importance of love enables a re-framing of the same-sex marriage debate. This chapter concludes with a discussion of alternative queer marriage ceremonies that challenge the conventions of marriage – such as exclusivity, union and completion. It reflects on the troubles that afflict both love and marriage though it also traces the potential for transformative difference inherent in each.

Chapter 9 returns to Plato and to Levinas reflecting on the love that grounds philosophy as well as ethics and politics. Through a conversation between Jean-Luc Nancy and Jacques Derrida the influence of Levinas on each is revealed and their differing elaborations of his ethics of love explored. Derrida expands Levinas' thought into a politics of hospitality, friendship and democracy 'to come'. Nancy moves in another direction founding his conceptions of community and culture on an erotic-ethical love that forms subjectivity as well as sociality. Lars von Trier's *Dogville* contributes to this conversation reflecting on the difficulties of conditional and unconditional hospitality in personal and political relations.

This book does not attempt to resolve love's troubles and paradoxes. Instead, it recalls and retells the many and divergent stories of love, reading not just the narratives but also the myths and codes, abstractions and figurations, structures, scenes, rhetoric, genre and techniques of the languages of love.

1

Sapphic and Platonic Erotics

Writing over two and a half thousand years ago, Plato points to the similarities between the experience of love and the desire for knowledge. The
arts of seduction are central in each case – to induce the beloved to accept
and reciprocate the lover's approaches parallels the art of charming the
uninitiated into the ways of philosophy. Plato's *Symposium*, perhaps the
most enduring and influential philosophical reflection on love, describes
not only the experience of erotic love but also the passions of the mind.
It reveals links between the erotics of sexuality and philosophical inquiry
and demonstrates how we are all, in the throes of erotic love, also lovers
of knowledge. It intertwines these experiences while also showing how
one may lead to the other.

Constructed as a series of stories of love recounted by a group of
friends during a drinking party, Plato's *Symposium* inaugurates a
philosophy founded on love. From Alcibiades' impassioned tale of his
unrequited love of Socrates, to Aristophanes' story of love as the reunit-
ing of souls cut asunder by the vengeful gods, to Socrates' account of
love as mediation and ascent, the *Symposium* not only paints varying
images of the relation between lover and beloved, it also reveals
how philosophy, like love, arises through the work of the passions. In
this account, philosophy is more than logical analyses and reasoned
arguments. It is an impassioned yearning for greater knowledge and
understanding.

Nor is Plato the only Greek figure to have left a legacy that continues
to affect how we think about love. The influence of Sappho, the Greek
Poet born on the island of Lesbos, has also endured. While most of her
work has disappeared or been destroyed, and what remains is now
largely in fragments, it continues to inspire artists and theorists who
reproduce, translate and attempt to emulate her poetry.

This chapter traces aspects of Plato and Sappho's reflections on love,
pointing to similarities and differences between their visions of Eros.
While the Platonic vision of love is commonly understood as a non-
sexual affectionate friendship, this belies the erotic origins evident

in Socrates' speeches. This passionate element, I will suggest, echoes Sappho's phenomenological account of erotic, embodied love.

SOCRATES SPEECH: LOVE AS INTERMEDIARY AND ASCENT

Plato's *Symposium* stages a conversation between a groups of friends after a feast at the house of Agathon during which each describes his theory of love through a eulogy to the god Eros. Socrates' speech, unlike the others, represents not his own views but those of Diotima; the priestess from Mantinea who Socrates explains is an expert on love (Plato 1994: 20c–d). Diotima instructed Socrates in the ways of love and he in turn passes on this knowledge to his assembled friends. Plato's text then is an account of a discussion within which another conversation is reported. This device – Socrates' reporting Diotima's teaching later written by Plato – enables, a 'commingling [of] the male and female voice' (Cavarero 1995: 93). It also foregrounds questions of authorship, origin, representation, and mediation. A written report of a conversation describing another conversation, we have no direct access to the words of Diotima as these are mediated through both Socrates' and Plato's memories and re-articulations of Diotima's teachings.

Mediation, iteration, indirection, then, are central to the dialogical structure of Plato's text, and as it turns out, are central also to Diotima's account of love. Diotima makes clear that Eros is not a god, is not beauty and wisdom, as earlier speakers had suggested, but is a seeking after beauty and wisdom, and a movement toward them. The story of the birth of Eros sets the scene. Conceived during a celebration of Aphrodite's birth, Eros is the child of Poverty and Plenty and has the characteristics of each parent (Plato 1994: 203b–c). Eros, like his mother Poverty, while not destitute, is poor: 'he never has any money, and the usual notion that he's sensitive and attractive is quite wrong: he's a vagrant, with tough, dry skin and no shoes on his feet' (ibid.: 203c). But like Plenty, his father, he desires knowledge, seeks beauty and value, and has 'courage, impetuosity, and energy' enabling him to successfully pursue his goals: 'hunting . . . knowledge . . . education' (ibid.: 203d). Love is a middle ground between ignorance and knowledge, between ugliness and beauty, need and fulfilment, mortality and immortality. Eros is a daimon (a spirit or messenger) who mediates between gods and mortals facilitating the search for beauty, wisdom and the good. Lacking these attributes, love desires and yearns to attain them. Love, then, is a lacking and a reaching for more that mediates and moves between opposites.

Interestingly, this description of love mirrors the image of Socrates himself who is renowned as the barefoot seeker of wisdom. Love is, like philosophy, the quest for knowledge and Socrates becomes, in Diotima's account, the emblem of both love and philosophy: 'behind the portrait of Eros, one cannot fail to recognise the features of Socrates . . . Eros, who is neither rich, nor beautiful, nor delicate, spends his life philosophising . . .' (Derrida 1981: 117).

If love is mediation and becoming, seeking and searching for wisdom, then philosophy, and Socrates as well – as the representative of Eros – lacking knowledge, beauty, and the good, desires and constantly inquires after truth and perfection. If love is a daimon between mortals and immortals, Socrates and philosophy too are mediators, messengers and communicators moving between the material and immanent human world and the immaterial transcendental world of beauty, wisdom and the good.

Like love, Diotima seems to say, philosophy lacks, desires and searches for the good. Like philosophy, love is a constant process of becoming that involves searching for more. While there is much debate about the relation between the beautiful and the good in Plato, in the *Symposium*, 'the beautiful is thought of as the quality by which the good shines and shows itself' (Ferrari 1992: 260). The search for beauty, wisdom and the good then are the objectives of love and philosophy, because, as Diotima explains, the attainment of these brings happiness (Plato 1994: 205a).

As Diotima's teaching proceeds, however, the image of love as the barefooted, philosophising seeker of wisdom is joined by another conception of love as creativity. This transition from seeker of wisdom to creativity is also a movement from a broader general description of love to a more focused, particular love. Love in general searches for the good, which is happiness, and this is manifest in particular cases in creative production or reproduction. 'Love's purpose', Diotima explains, 'is physical and mental procreation in a beautiful medium' (ibid.: 206b). Explaining further, Diotima continues: 'every human being is both physically and mentally pregnant . . . we instinctively desire to give birth, but we find it possible only in a beautiful medium' (ibid.: 206c). We desire procreation as a means to attain the good permanently; physical or mental offspring provide a form of immortality that ensures the continuation of our wisdom, good and happiness. Humans are all pregnant, physically and mentally, but to give birth we need to join with a beautiful and compatible other. This can produce a child but it can also, as Diotima explains, provide immortality through fame associated with creative productions of many types – artistic, poetic and political. This enables mortal beings to share in immortality, and 'it is immortality which makes this devotion, which is love, a universal feature' (ibid.: 208b).

Diotima goes so far as to suggest that mental creativity is superior to physical reproduction as it is more likely to ensure enduring fame. While physical reproduction results from the union of man and woman, the superior form of artistic, poetic and political creation results from union between men. Diotima explains that if a man's mind is filled with virtue:

> he longs to procreate and give birth . . . and he's particularly pleased if he comes across a mind that is attractive, upright and gifted . . . he takes on this person's education . . . together they share in raising their offspring. Consequently, this kind of relationship involves a far stronger bond and far more constant affection than is experienced by people who are united by ordinary children, because the offspring of this relationship are particularly attractive and are closer to immortality than ordinary children. (Plato 1994: 209 b–c)

Creative production then results from intimate relations between men; erotic unions between older men and younger men (which in ancient Greece are certainly acceptable and even, perhaps, superior to heterosexual relations) in which the older guide and mentor the younger (Halperin 1986: 60–80). Diotima is, therefore, not only asserting the superiority of mental procreation but also, by association, the homoerotic unions that facilitate their production.

Diotima, however, has not yet finished her account of love, and as her teaching continues she develops a third image to augment the barefoot, philosophising daimon and male homoerotic creativity – an ascending movement that leads to the good in general.

Diotima's description of love as ascent – as a ladder leading from a lower form of individual love of a particular beloved to a higher form of love of the good and the beautiful in general – is perhaps the most influential aspect of this speech. Having established that love, which produces ideas and creative works, is superior to love that simply produces children Diotima then explains to Socrates how this creative love can further evolve by climbing the ladder of love. This process starts from erotic love of a particular other and progresses through stages to an abstract love of the eternally beautiful. Love of a physically beautiful particular other person leads to appreciation of the physical beauty of many; then to recognition of attractive minds; and in turn to beauty in knowledge and wisdom; all of which progressively produces increasingly beautiful reasoning and thinking. Having perceived this 'everlasting loveliness' the final step in the ascent may be attained in which an appreciation and love of abstract eternal goodness is achieved. Diotima explains that at this stage the lover perceives not a particular, but a constant and lasting, beauty: 'he won't perceive beauty as a face or hands or any other physical feature, or as a piece of reasoning or knowledge, and he won't perceive it as being anything else either – in something like a creature of the earth or the heavens – he'll perceive it in itself and by itself, constant and eternal . . .' (Plato 1994: 211 a–b).

This account of love as contemplative ascent has influenced the Western philosophical tradition, Christian models that advocate love of the most high and of humanity as a whole, as well as literary and popular representations. However, this heritage is based on a particular interpretation of Diotima-Socrates' speech, which focuses on the ascent of love and reads this as a repudiation of erotics. Feminist philosophers, while critical of some aspects of this famous oratory, have emphasised other insights it offers into the nature of love, the role of gender, and the significance of carnality and sensibility.

EROS, GENDER AND FEMININE PHILOSOPHY

Luce Irigaray focuses on the intermediary role of love in her reading of Diotima's teachings. Diotima's love is a mediation moving between opposite terms but never reaching a static conclusion and always in a process of becoming. It is a dialectical movement, although as Irigaray explains, unlike the Hegelian dialectic in which two opposing terms, thesis and antithesis, are sublated or absorbed within a final third term that creates a synthesis, Diotima's love is never resolved. It is a third term moving between the ugly and beautiful, bad and good, ignorant and wise: 'The mediator is never abolished in an ineffable knowledge. Everything is always in movement, in a state of becoming' (Irigaray 1984: 21).

The intermediary nature of love also explains its relation with philosophy. Philosophy, like love, moves between ignorance and knowledge, and is a never-ending passionate pursuit of greater insight. Diotima's discussion, Irigaray suggests, reveals this relation: 'love is a philosopher and a philosophy. Philosophy is not a formal learning, fixed and rigid, abstracted from all feeling. It is a quest for love, love of beauty, love of wisdom, which is one of the most beautiful things' (ibid.: 24). Neither love nor philosophy has attained the beautiful and good. Both are barefoot, down-and-out vagabonds. But both are curious, fascinated and infatuated with their quest. Irigaray wryly comments that philosophers are more often perceived as learned, well mannered, and pedantic.

Diotima's linking of love and philosophy suggests another portrayal, in which the philosopher is 'a sort of barefoot waif who goes out under the stars seeking an encounter with reality, the embrace, the knowledge or perhaps a shared birth, of whatever benevolence, beauty, or wisdom might be found there' (ibid.: 24).

While Irigaray finds the image of love as mediating daimon productive, other aspects of Diotima-Socrates' speech trouble her. Irigaray contests the view that love is caused by the desire to procreate and attain immortality (ibid.: 27). She suggests that representing reproduction and the child as the motivation for love destroys the daimonic or intermediary character of love: 'love loses its daimonic character . . . Love has lost its divinity, its mediastic, alchemical qualities between couples of opposites . . . A beloved [the child] who is an *end* is substituted for love between men and women'. While the child could be born of love and allowed to 'germinate or ripen in the milieu of love' it has been made, instead, to represent love and to facilitate immortality and this, for Irigaray, is a failure of love. Irigaray concludes, 'A sort of teleological triangle is put in place instead of a perpetual journey, a perpetual transvaluation, a permanent becoming' (ibid.: 27). The production of a child, or of creative works, the creation of immortality through production or reproduction, is a teleological quest for immortality that replaces love as an 'immanent efflorescence of the divine of and in the flesh' (ibid.: 30).

Equally disturbing, for Irigaray, is the valorisation of same-sex love between men over love between women and men. In the *Symposium*, she writes: '. . . love between men is superior to love between man and woman. Carnal procreation is subordinated to the engendering of beautiful and good things' (ibid.: 31). As a result a hierarchy is established in which creative mental procreation is valued over reproductive birth. Mental procreation, associated with men and with love between men, takes precedence over physical birth and love of women. In Diotima's account the quest for immortality not only destroys daimonic love but also relegates women and biological reproduction to a secondary status facilitating male love and male procreative ascendancy.

Irigaray's commentary, while acknowledging the value of Diotima's daimonic vision of love disrupts and questions the subsequent reformulation of love as male mental procreation. While the homoeroticism of the *Symposium* challenges heterosexual dominance, Irigaray usefully points to the risks for feminine being and Eros that may arise. Nevertheless, within Plato's text itself the subordination of the feminine is already to some extent reversed by positioning Diotima as the teacher of Socrates. While ancient Greek homoerotics appears to have been founded on a pedagogical relation in which the older man instructed the younger, in the *Symposium* a woman takes the place of the older teacher and it is she who instructs Socrates, now positioned as the pupil. The *Symposium* then contains an internal, implicit and oblique critique of male homoerotic exclusion of feminine love by recognising Diotima's erotic lessons.

Moreover, the images of pregnancy, reproduction, birthing and parenting are central to Diotima's teaching placing feminine activities at the centre of love and of philosophising. Adriana Cavarero suggests that:

> It is not by chance that Socrates functions as her pupil and reports her discourse: Socrates is an expert in the maieutic method, the art of the midwife who does not 'insert' notions into the soul of the listener, but rather helps souls give birth to a truth that they already carry within them. (Cavarero 1995: 92)

Yet, in the end Cavarero, like Irigaray, is critical of Diotima-Socrates' account of love. For Cavarero, this description of male creative fertility involves a masculine mimicry of feminine reproduction that ultimately displaces and occludes the feminine. This 'mimesis of pregnancy' (ibid.: 94) involves a distinction between the body and soul and between physical birth of children and male mental birthing of ideas and creative works. Significantly, the latter is valued over the former so that this metaphor of 'male maternity . . . ends up disempowering and negating the female experience' (ibid.: 101).

While Irigaray and Cavarero caution us about the disempowering effects of Diotima-Socrates' representation of love, Wendy Brown suggests that Socrates disrupts the philosophical enterprise precisely by using the image of giving birth to ideas to challenge the agonism inherent in philosophical disputation. As Brown writes, Socrates, 'makes strange by making female the entire philosophical endeavour, thereby . . . divest[ing] philosophy and politics of the socially male qualities to which he objects' (Brown 1994: 173). Elaborating, Brown explains:

> In contradistinction to an agonistic context for philosophising, in which glory, reputation, and power are pre-eminently at stake in espousing wisdom, Plato locates philosophy in the realm of love, nurturance, and procreation. The birth and cultivation of new ideas are the natural product of a well-chosen union between two virtuous human beings. Philosophical truth is thus situated in the context of love, attachment, and desire for the Good. (ibid.: 171)

While Diotima-Socrates' speech has generally been read as a valorisation of mind over body, and of philosophic love of knowledge over embodied passion, this interpretation obliterates the metaphor of birth, and the significance of Eros in the dialogue. Socrates does not construe the acquisition of knowledge as a process of transmitting ideas and concepts from the mentor to the disciple, but as a nurturing that encourages the recognition of awareness and insight already latent within the novice. Instruction does not involve the mere provision of information but rather the work of the midwife who facilitates the birth of a wisdom already encrypted within those who seek it (ibid.: 166). This maieutic and maternal strategy, this metaphor of pregnancy and birth, challenge the more combative and agonistic styles of learning and politics based on a competitive acquisition of knowledge and power.

In addition, Diotima-Socrates' recitation establishes the centrality of love for philosophy and for learning more broadly. Beginning with an image of love as a lacking intermediary that searches always for beauty, knowledge and the good, Diotima-Socrates explains that the quest for knowledge is founded on desire. While the ascent appears to leave embodied erotics behind in favour of the more abstract pleasures of the mind, it is clear that the experience of Eros inaugurates philosophy.

Moreover, the Diotima-Socrates' account of love is not the final speech in the *Symposium*. Alcibiades' story of his love, and failed seduction, of Socrates offers a more embodied and personal perspective that augments Diotima-Socrates' account of philosophical love indicating the continuing significance of the erotic. Alcibiades has been absent during the earlier discussions but, arriving late and drunk, he offers his own account of love, overturning or inverting the more sedate earlier discourses.

ALCIBIADES' SPEECH: 'TEARS FLOOD MY EYES'

Interrupting the orderly elevation of love from daimonic mediation, through homoerotic creative production, to philosophising, disembodied love of the good, Alcibiades, garlanded in ivy and violets, drunkenly confesses his passionate, and ultimately unrequited, pursuit of Socrates. Alcibiades' personal story of love of Socrates brings the discussion back down to earth; back down to the everyday experience of rapture, longing, obsession, and also pain and despair. Inspired and transformed by his love, Alcibiades repudiates his dissolute lifestyle pursuing instead the Socratic way. Confiding his obsession he proclaims: 'Whenever I listen to him speak, I get more ecstatic than the Corybantes! My heart pounds and tears flood my eyes under the spell of his words' (Plato 1994: 215d–e).

Alcibiades eulogy of Socrates continues as he explains that it is not just Socrates' wisdom that is praiseworthy but, in addition, his bravery in battle, his stoicism in the face of hunger and cold, his indifference to wealth and privilege, and his resistance to sexual seduction. Using the excessive language of the obsessed lover, Alcibiades describes Socrates' power over him:

> I don't know if any of you have seen the genuine Socrates, opened up to reveal the effigies he has inside, but I saw them once, and they struck me as so divine, so glorious, so gorgeous and wonderful that – to cut a long story short – I felt I should obey him in everything. (ibid.: 216e–217a)

Alcibiades narrates his attempts to seduce Socrates. First, he contrives to spend time alone with him, believing that his beauty alone will enchant Socrates. He next invites Socrates to the gymnasium where they wrestle together – still with no perceptible effect. Dinner together is the next equally unsuccessful strategy. Finally, detaining Socrates through conversation till late at night, Alcibiades induces Socrates to stay the night. Realising that Socrates will not initiate an erotic encounter, Alcibiades reports that he said to Socrates:

> I think you're in love with me . . . You're too shy to bring it up in my company, so I'll tell you what I feel. I think it would be stupid of me not to gratify you in this and in everything else you want . . . (Plato 1994: 218c)

Socrates rejects Alcibiades unsubtle advances, however, accusing him of wishing to trade 'gold for bronze' – that is of wanting to exchange 'the semblance of beauty and get the truth in return' (ibid.: 218e). For Socrates, Alcibiades' physical beauty is not as valuable as his own understanding of truth and so the inducement into erotics is insufficient.

Yet, Socrates spends the night with Alcibiades who reports that while he wraps him in his arms, Socrates remains impervious to him:

> I put my thick cloak over him . . . and lay down under his short cloak. I put my arms around this remarkable man . . . and lay there with him all night long . . . And after all that, he spurned and disdained and scorned my charms . . . (ibid.: 219b–c)

Alcibiades' homage to Socrates is partly drunken rave, and partly a wounded jibe at Socrates for his rejection of him. Yet, it also conveys the entrancement and the anguish of love. Alcibiades is moved to tears; he is 'bitten by something with a far more excruciating bite than a snake' (ibid.: 218a). His experience of love is not the disembodied quest for knowledge but an embodied sensuous torment.

Alcibiades' speech is generally regarded as light comic relief following the more profound and serious Socratic image of philosophy as love of knowledge. Alternately, it is sometimes conceived as representing a choice that must be made between a generalised Socratic love of knowledge and particular erotic pleasures. These interpretations, however, ignore the complexity of the formulation of love in Plato's text. Rather than disregarding Alcibiades' story, or construing it as a choice, reading it in conjunction with Diotima-Socrates provides greater insights into the lived experience of love. Supplementing Socrates with Alcibiades reveals the multiple possibilities of love and its perplexing articulation of the carnal and the ethereal, of voluptuousness and torment. Abstracted love and passionate love are not wholly opposed in Plato's text but are instead interrelated: love of knowledge develops from erotic experience and while Socrates refuses Alcibiades advances this story demonstrates the erotic context of Socrates' contemplations. This entwinement of philosophic and erotic love emerges also in Plato's *Phaedrus*, which acknowledges the influence of the wise poet Sappho.

SAPPHO AND SOCRATES: THE HEART ON WINGS

Plato's *Phaedrus* like the *Symposium* speaks of love – though here in the form of a conversation between two friends, Phaedrus and Socrates. This text, like the *Symposium*, is also most often interpreted as representing a choice between abstract and embodied love. And, there is certainly evidence for this in Socrates speech in which love is depicted as a struggle within the soul between the charioteer and two horses; one obedient, the other defiant. The defiant steed, suffering the urgency of desire, wants to ravish at once the beloved while the charioteer and obedient horse attempt to control this wild desire (Plato 2002: 253d–254e). This image of a respectful, controlled desire struggling with uncontrolled urges may be discerned, also, in the two opposed speeches that Socrates presents in this text. In the first he condemns love for its deceitful and manipulative attempts to seduce the beloved; though he immediately repudiates this account representing, in the second speech, the importance of Eros as the origin of a higher love. The *Phaedrus* then may be interpreted as restaging the concerns of the *Symposium* between the good, evident in love of knowledge, and the disreputable ravages of erotic passion.

However, there is also evidence for an alternative reading; one that reveals the relation and oscillation between erotic love and the search for wisdom. Wendy Brown suggests that in both *Phaedrus* and the *Symposium* Socrates equates erotic and philosophic love pointing to the rapture that accompanies both experiences:

> [In *Phaedrus*] Socrates is speaking simultaneously of the experience of love of wisdom and love of another human being. Here, as in the *Symposium*, he is suggesting not merely similarity but potential identity or accord between

loving truth and loving a person. Pursuit of knowledge is, ultimately, an erotic endeavour and brings the pursuer to the same heights of frenzied rapture as love of a human creature does. (Brown 1994: 169)

In Socrates' discussion of love he explains that the wings of the soul atrophy when it descends from the heavens to the earth. The experience of love, however, nourishes the wings of the soul so that they unfurl and potentially enable a return to the higher realms. Here, Socrates equates the seeker of wisdom with the lover: each beholds beauty and this sight creates fever, throbbing and swelling:

Following this sight, the kind of change comes over him that you would expect from a shivering fit, and he begins to sweat and run an unusually high fever . . . His heat softens the coat covering the feather's buds, which had been too hard and closed up for wings to grow . . . the quills of the feathers swell and begin to grow from the roots upwards . . . his whole soul seethes and pounds . . . So the soul, as it grows its wings, seethes and feels sore and tingles. (Plato 2002: 251b–c)

Brown comments that this 'highly sexual' description refers to both the sensations of erotic desire and the experiences of the lover of wisdom.

Further evidence for this interpretation is suggested by the connections between Socrates' speech and Sappho's erotic poetry. While speaking of love, Socrates defers to the greater knowledge demonstrated by the poets: 'the fair Sappho, or Anacreon the wise' (ibid.: 235c). Sappho's influence on Socrates has been established with various commentators pointing to their similar phenomenological descriptions of the experience of desire. Socrates and Sappho both speak of the trembling, sweat and heat that overtakes the lover at the sight of the beloved. Page duBois suggests that this similarity indicates that Socrates is possessed by Sappho, demonstrating again the significance of female influences on his philosophies (duBois 1994: 148). But it is not just the sensations of the body that Socrates echoes but also the metaphor of the wings. Sappho writes:

. . . oh it
puts the heart in my chest on wings . . .
fire is racing under skin . . .
and cold sweat holds me and shaking
grips me all . . .
(Sappho 2002: fragment 31)

Yet Sappho's fragment also introduces something more into this description of the embodied effects of passion. For these bodily effects are incited by the poet's observation of her beloved as she speaks and laughs with a man who listens attentively. The poet's passion is incited, not just by the vision of her beloved but by the sight of her, sitting close, engaged with another admirer:

> . . . he . . . who opposite you
> sits and listens close
> to your sweet speaking
> and lovely laughing . . .
> (ibid.: fragment 31)

This may speak perhaps of an intertwining of jealousy with love or it may, as Anne Carson suggests, indicate the necessary triangulation of love (Carson 1986: 12–17). This is not just the re-enactment of the conventional love triangle but also the articulation of the three components necessary for love. If love is lack, as Diotima's account of Eros as the lacking child of Poverty and Plenty suggests, there needs to be not only lover and beloved but also that which comes between. Love desires what it lacks and its fulfilment would quench the passion of love. Love, thus, requires an obstacle that defers or displaces, preserving the lack and ensuring the preservation of desire. The beloved's companion is not simply a rival to be overcome but the principle of obstruction that keeps love alive.

There are, of course, many strategies employed in love to obstruct and so preserve love: the rituals of modesty that deflect the suitors' seduction through reference to the requirement for chastity; the erotics of flirtation predicated on a play between the promise of more and the denial of its fulfilment; the dating game of pursuit by the lover and reluctance, dissuasion or flight by the beloved. Perhaps Socrates and Alcibiades, too, know this game. Carson points out that though Alcibiades entices Socrates to his bed he also carefully wraps Socrates in a cloak before wrapping him within his embrace (Plato 1994: 219b–c). Cocooned in a coat, Socrates is already halfway protected from the Alcibiades' desires (Carson 1986: 22–3). While Alcibiades chastises Socrates for rejecting his advances, Carson suggests that Alcibiades has already ensured this outcome by placing the cloak between them. Yet, if Alcibiades is playing both the role of seducer and at the same time constructing obstacles to that seduction, Socrates is perhaps outwitting Alcibiades at this game. Seducing Alcibiades with his philosophic words, bringing tears to his eyes and a pounding to his heart, Socrates preserves and prolongs Alcibiades' adoration by playing hard to get. In another context, Phaedrus chides Socrates for precisely this behaviour. Socrates feigns unwillingness to speak of love and Phaedrus demands that he 'Stop playing hard to get' (Plato 2002: 236d). Aware that love is lack and that fulfilment will quiet the urgency of desire, Socrates thwarts Alcibiades' advances all the while stroking Alcibiades' passion. Not an outright rejection of Alcibiades, then, but an erotic strategy of evasion and deferral, Socrates keeps passion alive.

While Socrates equates erotic and philosophic love, Sappho focuses on the phenomenological particularity of the impassioned body, and this depiction provides lessons about the experiences and expressions of love. The 'sweet speaking' and 'lovely laughing' woman that the poet adores is not attending to her but to another. Her unavailability is, it appears, part of her attraction. This theme returns in fragment 105:

> as the sweetapple reddens on a high branch
> high on the highest branch and the applepickers forgot –
> no, not forgot – were unable to reach
> (Sappho 2002: fragment 105a)

Preserved only as a fragment of a longer poem, the comparison promised at the start is lost. Sappho's unresolved metaphor leads us to speculate about what unreachable thing might be compared to this high-branched apple. The lacking comparison emulates the lack of love and of learning. The sweet apple on a high branch might be compared with a girl unavailable to the lover. Socrates might have compared it with the highest branches of learning toward which we reach but rarely achieve full understanding.

This may be the allure of both love and learning – the apple, the girl, the philosophical concept, just beyond our reach, induces a yearning for more. Sappho's unresolved, incomplete epigram, promising an answer that it fails to deliver, reiterates this hunger. The reader, the lover, the thinker, all want more. And it is this irresolution and incompletion that stirs the desires of both love and thought. The processes of learning and of falling in love, then, exhibit this similarity: they are both founded on a lack that provokes a desire for more. In the process both produce an excitement, a delight, a shivering, that is, as Carson says, the feeling of being alive (Carson 1986: 70).

Recognising Sappho's influence on Socrates reveals aspects of his work overlooked in conventional interpretations. Rather than a rejection of erotic love or a choice between erotics and wisdom, Socrates may be indicating as well a complex intertwining of desires. Sappho depicts love, not as choice, but as a 'sweetbitter' sensation that overtakes and destabilises the self:

> Eros the melter of limbs (now again) stirs me –
> sweetbitter, unmanageable creature who steals in
> (Sappho 2002: fragment 130)

Eros is not sweet at first and bitter as it ends; nor is it sweet in one instance and bitter in another: sweet in philosophic love and bitter in erotic love for example. Instead, love is simultaneously bitter and sweet, the bitter frustrations and obstructions of love being the very cause of the lack and desire that incite sweet love (Carson 1986, 3–9). It is not only erotic love that is 'sweetbitter' in this way for philosophic love and love of learning in general also have their joys and distresses. The process of learning opens new perspectives, new ideas and new worlds but it also, tantalisingly and frustratingly, always offers the ineffable just beyond current understanding.

CONCLUSION

While Platonic love is traditionally read as a rejection of erotic love in favour of a higher form of philosophic love of the abstract good, or as a choice between erotics and love of wisdom, Socrates' tactic of simultaneous dissuasion and provocation might suggest, instead, a more complex entwining in which philosophic and erotic seduction are thoroughly enmeshed. This lesson about love may be inherited from Sappho whose poetry suggests that love as a yearning is augmented, rather than frustrated by, obstruction. Her lyrics trace the physiology of love revealing an embodied phenomenology of erotic love. For Sappho erotic love involves obsession, rapture and longing and reveals the bittersweet intertwining of excitement, distress, frustration, lack and joy. It ceaselessly reaches toward the ineffable, just beyond its grasp.

Insofar as Socrates listens to Sappho's lessons, then for him, too, love is the movement toward, rather than the final attainment of abstract and particular beauty. Love as mediation between lack and fulfilment would be extinguished by the attainment of the desired object. Love desires, reaches toward, and seeks the other: wisdom and the beloved. Love of learning is like erotic love: both are based on a lack and on a yearning for more and both involve a mediation between Poverty and Plenty, ignorance and wisdom, lack and fulfilment. Alcibiades' simultaneous passion for Socrates and for his wisdom, and the games of seduction and obstruction that Alcibiades and Socrates both employ suggest that seeking knowledge is not antithetical to, but rather facilitated by, erotic passions. Philosophic love, this suggests, is not the overcoming of the body: rather it is itself erotically incarnate.

2

Paradoxical Passions in Shelley and Nietzsche

௸

Mary Shelley, daughter of influential feminist philosopher Mary Wollstonecraft, wrote *Frankenstein Or The Modern Prometheus* in 1818. Reiterated and popularised in theatre, film, and song from James Whale's *Frankenstein* and *Bride of Frankenstein* (1931 and 1935) to hybrid adaptations such as *The Rocky Horror Picture Show* (1975) and *Blade Runner* (1982), *Frankenstein* evokes the horror of vengeful progeny and anxiety about misdirected passions. Not simply a living-dead horror narrative, *Frankenstein* also raises the spectre of tragic and unrequited love: searching in vain for friendship and rejected by a world repulsed by his difference, the creature reciprocates his persecution murdering those his creator loves.

Mary Shelley predates German philosopher Friedrich Nietzsche by fifty-plus years, is a novelist rather than a philosopher, and explores the horrors of monstrous life rather than the horrors of conventional moralities, but there are, nevertheless, certain affinities between Shelley's and Nietzsche's reflections on love. While *Frankenstein* appears to oppose family love to monstrous hatred, the novel could also be read as staging a complex entwining of Victor Frankenstein's saintly wife with his man-made monster. The idyllic familial love Elizabeth represents articulates with the heinous passions associated with the creature suggesting that the ordinary and the odious cannot be easily dissociated. This ambiguous imbrication of the monstrous and the conventionally romantic is also elaborated, through differing images and concepts, in Nietzsche's varying pronouncements on love. Nietzsche, too, reveals the paradoxes inherent in the love relation. Nietzsche reverses our conventional valorisation of romantic and familial love, in seeking a distant and futural love, while also exposing the convolution of mundane, ordinary love with the creative love of the future. Nietzsche and Shelley, then, each write of the dangers of love: the illusory enchantments of the romance of love and the paradoxical chiasmic intersections between mundane love and uncanny, miraculous and monstrous love.

MONSTROUS LOVE

> . . . I was disturbed by the wildest dreams. I thought I saw Elizabeth, in the bloom of health, walking in the streets of Ingolstadt. Delighted and surprised, I embraced her, but as I imprinted the first kiss on her lips, they became livid with the hue of death; her features appeared to change, and I thought that I held the corpse of my dead mother in my arms; a shroud enveloped her form, and I saw grave-worms crawling in the folds of flannel. (Shelley 2003: 59)

On the night that Victor Frankenstein finally gives life to his creature – created from the sutured bones, organs and flesh of corpses – he is beset by nightmare visions of his intended-wife and his dead mother. Kissing Elizabeth, he transforms her into the wormy corpse of his mother, mirroring the creature's transformation, at the moment of animation, from a wondrous scientific feat into a demoniacal monster. Frankenstein, horrified at his own creation, repudiates the creature, precipitating a cycle of murder, revenge and hatred. The creature seeks friendship and love but, rejected by Frankenstein and by humanity at large, vengefully murders or condemns to die the icons of innocence – the playing child and the sleeping girl. Frankenstein, convinced by the creature that his murderous rage will be placated by the creation of a mate, begins to form a female creature but finally dismembers her half-formed body believing that she will propagate a monstrous species that will ultimately threaten humanity. The creature murders in turn Frankenstein's friend, Clerval, and, on their wedding night his wife, Elizabeth, inciting the final arctic pursuit as Frankenstein seeks to avenge the deaths of his family.

The numerous interpretations of the Shelley novel have focused variously on the non-sexual (re)production of the monster; the homosocial and homophobic associations between Victor and his creation; the depiction of femininity in the novel; and the abject monster as metaphor for colonial anxiety about the racial other (Sedgwick 1985; Jacobus 1982; Spivak 1999). Feminist and queer theorists have remarked especially on the marginalisation of women in this text. Mary Jacobus observes that women are either passive victims or 'the bearers of a traditional ideology of love, nurturance and domesticity' (Jacobus 1982: 132). Eve Sedgwick cites *Frankenstein* as illustration of homosocial bonding between men that may also involve the homophobic negative desire expressed by Victor for the monster (Sedgwick 1985: 116–17). Both refer to the circulation of desire and eroticism and a mingling of opposing forces – of life and death, erotic and horrific, love and hate. These reflections on the positioning of femininity and the imbrication of divergent experiences pave the way for a more detailed investigation of the ambiguous relation between Elizabeth and the monster in this text and especially on the troubling of love that results.

Frankenstein is saturated with the problematics and dynamics of love: Frankenstein's for Elizabeth, for his friends and family, and also, ambivalently, for the creature; the creature's desire for a mate and for friendship; the contending images of idealised maternal love, maternal abjection and motherless existence. Strikingly and most obviously, familial love is juxtaposed against murderous hatred. Or so it, initially, appears.

At first glance familial love is represented in idealised terms: a halcyon vision of perfect felicity, harmony and virtue in which each relation is characterised by affection, adoration, tenderness and benevolence. Victor Frankenstein describes the love between his parents as 'devoted affection' (Shelley 2003: 34) and their love for him as demonstrated in 'my mother's tender caresses and my father's smile of benevolent pleasure' (ibid.: 35). Similarly, he wishes to 'protect, love and cherish' (ibid.: 37) his sister, Elizabeth. These unfailingly affirmative relations create an idyllic childhood. Victor, proclaims that: 'No human being could have passed a happier childhood than myself. My parents were possessed by the very spirit of kindness and indulgence . . . the agents and creators of all the many delights which we enjoyed' (ibid.: 39).

Yet, this vision of perfection is finally unsettling as all the relations merge and Elizabeth, especially, incestuously circulates from the position of sister to wife and mother thereby homogenising the feminine roles. Elizabeth, adopted as a child into the family as Victor's sister, is from the outset also positioned as his future wife and finally, in his nightmare vision, transmogrifies into his decaying mother. Elizabeth synthesises the feminine familial positions and, in so doing, also accentuates the equivalence between the various forms of familial love.

Within the family circle love, endlessly safe, comfortable and familiar, circulates monotonously, with parental love seemingly equivalent to filial love and to conjugal and sibling love. This equivalent faultlessness of each love relation and the unremitting sweetness Elizabeth brings to her rotating roles finally transforms Elizabeth into a robotic figure: an ever-replaceable empty idyll. Elizabeth anticipates the *Stepford Wives* (1975) playing a bloodless and vacant automaton who uncannily and monstrously repeats the formulaic family romance. Elizabeth, the emblem of perfect familial love, is an empty void – a de-animated, inhuman replicant.

This hyperbolic and mutating family romance is juxtaposed against the murderous creature and Victor's impassioned obsession, first with creating the creature and subsequently with destroying him. Victor's creation of the creature can be read as parthenogenetic – a motherless reproduction of the same, devoid of the difference of the sexual encounter. Yet, for Victor, the creature becomes monstrous, failing to repeat the same and embodying instead a difference that horrifies and fascinates.

In her interpretation of Shelley's text, Gayatri Spivak identifies a double reproduction in the creation of the creature. Not simply a metaphor for sexual reproduction, the creature also stands for the imperialist social mission of 'soul-making'. These are not, she suggests, in conflict but are articulated together in the womb of Frankenstein's laboratory:

> *Frankenstein*, however, is not a battleground of male and female individualism articulated in terms of sexual reproduction (family and female) and social subject-production (race and male). That binary opposition is undone in Victor Frankenstein's laboratory – an artificial womb where both projects are undertaken simultaneously, though the terms are never openly spelled out. (Spivak 1999: 133)

The *Frankenstein* story reveals the imbrication of sexual reproduction with the civilising mission that humanises the 'native', while it also echoes the horror evoked by the monstrousness of the resistant subaltern other. Frankenstein destroys the female creature, anxiously anticipating that she would reproduce 'a race of devils' (Shelley 2003: 170) who would threaten humankind, mirroring the colonialist fear of third world over-population and diasporic migration. While suggesting therefore that *Frankenstein* reflects colonial anxiety about the monstrous racial other, Spivak also contends that Shelley's novel equivocates allowing the monster to evade colonial capture. While the creature, at Frankenstein's deathbed, foretells his own demise, this anticipated narrative closure is rescinded by the novel's final image of the monster: 'He sprang from the cabin window . . . upon the ice-raft which lay close to the vessel. He was soon borne away by the waves, and lost in the darkness and distance' (ibid.: 225).

Having created the creature, Victor repudiates the monstrous difference of the monster, returning to the cloying familiarity of familial love. Yet, he craves, too, the adventure of difference, returning to and repeatedly confronting and pursuing the creature. While Victor appears to love Elizabeth and hate the creature, these seeming opposites are entwined with Elizabeth's saccharine automaton perfection becoming sinisterly monstrous, and the monster, despite his murderous passions becoming strangely empathetic as his thwarted search for companionship and resulting loneliness are revealed. (This sympathy for the creature, already evident in Shelley's novel, is perhaps accentuated in James Whale's 1931 film depiction. Some commentators have suggested that, as a gay Hollywood director, Whale's outsider perspective facilitates an identification with the persecuted creature resulting in a more sympathetic portrayal [Russo 1987].) The beautiful and the abject, the familiar and horrifying, no longer distinct, infect, exchange and replace each other. Elizabeth transforms into the mother's cadaver, which itself evokes the creature sutured together from the corpses of the dead. And in this strange chiasmic exchange, love and hate are also imbricated with Victor's love of Elizabeth equated with a horrified love of the cadaverous mother and finally transmogrified into an abjected and repressed love-hate of the creature.

The reversals and entwinings here are numerous. Elizabeth, as wife and mother represents a life-giving force; yet, in the nightmare dream she becomes the maternal corpse. The murderous monster is life-destroying yet he is the re-animation of the dead. The creature galvanises life and passion while Elizabeth, anodyne and passive, awaits death. Twisting the reversals further Elizabeth, as automaton, becomes monstrous and the creature increasingly expresses human emotions and desires. Elizabeth and the monster do not, however, simply exchange roles. Rather they entwine, suggesting that common ordinary love can transmute into difference, and that the different and seemingly abject other can fascinate and compel. Shelley's novel, then, opposes and then articulates idyllic love founded on similarity and monstrous love imbued with difference and ultimately, paradoxically, imbricates one with the other suggesting that similarity itself gives birth to or animates difference.

If Shelley explores the ambiguities of love, Nietzsche too articulates the contradictions and paradoxes of amorous life, and like Shelly reveals the entwining of difference and commonality in love.

PARADOXICAL LOVE

> I fear you when you are near, I love you when you are far; your fleeing allures me, your seeking secures me: I suffer, but for you what would I not gladly endure!
>
> For you whose coldness inflames; whose hatred seduces, whose flight constrains, whose mockery – induces:
>
> who would not hate you, great woman who binds us, enwinds us, seduces us, seeks us, finds us! Who would not love you, you innocent, impatient, wind-swift, wild-eyed sinner! (Nietzsche 2003: 241)

Friedrich Nietzsche, born some fifty years after Mary Shelley to a German Lutheran pastor who died when Nietzsche was four and a mother who outlived them both, grew up in a family of women. A brilliant student and professor of classics he suffered debilitating illnesses ending with complete mental or psychological collapse throughout the last ten years of his life. Nietzsche's theories are sometimes dismissed as incoherent ramblings partly, perhaps, because his ideas are so challenging and unconventional. He rejects the ideals of the Enlightenment, criticises democratic politics and Christian and utilitarian ethics, and valorises the unconscious passions over the rational side of human existence. His attitudes to women often appear misogynistic and he has been accused of anti-Semitism (mainly as a result of misrepresentations of his work disseminated by his sister, Elizabeth). Despite, or perhaps because of, his unconventional approach Nietzsche is able to challenge and disturb our most settled convictions forcing us to rethink taken-for-granted notions and assumptions.

Nietzsche's various fragmentary, aphoristic, proclamations on love appear at first contradictory and confused. In *The Gay Science* he writes that love is avarice, 'a lust for possession,' and 'the most ingenuous expression of egoism' (Nietzsche 1974: 88–9). But in the same aphorism he also proclaims that 'here and there on earth' we find a love that craves a higher shared ideal and this he calls friendship (ibid.: 89). Or again, in *Thus Spoke Zarathustra*, Nietzsche is critical of the 'bad love' of the neighbour but extols love of the distant and future: 'Higher than love of one's neighbour stands love of the most distant man and of the man of the future; higher still than love of man I count love of causes and phantoms' (Nietzsche 2003: 87). He also repudiates marriage as 'poverty of the soul in partnership' though he nevertheless identifies a 'holy' form of marriage (ibid.: 95–6).

While Nietzsche's account of love seems initially puzzling his work nevertheless deserves deeper reflection. Excavating beneath our generally romanticised idealisation of love Nietzsche attempts to explain the genesis of love insisting that it is motivated by greed and self-interest. Desire and lust, Nietzsche warns, are always for the new as we tire of existing possessions and crave new attractions, experiences and material goods:

> Gradually we become tired of the old, of what we safely possess, and we stretch out our hands again. Even the most beautiful scenery is no longer assured of our love after we have lived in it for three months, and some more distant coast attracts our avarice: possessions are generally diminished by possession. (Nietzsche 1974: 88)

While desire as attraction for the new is not too unsettling, Nietzsche extrapolates the consequence for love, revealing the exploitation inherent in benevolent love as well as in sexual love. The feeling of pity may incite a benevolent love and care for the other but, for Nietzsche, this is motivated by a desire to possess. We take advantage of the other's suffering to gain possession of her, though we disguise this by labelling it 'love'. Similarly, sexual love demands exclusive possession of the beloved, excluding competitors from the joys of this love and condemning them to 'impoverishment and deprivation', thereby revealing the 'wild avarice and injustice of sexual love'. Nietzsche concludes that while love has been 'glorified and deified . . . in all the ages' and perceived as 'the opposite of egoism' it turns out that love 'may be the most ingenuous expression of egoism' (ibid.: 89).

This description of sexual love as egoistic and possessive is commonplace enough (though Nietzsche's condemnation of pity and benevolence as a disguise for exploitative possession questions the belief in disinterested charity). However, while we may concede that love is born of egoism, Nietzsche now challenges this position, not to argue the opposite – that love is selfless – but to argue that through egoism love has the potential to create a bond based on shared desire for the new. Mutual possessive desire between lover and beloved makes possible a joint longing for the unknown, the undiscovered, the new and different. Nietzsche calls this friendship:

> . . . this possessive craving of two people for each other gives way to a new desire and lust for possession – a shared higher thirst for an ideal above them. But who knows such love? Who has experienced it? Its right name is *friendship*. (ibid.: 89)

Nietzsche avoids an antithetical or oppositional formulation of love – as egoism or selflessness, as selfish or caring, as avarice or generosity. Rather he questions the romancing of love as benevolent devotion revealing its inherent avarice and identifying the positive consequences and possibilities of a mutual yearning for more. This movement from greed and possessiveness to a sharing friendship appears contradictory but Nietzsche's genius lies, in part, in his ability to trace the complex paradoxes in human relation, so often overlooked or disguised by reductive formulations of love as either egoistic avarice or benevolent generosity.

Nietzsche's proclamations about love and friendship in *Thus Spoke Zarathustra* are, again, initially perplexing but also yield surprising insights. He advises that a friend must also be recognised as an enemy – 'If you want a friend, you must be willing to wage war on him' (Nietzsche 2003: 82) – indicating that friendship involves an interruption of, and even an opposition to, our preconceived ideas and beliefs. Friends do not unquestioningly uphold, reinforce and echo our attitudes but provide new perspectives and interrogate our presuppositions. In addition, Nietzsche warns us not to reveal all to our friends. We are not gods, not perfect, and we ought not debase our friends or ourselves by appearing naked and revealing all our imperfections: 'He who makes no secret of himself excites anger in others: that is how much reason we have to fear nakedness! If you were gods you could then be ashamed of your clothes!' (ibid.: 83).

Nietzsche's advice, on both counts, seems counter-intuitive. Many believe that friends who criticise us, who fail to provide unconditional support, are false friends. On the other hand we believe that true friends have no secrets and that friendship is sustained through openness. But these two beliefs are contradictory, for complete openness must also allow expression of difference and disagreement. Nietzsche advises both discretion and challenge within friendship as, for him, friendship aims at a creative, transformative life. For Nietzsche, friendship involves not only a mutual desire for the new and for difference, but this is, in itself, also a yearning for a different way of life beyond the mundane ordinary life of the masses. Nietzsche values the exceptional and creative 'Overman' or 'Superman' over the ordinary person who unquestioningly accepts the norms and conventions of her society. Nietzsche uses terms such as the 'herd' and 'sheep' to describe the masses of ordinary people who complacently accept conventional ethics, politics and customary behaviours and attitudes. The Overman or Superman, who he also calls the noble, is not a dictator or master concerned with controlling and exploiting the herd, but is a creative passionate person who questions and overcomes small-minded conventions, petty attitudes and vacuous beliefs.

A friendship founded on craving for difference is a friendship that strives to overcome mundane life in favour of creative, passionate life. To achieve this involves discretion – keeping the secret of ones own pettiness and vacuousness – and also invokes criticism of these tendencies in the friend. The aim is the overcoming of ordinary existence through friendship: 'You cannot adorn yourself too well for your friend: for you should be to him an arrow and a longing for the Superman' (Nietzsche 2003: 83).

Interestingly, Nietzsche restricts this joint craving for the new and different to the realm of friendship implying that sexual love cannot provide this experience. Nietzsche claims that women are incapable of friendship (ibid.: 83–4) indicating that women cannot participate in this shared love of difference and explaining why heterosexual erotic love cannot attain shared love, for women foreclose this possibility. Understanding

Nietzsche's attitude to women then is central to unravelling his complex theories of love, desire and friendship.

Nietzsche contends that friendship involving passionate, creative longing for difference – a friendship that he elsewhere calls 'star friendship' (Nietzsche 1974: 225) in contrast to mundane conventional friendship – is impossible for both slaves and tyrants. Further, he claims that woman is both a slave and a tyrant and that therefore woman cannot participate in friendship. Surprisingly, as we will see in the next chapter, Simone de Beauvoir concurs with Nietzsche's evaluation of woman in this regard. For Beauvoir, women's restricted social and economic roles create dependency on men, producing slavish and tyrannical behaviour as a means of control (Beauvoir 1997: 652–78). Nietzsche's reasoning about women's slavery and tyranny is less clear. He writes:

> In a woman, a slave and a tyrant have long been concealed. For that reason, woman is not yet capable of friendship: she knows only love.
>
> In a woman's love is injustice and blindness towards all that she does not love. And in the enlightened love of woman, too, there is still the unexpected attack and lightning and night, along with the light.
>
> Woman is not yet capable of friendship: women are still cats and birds. Or, at best, cows. (Nietzsche 2003: 85–6)

The status of the figure of woman in Nietzsche's text has been controversial with many commentators concerned about his often apparently critical comments about, and negative portrayals of, femininity. While this concern ought not be lightly dismissed, the complexity and ambivalence of Nietzsche's images of woman cautions against a too easy rejection of Nietzsche as an out-and-out misogynist.

Sarah Kofman's analysis of Nietzschean woman in her paper 'Baubo: Theological Perversion and Fetishism' provides a more sympathetic interpretation that suggests Nietzsche's ambivalence about woman reveals a troubled love rather than an abjection or despising of the feminine. Two points are central to Kofman's argument. First, Nietzsche does not class all women together and thereby accuse femininity in general of degeneration. Rather just as Nietzsche distinguishes between weak and strong men, so too he makes a distinction between degenerate and life-affirming women. Second, Kofman suggests that Nietzsche's affirmative philosophy can be read in association with the conception of woman as life-giving and life-producing. Kofman focuses on Nietzsche's reference to the Greek mythological figure, Baubo. Nietzsche writes: 'Perhaps truth is a woman who has reasons for not letting us see her reasons? Perhaps her name is, to speak Greek, Baubo?' (Nietzsche, qtd in Kofman 1988: 194).

In Kofman's reading of Nietzsche the world, like the woman, may deceive or rather elude us by maintaining a certain modesty or distance, by veiling the 'truth', but this is not a matter of regret. Rather to acknowledge the ambiguity of the world and of woman is an affirmative engagement with the plurality and multiplicity of existence. Summarising, Kofman writes: 'Mastery means to know how to keep oneself at a distance . . . not to refuse appearance but to affirm it and laugh, for if life is ferocious and cruel, she is also fecundity and eternal return: her name is Baubo' (Kofman 1988: 196).

In Greek mythology Baubo is a figure of laughter, affirmation, rebirth and renewal of life who guides Demeter in her search for her daughter Persephone. Demeter, distraught and melancholy following the abduction of her daughter by the underworld god, Hades, is induced to laugh by Baubo who, imitating labour and lifting her skirts, produces (or reveals an image on her belly of) Demeter's son Iacchus (otherwise also called Dionysus). Kofman speculates: 'By lifting her skirts, was not Baubo suggesting that she [Demeter] go and frighten Hades, or that which comes to the same, recall fecundity to herself?' (ibid.: 196–7). Kofman's argument here is that Baubo suggests to Demeter that she fight Hades' death using her fertility and fecundity. Baubo represents the possibility of life and the affirmative attitude that loves life, that enables Persephone's rescue from the realm of death, and that wishes for the eternal return of life. This concept of 'eternal return' is central to Nietzsche's philosophy, indicating a love of life – a love so passionate that we wish each moment of our life to return endlessly. This wish for eternal return is a test of our affirmation of life: rather than resent or regret our life we embrace life so that we would welcome the endless repetition of our life. Baubo affirms life through laughter but also by reminding Demeter that she can rescue her daughter from the underworld and thereby allow her life to return. Moreover, Kofman suggests that Baubo also represents the female sex organs that symbolise fertility, regeneration and 'the eternal return of all things' (ibid.: 197).

For Nietzsche, then, woman is a complex figure who cannot be reduced to one essence or representation. Sometimes affirmative, sometimes negative, but never ignored nor simply relegated to insipid traditional femininity, woman occupies an ambiguous and varied role in Nietzsche's text. For Kofman this indicates an ambivalence suggestive of strong emotion and great love: 'The maxims and arrows Nietzsche directs toward women: is not their severity the mark of this ambivalence? Are they not symptomatic of a deep love of women . . . ?' (ibid.: 199). Given Nietzsche's insistence that friendship involves criticising our

friends and challenging them to adopt the more creative and transformative life of the 'Overman' perhaps Nietzsche's critique of woman may
be read, not as hatred, but as an incitement to repudiate the subordinations of common life.

Kofman's analysis suggests that Nietzsche's attitude to woman is
complex – at times negative, at others affirmative, Nietzsche refuses to ide-
alise femininity or to homogenise the diversity of women's experiences and
lives. If Nietzsche refuses to consider the possibility of female friendship,
describing women as slaves and tyrants and denigrating them as cats, birds
and cows, as animal-like and perhaps herd-like, he has also called men
sheep and follows his dismissal of woman friends with a questioning of
man's friendly capacities: 'Woman is not yet capable of friendship. But tell
me, you men, which of you is yet capable of friendship?' Women may be
animal-like but men have a 'poverty' and 'avarice of soul' that restricts
friendship allowing only 'comradeship' between men (Nietzsche 2003: 84).

Nietzsche, then, disturbs all our most cherished beliefs: for him love
is founded on greed; friendship involves secrecy and antagonism; women
and men both are incapable of star friendship attaining only a servile
form of love and comradeship respectively. But paradoxically he also
proclaims that greed for the unknown, undiscovered and different can
breed a higher friendship that seeks the new. Moreover, despite his depiction of women as slaves, and as incapable of friendship, he also concedes
that the enslaved may yet unchain her friend: 'Many a one cannot deliver
himself from his own chains and yet he is his friend's deliverer' (ibid.: 83).
While the slavish cannot be friends, they can free their friends form herd-
like conventionalism, suggesting that friendship has its ambiguities. Not
a friend and yet a friend, the woman and the man both, may yet desire,
long for and seek a higher friendship beyond the restrictions of slavish
love and impoverished comradeship.

Nietzsche's fragmentary commentary on love and friendship has been
interpreted in different ways. Irving Singer, in his 1987 third volume of
The Nature of Love describes Nietzsche's conception of love as dialectical and suggests that this movement between opposing perspectives is
resolved in Nietzsche's later works where he conceives love as developing from passionate fatality to spiritualised love. Singer contends that the
seeming contradictions in Nietzsche's work may be overcome by identifying a progressive narrative whereby the dangers inherent in love are
superseded by a higher 'spiritualised' love (Singer 1987: 84). This devel-
opmental interpretation (that echoes in some respects the Socratic evo-
lutionary model) risks, however, obscuring the insights offered in
Nietzsche's formulations.

In contrast to Singer, Alexander Düttmann's interpretation of Nietzsche insists on the necessary paradoxes operating in the experience of love. Düttmann's Nietzsche conducts a genealogical investigation into the origins of love only to find hidden and disavowed beliefs, values and attitudes as the motivation of love. Nietzsche is especially scathing about women's motivations in love (as we have seen) though he is hardly less critical of the common man's attitude. Woman's love is, for Nietzsche, a 'finer *parasitism*' that exists 'at the expense of the host' (qtd in Düttmann 1993: 286). Love is not selflessness, as is commonly believed, but a self-interested egoism (ibid.: 292). Moreover, love, in Nietzsche's view, is an illusion created to fill our experience of lack (ibid.: 288). But paradoxically it is these very attributes, which we most vehemently deny, that can potentially become the basis of a joyous love characterised by abundance, creativity and transformation. If love is founded on a feeling of lack and deprivation this also inaugurates a 'wanting-more' that may be the basis of a 'divine' as opposed to a 'slavely' love (ibid.: 289). This 'wanting-more' is not to be understood as a desire for more love that would provide fulfilment and thereby overcome the experience of lack. Rather 'wanting-more' is a desire for more than this settled and self-satisfied love; it is a desire for 'transformation and metamorphosis'; it is a movement reaching beyond the sameness of the self toward the outside, the different, and the other. It is, Düttmann writes: '*the originary opening of otherness* which never has the stability of a fixed or a fixing Being' (ibid.: 294).

Düttmann adroitly identifies the productive paradox in Nietzsche's thinking on love. Lack creates a need for more which will not be satisfied by the inducements of a common, comfortable, stable, love-relation but will instead constantly search for a beyond, for a creative, transforming difference. Lack then leads to love as wanting-more. Moreover, this also produces an abundance and giving-away:

> If love wants more than love, it is characterised by a lack. Without lack there is no wanting-more that opens up to the other and thus creates and metamorphoses the other. Because of its essential lack, love is more than mere lack. Lack is the excess, the richness, the abundance and over-abundance of a love that gives itself away, a love that only exists in a metamorphosing giving-away of itself . . . (ibid.: 293–4)

But, in another convolution of the paradox, this wanting-more of love also means that love is associated with contempt. If love wants more, this indicates that love despises the present situation that it wants to escape. Love is a searching beyond the sameness of the self, beyond the common

situation. It is a rejection of this self-enclosed circle of the same and a
reaching beyond. Love, then, born of lack searches for more beyond the
mundane, paltry, ordinary-ness of sameness. Moreover, this love inaugurated by lack in searching for more creates abundance and unrestricted
giving-away.

Düttmann's formulation of Nietzschean love as a lack that leads to
wanting-more recalls elements of Plato's *Symposium*. Aristophanes' story
of love as the restoration to wholeness of the two halves of a self cut
asunder by the gods also suggests that love originates in lack and a searching for more. Diotima's account of love as the child of poverty and plenty,
and her formulation of a higher love found in the abstract good, also indicate a trajectory from lack toward fulfilment. Yet, Nietzsche diverges
from this conventional interpretation of the Platonic model for while
Aristophanes and Diotima identify a moment of fulfilment in the reunion
with the lost other half, and in the love of the abstract good, Nietzsche
insists on the endlessness of the movement toward difference. As
Düttmann observes, in Nietzsche's formulation 'love do[es] *not* lead the
wanting-more to a satisfying disappearance in the sublation of all movement' (Düttmann 1993: 307). Indeed, the 'restitution of an originary unity'
is the erasure of the movement of love rather than its continuing existence.

In 'The Second Dance Song' in *Thus Spoke Zarathustra* Nietzsche
pushes the paradoxes of love further still revealing the ambiguity of love.
Love is not a symbiosis, a union of two halves, a melding of two lives
into one, but an engagement of differentiation, even disagreement and
disenchantment, and perhaps also enemy combat. She who allures me
also repels. She, who seduces, induces hate as well as love: '. . . who
would not hate you, great woman who binds us . . . seduces us . . . who
would not love you . . .' (Nietzsche 2003: 241). The passions of love are
not consistent and uniform but multitudinous and unpredictable.

Nietzsche's 'unruly paragon [and] . . . sweet, ungrateful tomboy'
(ibid.: 241) becomes in the course of this aphorism, variously an owl, bat,
ambiguous tooth-baring, mane-bearing, creature, snake, witch who
seduces and eludes the 'sheepish' and meek pursuer who in frustration
cracks his whip. The creaturely transmogrifications of both seducer and
seduced are associated with the dynamic movement, exchanges and
strategies of seduction that cause each lover to dance, sing, flee, leap
and chase. And the cracking whip reaffirms that love is imbricated with
lack, despising and hatred that are intrinsic to the creation and transformation of the wanting more of love.

In 'The Second Dance Song' life (which is loved passionately and
returns eternally) is represented as feminine. This beloved life/woman is

however chimerical, monstrous and bestial suggesting a further aspect of love: not simply complex and paradoxical, love is also a shape-shifter, transforming lover, beloved and world. The beloved with hissing hair and crooked smile is concurrently a 'child-eyed sinner', 'unruly paragon', 'sweet, ungrateful tomboy', a bat and owl, who learns from dogs to 'bark and howl', a maned creature, a snake, a witch, a 'wanton companion'. The lover is at once 'sheepish' and a shepherd. The world is night and dark waters, populated by serpents and goldfish, caves, dales, hills, lakes and sheep. Importantly, though, shape-shifter love is inextricably bound to the lack, the despising, the greed, and the wanting-more that lays the ground for difference (Nietzsche 2003: 241–2).

LANGUAGES OF LOVE

In his reflections on Nietzsche's conception of love Alexander Düttmann suggests that the experience of love cannot be separated from the invention of love stories. He suggests that 'narratability is inscribed into love' (Düttmann 1993: 287). Indeed, Düttmann's analysis of Nietzschean love is premised on an interpretation of Nietzsche's theory of language. Reading Section 268 of *Beyond Good and Evil* Düttmann proposes that for Nietzsche language expresses and communicates common, repeated, ordinary experiences and sensations. As a result the unusual, dangerous and different is excluded from language and from social relations. Nietzsche's conception of language is ambiguous in that it can be read as suggesting either that common experiences produce a common language and a unified people, or that common experience is produced by the structuring of language to exclude difference and foreground commonality. Either way, though, Düttmann contends, the commonality of language is founded on a danger or threat that needs to be alleviated through efficient common communication. This threat or danger indicates a difference that is suppressed in common language. But the experiences of love and friendship may uncover difference and threaten commonality and unity. Nietzsche suggests that discovering that a friend or lover understands the languages of love differently threatens ordinary servile forms of love: 'One makes this same test even in the case of friendships or love-affairs: nothing of that sort can last once it is discovered that when one party uses words he connects them with feelings, intentions, perceptions, desires, fears different from those the other party connects them with' (Nietzsche 1986: 186).

Düttmann illustrates using the common utterance 'I love you' asking whether the need to announce one's love already indicates a lack or doubt within love that needs to be assuaged through the reassurance of the utterance. Speaking of love reveals the ambiguities of love and its association with lack, loss, danger and suspicion so that Düttmann suggests: 'It is impossible to speak of love without taking its contingency into account, since there is no love beyond contingency' (Düttmann 1993: 278).

Düttmann's discussion suggests a complex structure inherent to language. When I utter 'I love you' I immediately raise the spectre of a lack of love, of a misunderstanding about the meaning of the utterance, of differing experiences and sensations that are obliterated in the abbreviating processes necessary to the creation of languages.

Düttmann goes on to link this argument to the idea of love as paradox. He suggests that commonness (in language and in love) 'contains an unavoidable and irreducible alterity' and that 'Love and friendship are the common experiences that uproot the common' (ibid.: 283). If language involves communicating common experience and tends to obliterate the uncommon in identifying the common, and if love is communicated through this reduced expression, then both language and love may involve not only misunderstanding and miscommunication but also a difference or alterity that is repressed but nevertheless haunts language and love. Love and friendship expose this alterity when communication jarringly fails to express a common or shared understanding or experience. Düttmann concludes that 'Love and friendship are experiences of the most common *as* the most monstrous' (ibid.: 284).

Mary Shelley's *Frankenstein* reveals the inherence of the monstrous in common ordinary love. Elizabeth, as emblem of familial love, becomes monstrous both in her nightmare transfiguration into the worm-ridden maternal corpse and in her anodyne, android-like, passivity and perfection. The hyperbolic romancing of family disguises this difference or alterity – here figured as morbid and abject – so as to preserve the commonality that language and love each strives to produce. The figure of the creature reveals more explicitly this language effect. While Elizabeth represents the repression of the monstrous within the everyday, the creature overtly depicts the difference and danger that common language excludes. The creature hopes to be accepted into human sociality but is instead feared and repudiated. Pleading for a mate to assuage his loneliness the creature says to his creator, Frankenstein:

> Remember, that I am thy creature; I ought to be thy Adam, but I am rather they fallen angel, whom thou drivest from joy for no misdeed. Everywhere I see bliss, from which I alone am irrevocably excluded. I was benevolent and good; misery made me a fiend. Make me happy, and I shall again be virtuous. (Shelley 2003: 103)

Initially persuaded, Frankenstein agrees to create a female creature but finally, appalled at the thought, he breaks his promise. The creature, the different, the other, teeters for a moment on the edge of recognition and acceptance but falls back into the monstrous. The creature seeks to be 'linked to the chain of existence and events' (ibid.: 150) from which he is excluded. Peter Brooks reads this as a desire for representation in language as well as culture. The creature wishes for a resemblance that would be legible in common language, for as Brooks explains: 'Exclusion from this chain [signifying chain of language] could be the very definition of monsterism' (Brooks 1978: 593). Yet the exclusion of the creature does not safeguard commonality from monstrosity for as Elizabeth demonstrates monstrosity lurks within the ordinary.

Nietzsche's genealogical investigation of love – his uncovering of the history of that which appears ahistorical – suggests that this monstrosity of love is not a freakish Frankensteinian aberration but intrinsic to the movement of love. Love, the most common of experiences, exposes the uncommon, exceptional and monstrous that is difference and alterity. It is this transfiguring effect, this ambiguity and danger, that is the gate to 'the full bliss of love' (Nietzsche 1982: 135).

The paradoxes of language and of love emulate each other: each is founded on commonality, yet each is haunted by a repressed alterity. This might hint that love is not amenable to a purely rational, philosophical analysis. Rather love eludes interrogation emerging only through the discourses of love. Düttmann suggests that 'there is no strict boundary between love and the love story'. 'Love', he says, 'itself generates its own fiction and is nothing other than its story' (Düttmann 1993: 287).

3

Simone de Beauvoir's Desperate Housewives

◌

The hit TV series *Desperate Housewives* depicts red-haired Bree as the model retro-1950s housewife and mother who cooks gourmet meals and keeps the house in perfect order. This ideal is, however, gradually exposed revealing turmoil beneath the superficial harmony. Refusing to allow her all too human family to mar her perfect, shiny life, Bree denies their feelings and represses her own, smiling her way through marriage break-up, and her children's rebellions, papering over disharmony and distress. While for husband, Rex, married life is made intolerable by Bree's controlling behaviour – even packing his suitcase when he decides to leave – Bree's control is superficial and her acts often subterranean, manipulative and subversive. Lacking overt power, she controls by stealth (sabotaging the sofa so her husband is forced to return to the marital bed) and through shaming (removing her son's bedroom door as punishment after he visits a strip club). Bree is both a slave and a tyrant, manipulating those she serves and services.

Marc Cherry's 'darkly comic' TV series has been condemned by conservatives as an assault on morality and by some feminists as a celebration of old-time family values, while others have applauded its ironic commentary on suburban life and commented on the influence of Betty Friedan's *Feminine Mystique* (1973) and David Lynch's *Twin Peaks* (1990–1). If *Desperate Housewives* does provide a tongue-in-cheek critique of the rituals and mores of love, romance and family life, in the process and no less sardonically, it also twists and refigures the soap opera, the sitcom and the small-town film genres revealing the fears, hatreds and desperation behind the pretty gardens and superficially happy families. While the TV series represents the issues with a new ironic postmodern twist, the critique of the family romance and erotic love itself is not new, Simone de Beauvoir having explored these ideas over fifty years ago. Through *Desperate Housewives*, however, Beauvoir's views are given an unexpected contemporary setting and relevance. Interpreting *Desperate Housewives* (Season 1, 2004) through and against Beauvoir writings exposes the continuing subordinated situation of women in an era convinced that it has at last attained, or is certainly moving quickly toward, women's full equality and freedom.

The representations of both the married woman, and the mistress, in *The Second Sex* destroy our fantasies of princess weddings and happy-ever-after marriages. For Beauvoir the heterosexual couple are enchained in a master–slave dialectic of modern love. The man as autonomous sovereign breadwinner is trapped by the relative dependency of his partner, while the woman, limited by this dependency, 'makes a weapon of her weakness' (Beauvoir 1997: 500). While both men and women are constrained by this situation Beauvoir insists that women suffer greater subordination due to their restricted opportunities. While a genuine form of love is possible, Beauvoir argues that this can only be experienced between partners who are equally free and this she suggests would be impossible in situations of sexual inequality. Genuine love she says would be 'founded on the mutual recognition of two liberties' but until that future day when women and men are equally free love remains a 'mortal danger' that mutates women into slaves and tyrants and threatens their existence and freedom.

Beauvoir agrees with Nietzsche that woman, wanting to be possessed, gives herself unconditionally in love, while man takes possession but always remains a sovereign subject never giving all to his beloved. While we saw in the last chapter that Nietzsche does not consign all women to this denigrated and subordinated position, and that he recognises a positive and transformative femininity, nevertheless he does not provide an analysis or explanation of women's subordinate position. Beauvoir, taking up Nietzsche's suggestion that women and men understand and experience love differently, investigates this difference, further revealing the differing situations which constitute male and female love. This enables Beauvoir to identify the pre-conditions necessary for the creation of genuine love: equality, freedom, mutual recognition, as well as the shared reaching out toward a new and differing future (which may perhaps be equated with Nietzsche's 'wanting-more').

While Nietzsche reveals the paradoxes of love, I will argue that Beauvoir reveals the ambiguities of love – the indeterminate, uncertain and uncontrollable effects and affects of love. Simone de Beauvoir's cautionary representations of love may seem extreme or no longer relevant as women move towards greater equality. Yet Beauvoir's insistence on the significance of freedom, equality and mutual recognition in the love relation constitutes an important challenge to existing theories and the basis for a critique of theories founded on self-sacrifice, boundless generosity, and unconditional bestowal of love.

PHENOMENOLOGICAL EXPERIENCE

Simone de Beauvoir's *The Second Sex* (published in French in 1949 and in English in 1953) has been subjected to several waves of interpretation in the English-speaking world. At first denigrated for its sexual explicitness, *The Second Sex* soon became a founding text for second wave feminism. Widely read as an empirical account of women's subordination it was perceived as a rebuttal of biological determinism and as exploration of the socialised production of gender. In this early reception Beauvoir's claim that 'one is not born but rather becomes a woman' was interpreted as a rejection of biology in favour of socialisation in explaining the creation of gendered subjects. On the other hand, as Moira Gatens has pointed out, Beauvior was also criticised for giving too much weight to the role and influence of the body (Gatens 2003: 270–1). More recently, however, Beauvoir's text has been re-read as a phenomenological investigation of the lived experience of women and men that looks beyond the biological, social and psychological attempting instead to understand the meaning of embodied existence. The 'becoming woman' in this later interpretation of Beauvoir is understood as a rejection of the idea of woman as a 'fixed or completed reality' (Beauvoir 1997: 66) in favour of a conception of her as an open-ended process of transformation, interrelation and becoming.

As a phenomenologist, Beauvoir begins by questioning all preconceived knowledges, assumptions and prejudices about sexual difference and by examining the situations of women and men. This does not involve simply a description of experience but instead attempts to identify the characteristic ways of relating to the world and styles of embodied interaction with the world. Identifying the inherent qualities and modalities of experience involves, in part, contrasting similar and distinct events and objects so as to discern their features. Beauvoir uses this phenomenological approach in *The Second Sex* to investigate the issue of sexual difference, suggesting first of all that existing understandings of human experience are inadequate in that they ignore or misrepresent the specificity of women's experience. She explains women's 'situation' focusing on the embodied, lived experience of woman. Rejecting the many myths of femininity, and avoiding simply viewing the body as an empirical object that can be described objectively, she attempts instead to investigate the manner and character of the living body. Beauvoir avoids a deterministic or essentialist account of femininity by refusing to describe a fixed or static being and focusing instead on the living, changing becoming of woman. This approach suggests that sexual difference is not primarily a physical bodily difference but is instead a matter of styles – of differing ways of moving, gesturing and expressing experience – though these differing styles will be expressed through and partially arise from differing material bodies (Heinämaa 2003: 37–44).

The body expresses an attitude and a relation to the world including other people. However, the body's modes and expressions do not reveal a meaning hidden behind the physical body – as though an inner being was revealed through its manifestations in the body – but are intrinsic to the body itself. The smile I perceive in the eyes and on the lips of the other does not reveal an inner state. Rather joy is evident in the smile and arises through my engagement with the other. This challenges the conventional understanding of the mind–body relation. We normally understand the body as driven by an inner mind or soul that is expressed in the gestures and movements of the body. The phenomenological approach instead suggests that the mind cannot be separated from the body but rather suffuses the body, and that the surface expressions of the body are themselves the operation of personhood (ibid.: 39).

In Beauvoir's phenomenology the body is not just inert matter moved into action by the mind, like a machine moved by an energy source, but a unified style that arises from its being in the world, or rather, its becoming through its relations and engagements with the world. The body understood in this way develops a characteristic mode through its habitual actions, movements and gestures, so that different bodies are distinguishable by their modalities. The differences between women and men, then, are not simply physical but are stylistic, consisting of differing characteristic habitual styles of comportment and expression (Young 1990: 141–59).

All of this suggests that, as Beauvoir writes in *The Second Sex*: 'the body is not a *thing*, it is a situation . . . it is the instrument of our grasp upon the world . . .' (Beauvoir 1997: 66). But as Beauvoir also makes clear, the body is not only an instrument (this would be just one aspect of the way we perceive the body) but is also affective. That is the body lives the experience of joys and fears, wonder and sadness. Perceiving the body in this way – as an affective, characteristic and habitualised style of existing – allows the question of woman to be approached differently. Rather than asking 'what woman is', as though we could define her by describing her essential features, it allows Beauvoir instead to ask 'how woman is' (Heinämaa 2003: 70). Woman would not then be defined by physical attributes such as womb and breasts but would be perceived in terms of her way of being in the world – her temporal and spatial and relational modes of becoming: 'the terms that characterise the fundamental connections between women are not nouns such as female vulva, or womb, but adverbs: that is, the expressions that specify verbs' (ibid.: 68).

This is not to ignore the body, but to enable a different perception of the body. The body is not merely biological, nor is it simply an instrument; rather the body is my existence, experience and being in the world. Yet the body can also feel alien to me disrupting an absolute unity of self and body. This experience of the body as an alien obstacle becomes evident, for example, in illness when my body thwarts my intentions confining me to a bedridden existence against my desire for movement, work, play, pleasure and activity. While all bodies may be experienced as alien in this way, for Beauvoir, women's bodies can be particularly strange or estranged. Menstruation, pregnancy, lactation, childbirth all foreground the dual modes of the body as both myself and somehow other. In the experience of pregnancy, for example, the foetus is both 'an enrichment and an injury', 'a part of her body, and . . . a parasite' (Beauvoir 1997: 512). This equivocal experience of being one with the foetus and yet separated from it undermines self/other and subject/object dichotomies epitomizing the ambiguity of the lived body: 'in the mother-to-be the antithesis of subject and object ceases to exist: she and the child with which she is swollen make up together an equivocal pair overwhelmed by life' (ibid.: 512).

Beauvoir has been criticised for her apparently negative portrayals of women's bodies but this obscures Beauvoir's attempt to understand the double aspect of the body as both means by which we live in the world and also at the same time a limitation on our possible experience. The body limits my possibilities while it also facilitates them and while women and men both experience this double aspect of embodied existence it is more evident, and is experienced more intimately in the lived situation of the woman (Heinämaa 2003: 71).

One of the insights of Beauvoir's philosophy is the ambiguity that we experience as a result of experiencing the body as both the means and the limitation on our engagement with the world. In addition though, there is also a more fundamental ambiguity at the heart of existence. Beauvoir identifies two attitudes to our own existence. In the first we are aware of our being and our existence within an inter-subjective world; we perceive the world and our selves within it; we are exposed to the world and the world is disclosed to us. In the second we insist on the my-ness of the world; we impose ourselves on the world and on others appropriating it as our determination of it. Beauvoir writes: 'There is an original type of attachment to being which is not the relationship "wanting to be" but rather "wanting to disclose being" . . . [in which] man makes himself present to the world and makes the world present to him' (Beauvoir 1994: 12).

These two attitudes, of disclosure and of domination, structure our existence creating an ambiguity in our attitude to and relation with others and the world. Debra Bergoffen explains: 'The moments of revelation [wanting to disclose being] and appropriation [wanting to be] contest each other. They are also bound to each other. Their contested bond is the ground for what Beauvoir calls the ambiguity of the human condition' (Bergoffen 1997: 77).

Ambiguity is also evident in Beauvoir's formulation of immanence and transcendence. Immanence is associated with an animal-like existence that is tied to bodily life. Transcendence involves a reaching beyond this corporeality and an engagement with the world. For Beauvoir, women are constrained to a life of immanence through their association with the bodily functions of reproduction and birth and the activities of caring for others. Men, free to engage in the public worlds of work, politics and community, are able to engage with and transform the world transcending the limits of immanence in the body. However, for Beauvoir women may also choose transcendence though there are social and political constraints on this choice limiting, but not totally destroying, women's options. For Beauvoir, we always have a degree of freedom that enables us to choose how we express and pursue our embodied situations: we have, at least to some degree, a choice between immanence and transcendence. For Beauvoir then there is an ambiguous freedom that despite limitations enables us to create and pursue life projects beyond the constraints of immanence.

In *The Second Sex* Beauvoir explains how, historically, women have been confined to a life of immanence. She investigates biological, psychological and historical accounts of this situation but while these provide some insight, Beauvoir concludes that they cannot wholly explain women's subordination. Instead, she proposes that sexual inequality arises from repeated, larger and smaller, acts of aggression and oppression. While Beauvoir suggests that women's reproductive role contributes to women's marginalisation it is not the origin or cause but rather a justification for the exclusion of women. Beauvoir instead suggests that women's subordination has become habitualised and normalised through the endless reiteration of the sexual hierarchy (Heinämaa 2003: 104).

Through repeated acts of subordination women are confined to immanence, not through necessity, but through culturally habituated behaviours (see Deutscher 2006 for a detailed discussion of the multiple conceptualisations of repetition in Beauvoir's work). Beauvoir does not deny that objectification of the other person occurs in self–other relations. We may perceive the other as a non-intentional thing and fail to recognise their subjectivity. However, she does suggest that objectification is not the only mode of relation: experiencing ourselves as subjects we attribute this to others and additionally in desiring to communicate our subjectivity we call upon the subjectivity of the other.

However, in male–female relations Beauvoir suggests there is a habituated forgetting or occlusion of women's subjectivity so that women become fixed in objecthood. They are not only objects occasionally but permanently and so become property, matter and a resource for exploitation:

> . . . when a woman is given over to a man as property, he demands that she represent the flesh purely for its own sake. Her body is not perceived as the radiation of a subjective personality, but as a thing sunk deeply in its own immanence; it is not for such a body to have reference to the rest of the world, it must not be the promise of things other than itself: it must end the desire it arouses. (Beauvoir 1997: 189)

The consequences of this situation are for Beauvoir disastrous for women's lives in general and for the love relation in particular. In the second volume of *The Second Sex* Beauvoir examines women's 'situation' or her embodied lived experience devoting a number of chapters to women's erotic and amorous relations. She examines the experience of sexual initiation as well as those of the wife, the mistress, the prostitute, and of the lesbian, concluding in each case that sexual inequality constrains women's possibilities and damages love relations. Nevertheless, Beauvoir insists that women retain an ambiguous freedom, within the limits of her concrete situation, to reject her subordination and to seek authentic love.

BEAUVOIR'S DESPERATE HOUSEWIVES

In her examination of 'The Woman in Love' Beauvoir refers to Nietzsche's reflections on the differences between women's and men's experiences of love and while she agrees with his observations she clarifies that these differences are not biological or natural but arise from differing 'situations'. Man, as the transcendent creature, is able to extend his relations with the world and to transform his world. Woman, relegated to immanence, is unable to achieve self-realization through actions in the world and as a result seeks an indirect, vicarious, transcendence through her male lover or partner (Beauvoir 1997: 653). Even when mutual love exists, Beauvoir argues, there remains a difference in the feeling and experience of love for man and woman. Man 'justifies himself' and lives in the world as a subject independently of her. Woman, on the other hand, requires him for her existence – if not for her physical and economic well being then certainly in order to gain a sense of identity and an indirect transcendence (ibid.: 670).

As Beauvoir argues, however, if woman is dependent on man for her sense of being, or subjectivity, she thereby becomes trapped in a situation that is partly of her own making. Beauvoir reveals the ambiguity of this situation describing how woman's freedom is limited by her situation; but also insisting that she nevertheless retains an ability to either accept these constraints or repudiate them. Woman is 'doomed to immanence,' 'shut up in the sphere of the relative' and 'habituated to seeing him as a superb being whom she cannot possibly equal.' Yet she also 'chooses to desire her enslavement' and 'will try to rise above her situation as inessential object by fully accepting it' (ibid.: 653). Beauvoir suggests that even when women have the opportunity to seek independence they often prefer dependency, as 'it is agonizing for a woman to assume responsibility for her life' (ibid.: 655). Boys, she says, are trained to assume responsibility and to see themselves as sovereign subjects; girls encouraged to 'follow the easy slopes' so that seeking her own liberty becomes disconcertingly arduous.

The excessive measures to which the *Desperate Housewives* resort to retain or attract their men at once testifies to this dependency imperative but also gently satirises and ridicules this situation through exaggeration and caricature. Bree, the uptight anachronistic 1950s white-picket-fence wife, tries to win back her man by arriving, clad only in a fur coat and lingerie (reprising the classic seduction exemplified by Liz Taylor in the 1960 film *Butterfield 8*), at her husband's hotel room, only to be distracted mid-seduction by a falling burrito that threatens to mess the carpet (Season 1, Episode 6). This scene does not simply reproduce the tired old traditional seduction scene, but, by juxtaposing it with housewifely obsession with cleanliness and order, gently sends up and mocks both these stereotypes. The contradiction between sex-goddess and perfect homemaker is revealed, allowing a questioning of both idealised feminised roles. The obsession with 'catching' the man is especially evident in the competition between Edie and Susan over Mike. Blonde bimbo Edie, and sweet single-mom Susan vie for the attentions of new neighbour Mike, leading to a series of misadventures: house fires, canine choking, missed dates and misunderstandings (Season 1, Episode 2). But here again the stereotyped representation of women fighting over a man is parodied rather than sanctified. 'Good girl' Susan is pitted against 'sultry' Edie and both characters are cartoon-like caricatures of this conventional Madonna/whore dichotomy. By exaggerating the stereotypes, the stereotypes are themselves rendered bizarre and unlikely, undermining their credibility.

The TV soap explores the varying desperate strategies that women employ to attract men and, rather than normalise and extol, it parodies gesturing to the outlandish oddity of conventionalised courting conduct. If Beauvoir provides a phenomenological account of women's obsession with, devotion to, and worship of love, *Housewives* denaturalises love, making it strange, by using farce to reveal the bizarre behaviours inherent in the sexual relation.

For Beauvoir, women's acceptance of immanence and attempt to disguise this by seeking indirect transcendence through her male partner is a form of annihilation. In taking on the role of the second sex woman looses her freedom and her subjectivity – though, Beauvoir concedes, woman desires and hopes to be rescued from her plight by her lover and thereby achieve salvation. Beauvoir compares woman's worship of her lover with religious devotion:

> . . . this dream of annihilation is in fact an avid will to exist. In all religions the adoration of God is combined with the devotee's concern for personal salvation; when woman gives herself completely to her idol, she hopes that he will give her at once possession of herself and of the universe that he represents. In most cases she asks her lover first of all for the justification, the exaltation, of her ego. (Beauvoir 1997: 656)

Woman's attempt to find herself through the other though is fraught. Beauvoir suggests that in the sexual relation both women and men (but more frequently women) can be treated as an 'instrument' by their partners. She is often the carnal object, or the prey in the game of seduction, and this, far from recognising her subjectivity, turns her into a thing. Yet, as a thing, she craves even more the attentions of her partner to reassure her of her existence (ibid.: 658).

Of course, women also play the seduction game setting out to entice and enchant her object of desire. Her strategies, however, differ from that of man: she adorns her body and gives her body; he evaluates and takes her body. Housewife Susan anticipating Mike's arrival dresses in the conventionally seductive attire of lingerie and Mike's appraisal and affirmation (in an earlier scene) of her naked body provides the recognition she demands. This earlier scene recalls the naked-in-the bushes scene in the 1946 Frank Capra small-town film *It's a Wonderful Life*. Susan looses her bath towel in the yard and hides as Mike walks by. Pretending to be oblivious he confirms a planned date, adding jokingly 'I assume the dress is casual' (Season 1, Episode 3). The similar scene in *Wonderful Life* has the disrobed Donna Reed hiding in the bushes as her date James Stewart jokingly ponders his options. The gentlemanly gallantry of the earlier film is undercut in the satirising TV series when Mike admits that he sneaked a peak though he is redeemed as a suitable suitor by complementing Susan: 'And for what it's worth, wow!' he proclaims. Through her body Susan receives the affirmation and recognition she desires.

Of course to suggest that woman is simply and only objectified would be to gainsay the pleasures, the ecstasy and the transcendence that can be experienced in the sexual encounter, as Beauvoir acknowledges (Beauvoir 1997: 659). Moreover, woman can also reverse convention and treat her partner as a mere instrument – and Beauvoir does not deny this possibility either. Finally, of course, the pleasures inherent in passivity, in objectification, in conventional strategies of desire and seduction ought not be overlooked or denied. Yet, Beauvoir's suggestion is that too often women become trapped in the role of object and in the situation of immanence, undermining her ability to participate in transcendence.

Beauvoir's further point is that having turned to man, as the means to attain an *ersatz* transcendence, woman then becomes both a slave and a tyrant in the sexual relation. Hoping to maintain his attachment she makes herself his slave and fearing the loss of his devotion she becomes a tyrant. She serves him, Beauvoir writes, so that 'she will be integrated with his existence, she will share his worth, she will be justified' (ibid.: 660). Having lost her sense of self and seeking validation through the other she attempts to become one with him; to create an 'identification with the loved one' (ibid.: 663) through the union of their two selves into one. Beauvoir cites Catherine's love of Heathcliff in *Wuthering Heights* as illustration:

> 'I am Heathcliff,' says Catherine in *Wuthering Heights*; that is the cry of every woman in love; she is another incarnation of her loved one, his reflection, his double: she is *he*. She lets her own world collapse in contingence, for she really lives in his. (ibid.: 663)

One of the outcomes of her worship of, and dependence on, her male lover is that he must inevitably disappoint her idealisation of him and it is a 'searing disappointment' when she discovers his failings. The woman perceives her lover as either divine or bestial, refusing to recognise his mundane humanness. For the woman trapped in this form of inauthentic love, Beauvoir writes, 'A fallen god is not a man: he is a fraud' (ibid.: 665). Old-fashioned housewife Bree personifies this contradiction. She initially worships her husband and attempts to secure her marriage through manipulation and control. But when she discovers her husband's 'failings' – his fetishist bondage fantasies that he satisfies with a neighbour who has a secret life as a home-based sex worker – her contempt and wrath are deadly. Following his first heart attack Bree tells Rex that she's going to engage a divorce lawyer to 'eviscerate' him adding: 'I'm glad you didn't die before I had a chance to tell you that' (Season 1, Episode 10). On a relationship rollercoaster Bree subsequently attempts to reconcile with Rex by dating their local chemist, George, hoping to make Rex jealous and so re-animate his original love and desire, but the antagonism, manipulation and mistrust only intensify. Rex's final and fatal heart attack, precipitated by George tampering with Rex's heart medication, leaves Bree cold and detached – a state she justifies by the need to support Rex's grieving mother.

For Beauvoir, Bree's vindictive behaviour would be explained in relation to her original unrealistic idealisation: her worship of her husband as a god means that his failure will be regarded as absolute evil. 'If he is no longer adored, he must be trampled on' (Beauvoir 1997: 665): if he is no longer superhuman than he must be inhuman.

Nevertheless, Bree's dependence on him results in one more attempt to secure their relationship and her flirtation with George would also be for Beauvoir a predictable strategy of inauthentic love. If the man's love wanes the desperate woman lover pretends to reassert her independence by flirting with another. She hopes thereby to arouse jealousy and inflame passion (ibid.: 675). Such strategies are fraught. This indifferent lover seeing through the strategy may be further alienated. Or he may, believing the flirtation genuine, see it as a justification for his escape. The flirting woman is caught in a double-bind for her strategy to regain her love may well instead destroy the remnants of love (ibid.: 675)

But this desperate strategy is not the only ambiguity, paradox or contradiction within the situation of inauthentic love. For Beauvoir, inauthentic love is based on paradox. In loving her partner as a god what the woman worships is at least in part his freedom and transcendence. Yet, in binding him to her she undermines this transcendence. 'This is the torture of impossible love,' Beauvoir writes, 'the woman wants to possess the man wholly, but she demands that he transcend any gift that could possibly be possessed: a free being cannot be *had*' (ibid.: 668). Moreover, woman's servility also creates a paradox. She hopes to serve her idealised master, yet in doing so she becomes dependent on him and even a burden (ibid.: 671).

It is not, however, only the attributes and actions of the woman that creates these amorous contradictions. Man, too, contradictorily, wants to own absolutely, to possess and to control, his partner but he also wants her free and distant so as to maintain her mystery and allure: '. . . he wants his mistress to be absolutely his yet a stranger; he wants her to conform exactly to his dream and to be different from anything he can imagine, a response to his expectation and a complete surprise' (ibid.: 674–5).

Both man and woman become trapped in the irreconcilable contradiction, the Catch-22, of love. Woman tries to become what her man desires and in so doing loses that which had constituted her allure – her freedom, her difference, her unexpected alterity: 'Giving herself blindly, woman has lost that dimension of freedom which at first made her fascinating' (ibid.: 675).

The underlying paradox of inauthentic love, however, occurs at the outset. In giving herself to her partner the woman hopes to achieve freedom and transcendence through him. Yet this act is precisely the destruction of freedom and transcendence. She becomes dependent, passive, reliant and trapped in immanence and thereby annihilates her own transcendence.

Beauvoir's argument seems to suggest that at least for woman, and possibly also for man, love is an inevitable bondage. Each is trapped by the paradoxes of love – though man at least is less likely to orient his life exclusively around this relation. However, Beauvoir's account of love also allows the possibility of a genuine experience of love in which each lover would approach the other from a position of equal freedom – and each would recognise the freedom of the other. On this basis each partner could move towards transcendence, could engage with and transform the world and remain open to new, different and transforming futures:

> Genuine love ought to be founded on the mutual recognition of two liberties; the lovers would then experience themselves as self and as other: neither would give up transcendence, neither would be mutilated; together they would manifest values and aims in the world. For the one and the other, love would be a revelation of self by the gift and enrichment of the world. (Beauvoir 1997: 677)

When equality is present, Beauvoir suggests, the erotic encounter provides a pleasure involving flesh and spirit, subject and object, self and other. This embodied and equal love overcomes the sacrificial gift offered in inauthentic love, transforming it into a 'generosity of the flesh' (Diprose 2002: 86; see also Vintges 1996 and Bergoffen 1997 for astute discussions of the relation between love, erotics and ethics in Beauvoir). Where there is equality, Beauvoir writes:

> . . . if he lusts after her flesh while recognising her freedom . . . her integrity remains unimpaired while she makes herself an object . . . under such conditions the lovers can enjoy a common pleasure, in the fashion suitable for each, the partners feeling the pleasure as being his or her own but as having its source in the other . . . Under a concrete and carnal form there is a mutual recognition of the ego and of the other. (Beauvoir 1997: 421–2)

Surprising as it may at first seem we may detect moments of this more fulfilling and enriching love even among the *Desperate Housewives*. Gabrielle, a 'trophy' wife kept by her husband, Carlos, appears at first to be a bimbo-in-bondage to her marriage. But, as soon becomes apparent, she refuses to acquiesce to his expectation that she become the perfect docile grateful wife and immediately embark on baby-making. Defying his insistence that she produce children she pursues an affair with their young gardener John. She does not worship Carlos as a god, does not enslave herself to him, and pursues her own pleasures and interests against his orders and wishes. Their marriage is certainly not a perfect genuine and free love but nevertheless struggling within a limited situation to create her own life and follow her own desires, Gabrielle refuses to be trapped in the passive dependent constraints of immanence. Moreover, in her affair with John a moment of genuine love may be glimpsed. John's gift of a single rose (clichéd as it is) signifies for Gabrielle a more genuine attachment that Carlos's gift of a new sports car (Season 1, Episode 2). While there are inequalities in both Gabrielle's relationships what characterises both is her desire for freedom, and in the affair with John she hopes too for his freedom, encouraging him to give up his gardening business to pursue further education despite the threat this represents for their relationship.

Bringing together Beauvoir's 1949 French philosophical text with the 2004 USA popular TV soap discloses the ongoing relevance of Beauvoir's work and perhaps provides a framework for reading and contextualising the desperation of the housewives. The comparison reveals connections between these two texts, but there are also differences in these portrayals of desperate love. Beauvoir's account is a phenomenological analysis of differing situations of women and men and the resulting divergent styles of their love relations. *Desperate Housewives* does not represent a phenomenology of love but rather focuses on the surface performances of love and on the influence of earlier love stories on current love relations. The Bree character re-enacts Elizabeth Taylor's classic *Butterfield 8* seduction scene; Susan and Mike mimic, though they also transform, the naked-in-the-bushes scene from *It's a Wonderful Life*. Though each text reveals the constraints, the ambiguities, and the desperation of love, each gives a different account of this situation. For Beauvoir women's immanence constrains and distorts her love relations, for *Desperate Housewives* love is created through cultural codes that repeat the constraints and limitations on gender relations and loving engagements. These differences, already evident in the comparison of *The Second Sex* and *Housewives,* becomes more evident still through a reading of Beauvoir's novel *She Came to Stay*.

THE AMBIGUITY OF LOVE

She Came to Stay explores the changing experiences, perceptions and emotions of the protagonist Françoise as her love relation with Pierre is transformed from a conventional coupling into a *ménage au trois* with Xavière's entry into their lives. While the lesbian erotic love between Françoise and Xavière is only implicitly hinted at and the physical desire between Pierre and Xavière never fully consummated varying forms of obsessional, devotional, genuine and slavish love circulate between the trio. Françoise at first conceives her relation with Pierre as a unity. Pierre says to Françoise: 'You and I are simply one. It's true, you know. Neither one of us can be defined without the other' (Beauvoir 1999: 25) and Françoise affirms this perception: 'We are simply one' (Beauvoir 1999: 26). But Xavière disrupts this unity and ultimately threatens not just Françoise's relationship with Pierre but also Françoise's consciousness itself. Françoise feels her connection with Pierre destroyed: 'She turned to Pierre; she needed to regain contact with him, but she had separated herself too completely. She could not succeed in attuning herself to him. She was alone' (ibid.: 285). Confronted by the evolving relation between Pierre and Xavière, a relationship that attempts to exclude her, Françoise at first attempts to subsume her needs, to repress her anguish, in order to enable their idealised trio to flourish. Finally however she feels negated, diminished, destroyed by this ongoing self-denial:

> On many occasions she had been stabbed by jealousy. She had been tempted to hate Pierre, to wish Xavière ill; but, under the futile pretext of keeping herself pure, she had created a void within herself. In contrast, Xavière, with calm audacity, chose to assert herself to the utmost. As recompense she had a definite place in the world, and Pierre turned to her with passionate interest.

Françoise had not dared to be herself, and she understood in a passion of suffering, that this hypocritical cowardice had led her to being nothing at all. (Beauvoir 1999: 287–8)

Françoise feels Xavière as a 'hostile presence' not only because Xavière attempts to usurp her in Pierre's affections but also more generally. As Françoise continually negates herself in favour of a utopian ethical love between three, Xavière manipulating this situation for her own ends asserts herself until: 'The entire universe is engulfed in it [Xavière's consciousness], and Françoise, forever excluded from the world, was herself dissolved in this void' (ibid.: 291).

In her relationship with Pierre there was mutual recognition so that Françoise does not find Pierre's separate consciousness threatening, but Xavière refuses to recognise, to acknowledge, Françoise's subjectivity transforming her into an instrument, and object, of Xavière's manipulation. Françoise begins to perceive this situation in a discussion with Pierre:

'The moment you acknowledge my conscience, you know that I acknowledge one in you, too. That makes all the difference.'
'Perhaps,' said Françoise . . . 'In short, that is friendship. Each renounces his pre-eminence. But what if either one refuses to renounce it?'
'In that case, friendship is impossible,' said Pierre.
Xavière never renounced any part of herself. No matter how high she placed someone else, even if it amounted to worship, that person remained an object to her. (Beauvoir 1999: 301–2)

Beauvoir's novel is prefaced by a quote from Hegel: 'Each consciousness seeks the death of the other' and it ends with Françoise murdering Xavière who had herself been annihilating Françoise's subjectivity. Beauvoir elaborates Hegel's claim that we all attempt to subjugate others illustrating this through the battle between the two women. This is not, for her, simply a fight over a man but a contest for recognition. Each seeks recognition by the other: the failure to gain recognition threatens subjectivity creating a mutual contest with each seeking the other's recognition. Xavière refuses to recognise Françoise and this is itself already to annihilate Françoise as a subject. Françoise's murder of Xavière then may be read as a form of self-defence against Xavière's annihilating refusal to recognise her friend.

However, the novel also explores the situations in which each subjectivity engages with rather than obliterating the other. The relationship between the two women is not just a struggle for recognition and for domination but is also, ambivalently, a relationship of love. At the outset

Françoise feels affection for the younger woman and this gradually transforms into a passionate love. Referring to the relationship between Pierre and Xavière, Françoise declares her own love from Xavière: 'A closely united couple is something beautiful enough, but how much more wonderful are three persons who love each other with all their being . . . Because, after all, it is certainly a kind of love that exists between you and me' (Beauvoir 1999: 210) There is love between the women but there is also antipathy and struggle for recognition.

The relationship between Françoise, Xavière and Pierre demonstrates the ambiguity that for Beauvoir structures human existence. Françoise's experiences this ambiguity in her changing attitudes toward the threesome she forms with Xavière and Pierre. Françoise moves between an attitude of openness and disclosure, 'wanting to disclose being', and an attitude of domination or appropriation, or 'wanting to be'. Initially, she welcomes Xavière enjoying her friendship and encouraging the emerging friendship between Xavière and Pierre. But the other aspect of human experience – the wish to assert oneself, to possess and control the situation and others in it, shadows this openness and engagement.

Françoise's reflections on her relationship with Xavière suggest a battle for recognition between them with the latter seeming to reject and to ignore and to negate the former's subjectivity. But there is also a welcoming and generous engagement that represents the inter-subjective disclosure that animates life. Françoise is caught in this ambiguity – wishing for a loving engagement, Françoise is thwarted by the world's and Xavière's resistance. This simultaneously reveals the separation and distance between the self and the world, which constitutes difference of the other, and also provokes Françoise's other attitude that wants to dominate and so to 'be'.

Beauvoir's novel then reveals the ambiguity that conditions not just human subjectivity but also the love relation. In *The Second Sex* this vacillation and paradox was associated with the ambiguous freedom that enables a limited choice between transcendence and immanence. While for Beauvoir women are often caught up with the immanence of reproductive embodied existence, this may be resisted enabling an engagement with the world more broadly. Despairing of this possibility, women may seek a second-hand transcendence through the love relation. This false transcendence though only makes the woman more dependent and desperate resulting in subservience or tyranny. This choice is, for Beauvoir, a form of false consciousness as despite the limitations on her freedom, the woman may choose transcendence so that she may become an equal in the love relation. This would create an authentic love that enables the pleasures of love and erotics to be mutually experienced and shared.

In *She Came to Stay* the ambiguity of love is further disclosed. Subjectivity is founded on an ambiguous relation between 'being' and 'disclosing'. The disclosing openness to the world facilitates the possibility of love: through this aspect of subjectivity we engage with, enjoy, and perceive the world and the other in their difference. But the self also attempts to assert itself as a 'being,' to have mastery, control and possession and this creates conflict with the world and the other. Love stumbles and disintegrates when each consciousness insists on being recognised by the other as this autonomous master. In *She Came to Stay* the failure of love between Françoise and Xavière is not just a result of their jealous contest for Pierre. It is also a result of the ambiguity of subjectivity and love – an ambiguity that moves between the joy of engagements and the defensive isolation of being autonomous.

While Beauvoir's stories of love and the TV series *Desperate Housewives* both examine the rituals, changing conventions and challenging re-conceptualisations of love, these partial affinities should not negate the equally significant differences between these works. Unlike Beauvoir's stories, *Desperate Housewives* is not a phenomenological examination of the subject and her relations with others, nor of the ambiguity that disturb our identities and our loving identifications. The narrative remains focused on the externally observable actions, conversations, and experience of the characters who are caricatures, not complex ambiguous or nuanced personalities. Bree is the strait-laced traditional housewife, Edie the Barbie-body party-girl, Susan the innocent and sweet girl-next-door, Gabrielle the spirited Latino, Lynette the harried stay-at-home mother. Instantly recognisable stereotypes, these cutout figures are used not to reveal the complexity of subjectivity but to establish and then challenge our conventional categorisations, prejudices and assumptions.

Desperate Housewives focuses on the surface performance or performativity of the characters and explains the characters' love relations, not through the ambiguous freedom offered in immanence and transcendence, nor through the struggle between revelation and appropriation, but through the iteration and repetition of images and stories of love that influence and shape subsequent love relations.

In *Desperate Housewives* the focus on consciousness is replaced by a focus on performativity – on external actions and behaviours. In addition *Desperate Housewives* positions this performativity within a discourse, a history, a culture, a language, which all act upon and influence the performative subjectivities of each character. Each character is a stereo-typed image of femininity constructed by cultural technologies – film, theatre, TV, novels – and cultural codes, rituals and practices. Bree acts not just as a result of inner reflections and calculations but, influenced by a cultural repertoire, iterates the seduction scenes of earlier films when she tries to regain the desires of her estranged husband. Susan and Edie are not just two consciousnesses locked in struggle but perform the cul-tural stereotypes of cat-fighting, bitchy jealous competition for a man. The homes used in the series recall the white-picket-fence staging of earlier feel-good family sitcoms, and small-town films with the *Leave It To Beaver* TV home reprised for Mary Alice's family. This reprising of the past is not nostalgia, nor is it simply parody. Rather *Desperate Housewives* reveals how earlier stories, images and rituals of familial and erotic love infuse and produce our current fantasies and behav-iours. Love, here, becomes not an inner state but a culturally narrated performance.

The Second Sex, She Came to Stay, and *Desperate Housewives* all disrupt our romantic visions of love. Beauvoir achieves this in *The Second Sex* through a phenomenological account of the slavery and tyranny that lie behind unfree, unequal love. In *She Came to Stay* the dream of unity with the other, and the hope for an ethical generosity between lovers is questioned by the revelation of the fraught ambiguity between disclosure and appropriation, or between 'disclosing being' and 'wanting to be'. Love and friendship may arise through mutual openness and recognition between subjects, but refusal to acknowledge the other, instead treating the other as object, thereby destroys the possibility of love. *Desperate Housewives* also destabilises the myths of love. Love, here, is not associated with the ambiguity of human subjectivity but is a reiteration, a mimicry, a performance of the stories and fables, the images and depictions, the fairytale and Hollywood romancing of love. This is not to suggest that the loves of the 'housewives' are insincere but rather to suggest that this TV series recognises that our identities and our rela-tionships are shaped and formed through the narratives that form our cultural understandings of love. In this perspective, love as we live it is a love story – a story we are given, but a story that, through reiteration, we can also transform.

4

Levinas: Love, Justice and Responsibility

∞

Ethical frameworks are generally formulated on the basis of reason, duty, or the greatest good; or even, for some, in terms of self-interest. Love seems to have little direct relevance here. Yet, the relation of love emerges as a crucial element in the ethical reflections of the French philosopher, Emmanuel Levinas. For Levinas the personal, ethical and political relation between the self and the other is central: these relations are founded on or conditioned by love. For Levinas the inter-human relation, named by him the face-to-face relation, is the most important philosophical issue – the first issue that philosophy should address. The face of the other calls the self to take responsibility for the other so that we are all and each responsible for the other, even before ourselves. The face-to-face relation reveals our responsibility to put the other's needs before our own.

This formulation of our ethical responsibility is intertwined in various crucial ways, in Levinas's work, with both the issue of love and that of sexual difference. For Levinas all ethical social relations are an expression of love. He even suggests that 'responsibility for my neighbor . . . is . . . the harsh name for what we call love of one's neighbor' (Levinas 1998b: 103). This claim reveals a link between Levinas's ethics and his reflections on love. In addition, Levinas investigates and articulates various other forms of love – and these, it turns out, are all related in some way to the selfless, ethical, love of the neighbour. Throughout his works Levinas discusses not only ethical love but also maternal, erotic, and paternal love. Intrinsic to these varying conceptualisations is the issue of sexual subjectivity and sexual difference. Levinas's intricate analyses reveal or postulate new perspectives on the phenomenology of love and also elaborates these in relation to the intersecting issues of ethics, politics and sexual difference.

Hiroshima, mon amour (directed by Alain Resnais and written by Marguerite Duras), does not replicate but supplements Levinas's ethics. It stages aspects of the Levinasian formulations of ethics and love – and also challenges the limitations of his approach. It depicts a love affair, between a French woman (Emmanuelle Riva) and a Japanese man (Eiji Okada), that is also an ethical engagement and a political commentary. Framed by the recent history of Hiroshima, and conscious of the impossibility of representing the enormity of these events, the film develops an oblique critique of war through a story of love. Through the erotic affair the relations between erotic love, selfless ethics and justice are evoked, reformulating and recasting Levinas's phenomenological account.

While Levinas's conceptions of ethics and love create new possibilities for understanding the complex relation between politics, ethics and erotics, some feminist theorists have been troubled by his representations of femininity and of the erotic and maternal relation. These depictions are disquieting. Yet, they also provoke a rethinking of the occluded role of both the feminine and love in political and ethical theory. Levinas's work opens up new possibilities for expanding our understanding of love and its significance not only for personal life but also for public exchanges and relations.

ETHICS AND LOVE IN THE FACE-TO-FACE RELATION

Ethics may be read as an elaboration of the centrality of love in the inter-human relation. The face-to-face relation – the relation to the other – demands that we take responsibility for the other, care for the other, and prioritise the other's needs. While this demand, inherent within the encounter with the other, can be ignored – so that for example we can refuse to provide for the other, even murder the other – nevertheless human sociality rests on recognising the demand for care, generosity and selfless love, conveyed in the face-to-face encounter.

In *Totality and Infinity*, Levinas argues that the ethical relation is fundamental. We are not first of all isolated individuals who then form ethical and political bonds with others. Rather we are, from the outset, individualities or singularities who are immersed within sociality. The human community or 'human city' is formed through a 'primary proximity' of 'individualities whose . . . singularity consists in each referring to itself' in which there is 'responsibility for oneself and for the Other' (Levinas 1969: 214). This primary proximity that constitutes sociality does not mean that we are reliant on the other to give us existence. We do not approach the other with empty hands but instead offer her or him our plenitude.

Levinas describes the plenitude we each experience, and which we offer to the other in the ethical relation, by revealing how we exist within, and live from, the elements and materials of the world. We are nourished by our encounter with the world: Levinas describes this as 'liv[ing] from "good soup," air, light, spectacles, work, ideas, sleep, etc. . . .' (Levinas 1969: 110). This 'living from . . .' not only involves nourishment and ful-filment of need but also enjoyment and love of life. Already, at this point in his articulation of the ethics of love of others, he points to a love of the world that forms the basis for love of, or responsibility for, others. He writes: 'Life is *love of life*, a relation with contents that are not my being but more dear than my being: thinking, eating, sleeping, reading, working, warming oneself in the sun' (Levinas 1969: 112). Levinas adds: 'At the beginning there is a being gratified, a citizen of paradise . . . Already and henceforth life is loved . . .' (Levinas 1969: 144–5).

This concept of 'living from . . .', enjoyment, and pleasure in life is supplemented by discussion of home or dwelling place. In the dwelling or home we retreat from the world, reflect on our experiences, and engage in recollection. This process of recollection enables 'a greater attention to oneself, one's possibilities, and the situation' (Levinas 1969: 154). The dwelling, as a place of refuge, also facilitates our subsequent labour in the world. It is only from the security offered by the home that we are able to act on and transform the world utilising it for our suste-nance. Central to Levinas's discussion of the dwelling place is the role of another inhabitant of the home who Levinas describes as 'the Woman'. Levinas writes: 'the other whose presence is discreetly an absence, with which is accomplished the primary hospitable welcome which describes the field of intimacy, is the Woman. The woman is the condition of recol-lection, the interiority of the Home, and inhabitation' (Levinas 1969: 155). (This controversial representation of femininity will be discussed further below.)

Levinas follows this discussion of living from the plenitude of the world, love of life, and the security and intimacy of the home, with his account of the ethical relation, which is the face-to-face relation. This aspect of Levinas's work is perhaps the best known and most discussed. It is also in some ways the most challenging and confronting, for Levinas insists that the face-to-face relation calls on us to give to the other before ourselves. We must go hungry, homeless, unclothed, before we see the other deprived. More startlingly still this is not a reciprocal relation. Levinas is not envisaging that the other would also prioritise our needs. Rather we are to have no expectation of a returned generosity from the other. Instead, we treat the other as at once the most high who always precedes us and has priority over us and at the same time the most destitute and therefore the most in need of our assistance. Levinas writes: 'The Other qua Other is situated in a dimension of height and of abasement – glorious abasement; he has the face of the poor, the stranger, the widow, and the orphan, and, at the same time, of the master called to invest and justify my freedom' (Levinas 1969: 251). The result of this is that I become a hostage to the other's needs: 'I am responsible to the point of being a hostage for him' (Levinas 1998a: 59).

A central feature of Levinas's formulation of the ethical relation is that in the relation between the self and the other, the alterity of the other is always maintained. This involves recognising the other's difference and avoiding subsuming the other within my experiences, understanding and categories. Prioritising the other involves accepting that I cannot impose my perceptions on the other. It involves allowing the other her differences, her alterity or otherness. Moreover, this difference of the other should not be understood as simply the opposite of the self or as a dialectical differentiation from the self. As Levinas explains, the relation to the other should not be understood through 'the logic of contradiction, where the other of A is the non-A, the negation of A' nor through a 'dialectical logic, where the same dialectically participates in and is reconciled with the other in the Unity of the system' (Levinas 1969: 150). Instead the other is, for Levinas, a separate being constituted in her own terms.

Readers of Levinas may object that his description of our ethical responsibility is unrealistic because the demands of the ethical relation, formulated in this way, could never be fulfilled. However, while Levinas's ethics may be utopian in the sense that it is never fully achievable, it nevertheless represents an ideal toward which we may ceaselessly reach. In addition, it is important to recognise that in certain limited ways this ideal is already at least partially lived out in everyday life and experience. Within family structures the needs of the infant or child are prioritised, enabling the survival of this totally dependent being. In welfare states, the needs of the destitute are often recognised – perhaps not sufficiently, but at least to some extent. Through extended families, community networks, and state funded agencies, the needs of children and infants, of the dependent elderly, of single parents, of those who are ill or have disabilities, and of those unable to work, are (at least partially) met. Welfare states, charitable organisations, and overseas aid all provide a faint glimmer of the Levinasian requirement that we prioritise the needs of the other. While these are too often inadequate, while they may be motivated in part by a concern to secure us against destitution in our own unpredictable futures, and may require some sort of reciprocity such as gratitude or attempt by the needy to attain self-sufficiency, they nevertheless rest on an element of responsibility for the other. Moreover, it is not just the community and the state that enact a Levinasian responsibility. Individual acts also express this ethical attitude. Opening a door for a stranger or friend; relinquishing a seat for someone less able; risking life to save another in danger: these mundane and courageous acts all express to some degree Levinasian ethical responsibility.

This representation of ethical responsibility for the other – who we envisage as the most high and at the same time the most destitute – is founded on a conception of disinterested love. While he explains that he recoils from the word love because it is 'worn-out and debased' (Levinas 1998b: 103) Levinas nevertheless explicitly connects ethics with love:

> From the start, the encounter with the Other is my responsibility for him. That is the responsibility for my neighbor, which is, no doubt, the harsh name for what we call love of one's neighbor; love without Eros, charity, love in which the ethical aspect dominates the passionate aspect, love without concupiscence. (Levinas 1998b: 103)

Furthermore, while Levinas understands the ethical relation as a relation between the self and one other person he also acknowledges and discusses situations involving more than two individuals. This political relation is not secondary to the ethical relation but is already present within it as '[t]he third party looks at me in the eyes of the Other' (Levinas 1969: 213). As soon as a third person enters the picture the absolute responsibility for the other becomes more complicated as I must then make judgements about the competing needs of the two, three or many others. This is now a question of politics and of justice for Levinas (Bernasconi 1991, 1999; and Critchley 1992). Nevertheless, even in this situation in which judgement is necessary, and justice is the basis for this judgement, love continues to have a role. While Levinas explains that 'primary sociality . . . is in the rigor of justice which judges me and not in love that excuses me' (Levinas 1969: 304) he also insists that justice is tempered by love. Or to put it another way, that politics is never entirely separable from ethics. Levinas emphasises the ongoing importance of ethical love in guiding and overseeing the judgements of justice: 'Justice comes from love. That definitely doesn't mean to say that the rigor of justice can't be turned against love understood in terms of responsibility. Politics, left to itself, has its own determinism. Love must always watch over justice' (Levinas 1998b: 108). So even in political decision-making, love continues to play a role.

We can now see that all aspects of human existence are informed by some experience of love in Levinas's framework. 'Living from . . .' the plenitude of the world involves a love of life. The relation with the feminine being of the home is a relation of hospitality, welcome and intimacy – a relation that suggests a nurturing love. The ethical relation involves taking responsibility for the well being of others and this is founded on a demanding and generous love. Finally, even the political relation of justice is informed by love so that justice is tempered by love.

There are various forms of love evident in these descriptions of love. The love of life is an experience of pleasure; that of the home is associated with a form of maternal or nurturing love; and ethical love is selfless and is expressed through responsibility for others. In addition, Levinas also describes the voluptuous experience of erotic love.

EROTIC LOVE, THE FEMININE AND THE FUTURE

Levinas acknowledges the importance of erotic love for the subject and ultimately for inter-human relations. He suggests that erotic love is both the enjoyment of pleasure and also a concern for the other. For Levinas: 'To love is to fear for another, to come to the assistance of his frailty' (Levinas 1969: 256). At the same time, though, love involves an egoistic satisfaction of need: 'Love does not transcend unequivocally – it is complacent, it is pleasure and dual egoism' (Levinas 1969: 266).

For Levinas then, erotic love involves a transcending of self in reaching toward the other and caring for the other (otherwise it would revert to sexual desire) but also a fulfilment of pleasures, creating a form of immanence through the satisfaction of desire. Levinas's erotic love involves both transcendence and immanence; both concern for the other and satisfaction of need (Levinas 1969: 254–5).

'Voluptuosity, as the coinciding of the lover and the beloved, is charged with their duality: it is simultaneously fusion and distinction' he explains (Levinas 1969: 270). This ambiguity of erotic love that Levinas stresses involves both the care and responsibility that characterises ethical love and a return of the carnal enjoyment, pleasure and 'love of life' evident in 'living from . . .' the elements and materials of the world. In developing this complex formulation of erotic love, Levinas indicates that erotic love is not simply a self-interested use of the other in order to gain sexual satisfaction. Rather, love also cares for and reaches toward the other (Bloechl 1996: 2). On the other hand, however, erotic love is not reducible to an ethical love that ignores entirely the needs of the self in fulfilling responsibility toward the other. Instead erotic love entwines carnality with responsibility. As a result it goes beyond both self and other toward a future, toward an obscure and remote distance.

Levinas uses the metaphor of paternity, or reproduction of a child, to indicate what this future might involve (Levinas 1969: 267), though this concept of erotic love transcending the immediate should not be reduced only to this metaphor of fecundity and reproduction. The metaphor of paternity – of reproducing oneself in the future – is invoked by Levinas to indicate the way in which the interlacing of carnality and responsibility produces future possibilities beyond the couple. This may be a child or it may be the movement toward the future and toward transcendence. Moreover, Levinas uses fecundity and paternity as metaphors for multiplicity so as to refute the traditional philosophical conception of the subject as a self-contained individual or monad. He argues that fecundity engenders multiplicity (Levinas 1969: 273), so that while western philosophy conceives the subject as a monad (Levinas 1969: 274), for Levinas paternity demonstrates that the subject is not a monad but a multiplicity (Levinas 1969: 277).

While Levinas emphasises the conjunction of the carnal and the ethical in erotic love – and underlines also the significance of the future emanating from this concatenation – he also stresses the significance of the immediate enjoyment of carnality in erotic love. This enjoyment of erotic love is expressed through immodesty, profanation, caress, exorbitant exhibitionism, nudity, tenderness and voluptuosity. The erotic experience returns us to our materiality – 'ultramateriality' Levinas calls it (Levinas 1969: 256). We are absorbed by the sensations of the body and by our contact with the other's body. We withdraw into, and are engrossed by, these sensations experienced through the caress. But the caress also transports us beyond this experience of the sensible, dissipating our constitution as a subjectivity or identity. Levinas writes: 'In the caress, a relation yet, in one aspect, sensible, the body already denudes itself of its very form, offering itself as erotic nudity. In the carnal given to tenderness, the body quits the status of an existent' (Levinas 1969: 258). It 'sweeps away the I' (Levinas 1969: 295) and at the same time undermines the subjectivity of the beloved whose 'face fades' and who 'quit[s] her status as a person' (Levinas 1969: 263). Swooning, caressing, vulnerable and mortal (Levinas 1969: 259) both lover and beloved are transported beyond being into a non-being through the experience of erotic love.

Levinas's description of erotic love suggests an entwining of egoistic pleasure and selfless engagement with the other in the sexual relation. Yet, increasingly in his later work, Levinas insists on a separation of erotic and ethical love. This insistence is however belied by his descriptions of these forms of love.

HIROSHIMA, MON AMOUR: ARTICULATING ETHICS, POLITICS AND EROTICS

In his later work Levinas demarcates the erotic and the non-erotic. For Levinas non-erotic love is primary and is distinct from Eros. He insists that:

> I am definitely not a Freudian; consequently I don't think that Agape comes from Eros . . . Agape is neither a derivative nor the extinction of love-Eros. Before Eros there was the Face; Eros itself is possible only between Faces . . . In *Totalite et Infini* [*Totality and Infinity*], there is a chapter on Eros, which is described as love that becomes enjoyment, whereas I have a grave view of Agape in terms of responsibility for the other. (Levinas 1998b: 113)

Levinas distinguishes between particular erotic love (Eros) and self-less love of humanity (Agape) and he indicates that it is Agape that is central to the ethical relation. The responsibility for the other, experienced in the face-to-face relation, is an expression of non-erotic love for the other. Levinas emphasises that this should not be understood as an easy sentimental affair but as exacting and uncompromising for, he writes: 'there is something severe in this love; this love is commanded' (Levinas 1998b: 108).

While Levinas insists on the distinction between ethical love (Agape) and erotic love (Eros) his description of erotic love nevertheless indicates that the two are interrelated. Erotic love involves an intricate interweaving of the corporeal pleasures and love of life associated with 'living from . . .' the elements with an ethical love expressed through the face-to-face relation. The face of the other is not absent in erotic love: 'the chaste nudity of the face does not vanish in the exhibitionism of the erotic' (Levinas 1969: 261). Rather it is presupposed and transformed in voluptuous love becoming laughter, play and enjoyment (Levinas 1969: 264).

While Levinas increasingly insists on the demarcation of Eros and Agape, Stella Sandford argues that they remain enmeshed. Not only does erotic love presuppose the ethical but, in addition, Levinas's descriptions of ethical love are saturated with erotic images. The ethical engagement with the other emerges from a proximity that is described in visceral terms, putting in question Levinas's segregation. Sandford writes:

> Over and over, Levinas asserts . . . that this intensely affective ethics is not eros . . . And yet, despite these disclaimers, it is remarkable that the descriptions of ethical proximity – or the *symptoms* of ethical proximity, one might say – are clearly and powerfully erotic in nature. (Sandford 2000: 119)

Illustrating this Sandford points to Levinas's descriptions of ethical proximity as 'the almost unbearable hypersensitivity of the skin responding to the merest brush', and as 'a getting under the skin, being obsessed by the Other despite oneself' (Sandford 2000: 119). Levinas, she continues, even equates this obsessive modality with the 'shuddering' that in Plato's discussion of love is described as overtaking the lover when he sees the beloved. Sandford identifies a connection between Plato and Levinas here. Just as Plato is conventionally understood as transcending erotic love in the quest for an abstract love of the good, so, too, Levinas wants to distinguish erotic love from selfless ethics (Sandford 2000: 92–109). Yet, as we saw in Chapter 1, Plato's ascent toward love of the good is founded on erotic attachment that it never fully discards. Levinas attempts to separate Eros from Agape because, for him, erotics involves egoistic enjoyment while ethical love is a selfless responsibility for the other. Yet, his discussions also indicate an enmeshing of the two that puts in question his bifurcation.

Alain Resnais's and Marguerite Duras's film *Hiroshima, mon amour* extends this conjoining of love, articulating not only the erotic with the ethical but also with the political. In the course of a love affair between a Japanese man and a French woman, the woman recounts the story of her first love. During the Second World War, she, very young, less than twenty, has a secret affair with a German soldier – that is, with the enemy. On the day of the Liberation he is shot and killed. Risking her reputation, she cradles him as he dies in the public square of her home town, Nevers. She is denounced, her head shaved to mark her as a traitor, and confined to the cellar of her home, where her grief and her rage turn to madness.

This death scene expresses Levinas's ethical responsibility: the young woman exposes the secret of their love by publicly holding him and grieving his death. Prioritising her lover, even in death, she risks and suffers being reviled as a traitor. But it is not just her act that is ethical. The film itself, in staging this scene, is a condemnation of the senselessness of war. It privileges ethical responsibility to individual others over the law of the state and the inhuman distinctions between allies and enemies. Duras writes in her script notes: 'The absurdity of war, laid bare, hovers over their blurred bodies' (Duras 1961: 87): the blurred bodies of the dying and the grieving lovers.

Here erotic love is entwined with ethical love. The young woman's ethical refusal of the unethical requirements of war is motivated by an erotic love that 'fear[s] for another . . . [and] come[s] to the assistance of his frailty' (Levinas 1969: 256). While Levinas attempts to separate erotics and ethics his own descriptions undermine this strategy and *Hiroshima, mon amour* reveals how the two are imbricated. In this film it is the experience of passionate, obsessional, devoted love for a particular other that grounds and informs the selfless ethical love of every other.

Hiroshimam, mon amour, however, extends this lesson further, creating a link between erotics and politics. The film opens with a scene of love between the Japanese man and the now older French woman – two bodies entangled, caressing, skin-to-skin. Marguerite Duras explains in her script that these entwined bodies are 'drenched with ashes, dew, or sweat . . . deposited by the atomic "mushroom" as it moves away and evaporates' (Duras 1961: 15). The love scene is intercut with documentary footage of Hiroshima after its destruction by the atomic bomb, and with scenes of the hospital, the museum and the monuments that mark this event. Across these juxtaposed images of love and death the French woman and her Japanese lover talk. She claims that she's seen everything in Hiroshima and understands everything. She knows about the 200,000 dead, the 80,000 wounded, the burned iron, shattered stones, the hair and skin burned, scarred and peeled away. He responds that she saw nothing: that she knows nothing. Challenging her claim to know, he indicates that reciting facts and figures cannot express or capture the extent or the extremity of Hiroshima's suffering. Duras writes in her synopsis: 'Impossible to talk of Hiroshima. All one can do is talk about the impossibility of talking about Hiroshima' (Duras 1961: 9). This film is not a documentary about Hiroshima for this would fail to express the experience of Hiroshima. It is the story of the lovers, for it is only through the lovers' story that Hiroshima may be approached. This gesture signifies the impossibility of knowing, seeing, talking about, documenting, Hiroshima – though it also indicates the ethical necessity of talking about this impossibility.

Going beyond Levinas's articulation of ethics and politics this opening scene suggests that the political is already present even in the erotic. The voluptuous movement of the lovers is not only a relation of bodies but also of histories, communities, and tragedies. The intercutting between the lovers' embrace and scenes of Hiroshima suggests the presence of the third (or of the political) within erotics. While for Levinas ethical love tempers political justice, this film raises the possibility that erotic love may also modify the ethical and the political.

At the end of the film, the lovers, nameless to this point, name each other. She calls him Hiroshima. He calls her Nevers. This act has been criticised for leaving them without personal names (and by implication faceless) and the film as a whole censured for supplanting Hiroshima with Nevers, thereby occluding the story of Japan with that of Europe. This, it is suggested, undermines Levinasian ethics by obliterating the name and face and experience of the other, thereby denying her or his alterity (Baker 1999: 387–406). Yet, the enmeshing of erotic, ethical and political love may be read instead as an elaboration of Levinasian ethics. The couple, in naming each other Hiroshima and Nevers, acknowledge the presence of the third or of the political even within their erotic relation. Erotics here does not negate ethics and politics but embraces the multiplicity of the other lover who is not just a body but also a subjectivity engaged in a sociality. The film does not obliterate Hiroshima but attempts instead to reveal the horror of Hiroshima through the eyes of those who love.

Despite Levinas's attempts to distinguish erotics and ethics, his own descriptions reveal an imbrication between Eros and Agape. *Hiroshima, mon amour* gestures to this entwining including also the political within this loving interrelation. While Levinas provides a compelling description of erotic love and its ambiguous relation with ethical love, his work is not without its problems. Many feminist philosophers have expressed concern about the way in which Levinas articulates sexual difference within his theory of ethics and love. For some, Levinas infantilises the feminine in his discussion of her role within the erotic relation and reproduces a rather limiting positioning for her as both the feminine other of the home and as the beloved within the erotic relation. For others, Levinas in effect subordinates the feminine by prioritising the other within the ethical relation over the feminine other of the erotic relation.

DISPLACING THE FEMININE WITH THE ETHICAL OTHER

Writing in the late 1940s in response to Levinas's early work, *Time and the Other* (first published in 1947), Simone de Beauvoir is the first feminist philosopher to take issue with Levinas's account of the feminine other. In a long footnote in *The Second Sex* Beauvoir quotes Levinas at length and argues that his description of the feminine as 'mystery' and as the opposite of consciousness or ego is 'a man's point of view' and 'an assertion of masculine privilege'. Beauvoir uses Levinas as evidence of her argument, central to *The Second Sex*, that woman:

> . . . is sex – absolute sex, no less. She is defined and differentiated with reference to man and not he with reference to her; she is the incidental, the inessential as opposed to the essential. He is the Subject, he is the Absolute – she is the Other. (Beauvoir 1997: 16)

But while Beauvoir's argument about the secondary nature of woman's status is generally convincing her use of Levinas as evidence for this is questionable. Levinas argues that woman is Other not in the sense of being secondary to man (as the opposite or complement of man, understood as the primary term) but in the sense of being irreducible to man (that is, of having her own status that is not determined in relation to man). The quote from Levinas that Beauvoir uses makes this clear. In part it reads:

> . . . the feminine represents the contrary in its absolute sense, this contrariness being in no wise affected by any relation between it and its correlative and thus remaining absolutely other. Sex is not a certain specific difference . . . no more is the sexual difference a mere contradiction . . . Nor does this difference lie in the duality of two complementary terms, for two complementary terms imply a pre-existing whole . . . (Levinas, quoted in Beauvoir 1997: 16)

While Levinas hopes to indicate that the feminine should not be reduced to the compliment, supplement or opposite mirror reflection of man, and should instead be respected in her absolute alterity or absolute difference, Beauvoir reads him as making woman secondary to man. Nevertheless, there are elements of Levinas's account of the feminine that are troubling and that require further investigation. Luce Irigaray, like Beauvoir, questions Levinas's descriptions of the feminine though she elaborates and extends this earlier critique.

Like Beauvoir, Irigaray argues that in Levinas's work the feminine is man's negative reflection. The feminine, she suggests, 'appears as the underside or reverse side of man's aspiration toward the light, as its negative'. Like Beauvoir she asserts that woman is represented from 'the point of view of man' (Irigaray 1991: 109). Focusing on Levinas's account of the erotic relation in *Totality and Infinity*, Irigaray argues that woman functions merely to 'sustain desire' to 'satisfy hunger' and to 'renourish . . . a "future event" ' (ibid.: 110). As a result, woman as other is lost and man's erotic love is reduced to an 'autistic, egological, solitary love' (ibid.: 111). Further, Irigaray suggests that in Levinas's account the woman as other is replaced by the son who functions simultaneously as other and as reproduction of the self. In abandoning woman for the son, Levinas, Irigaray suggests, 'clings on once more to this rock of patriarchy' (ibid.: 113).

For Irigaray, Levinas destroys woman's alterity by reducing her to a negative reflection of man and to an object which functions simply to fulfil his desires. Woman in Levinas's account is reduced to flesh because as Irigaray makes clear 'the woman is reduced to animality, perversity, or a kind of pseudochildhood' (ibid.: 116).

While Irigaray reveals the pitfalls of Levinas's representation of the feminine she also develops his concept of the erotic caress elaborating its positive potentiality (see Vasseleu 1998: 109–28; and Deutscher 2002: 150 on Irigaray's debt to Levinas). Irigaray suggests that the caress can either 'open a future' and facilitate a new becoming or it can relegate the other to animality (Irigaray 1993: 187–9). The danger of the caress is that it can plunge the (feminine) other into profanity; on the other hand it can nourish and enable transcendence, freedom and becoming. Irigaray's central concern about Levinas's account of the erotic is that he distinguishes between the lover and the beloved and assigns a sex to each role – the lover is male and the beloved is female. As a consequence the subjectivity of the woman in the erotic relation is undermined and she is at the mercy of the lover:

> . . . to define the loving couple as a male lover and a *beloved woman* already assigns them to a polarity that deprives the female lover of her love. As object of desire . . . the woman is no longer she who also opens partway onto a human landscape . . . Leaving him, apparently, the whole of sensual pleasure . . . (Irigaray 1993: 205–6)

To overcome this danger Irigaray uses the terms 'woman lover' as well as 'beloved man' to indicate that each can take either role and that love involves a reciprocity between subjects:

> . . . I wanted to signify that the woman can be a subject in love and is not reducible to a more or less immediate object of desire. Man and woman, woman and man can love each other in reciprocity as subjects . . . The description of pleasure given by Levinas is unacceptable to the extent that it presents man as the sole subject exercising his desire and his appetite upon the woman who is deprived of subjectivity except to seduce him . . . (Irigaray 1991: 115)

Tina Chanter identifies further problems with Levinas's account of femininity. For Chanter, Levinas does at first create a central role for the feminine but in his later work this is elided. In his earlier book *Time and the Other*, Chanter explains, Levinas had conceived of the feminine as emblematic of absolute alterity. However, in *Totality and Infinity* it is the ethical face-to-face relation that represents the relation to the absolute other and woman is now relegated to the feminine other of the dwelling and of the erotic relation. This sidelining of the feminine continues in *Otherwise Than Being* where woman does not appear at all except through her role as mother – and her maternity is used as a metaphor for ethical, selfless, giving without return (Chanter 1995: 196–224). Moreover, Chanter points out that woman is not only occluded in this transition but she is also restricted to stereotypical roles confining her to the arenas of the erotic, the home, and the maternal (ibid.: 199).

While Levinas's theories of ethical love and erotic love are not unproblematic in relation to sexual difference, some theorists have attempted to defend Levinas against these criticisms. Claire Elise Katz, for example, argues that Levinas's phenomenological account of erotic love is indebted to both Franz Rosenzweig's *Star of Redemption* and to the *Song of Songs*. She suggests that in both these texts it is clear that the beloved and the lover are not distinguished by their sex but rather by their roles – the lover is active and gives while the beloved receives. She argues that 'The logic here is less a logic of "genders" than it is a logic of "positions" ' (Katz 2001: 126). This, she argues, is also discernable in Levinas's text as he often refers to, the beloved, in the male pronoun.

While Katz's attempt to rescue Levinas from the more critical accounts outlined above is both perceptive and useful in providing an alternate reading of Levinas's work, this reinterpretation also raises problems. If lover and beloved can be either male or female what would this imply about sexual difference? (The same question may be asked of Irigaray in relation to her insistence that lover and beloved can be reconceived as both male and female.) While Levinas's account of sexual difference is undoubtedly problematic, as the above critiques make evident, this attempt to remove sexual difference by making male and female equivalent in the erotic relation risks reintroducing sameness into Levinas's text – and sameness is the very thing that Levinas seeks to eschew in his ethics of alterity.

Perhaps another direction is needed in rethinking the difficulties raised by Levinas's articulation of ethical difference and sexual difference. Instead of insisting on an exchangeability of roles in the sexual relation it may be more productive to question the neutrality and eventual masculinisation of the ethical relation. Cathryn Vasseleu's discussion of Levinas perhaps most clearly articulates this approach. She reveals the way in which Levinas assumes that the difference inherent in the ethical relation is neutral or asexual. This neutrality inevitably falls back into the dominant conception of humanity as man – though it disguises this masculinity of the ethical relation. While Levinas retains sexual difference within the erotic relation this is secondary to the primacy of the seemingly sexually indifferent ethical relation. Vasseleu writes:

> The problem which confronts Levinas here is that in the name of ethics he reinstates sexual neutrality in all its masculinity as the human paradigm. His solution, which in no way engages with this problem, is to maintain that humans are sexual beings, but this sexuality is secondary to a transcendental humanity. (Vasseleu 1998: 111)

Jacques Derrida also addresses this issue in his paper 'At This Very Moment in This Work Here I Am'. Here, Derrida interrogates Levinas's prioritising of ethical difference over sexual difference. He writes:

> . . . E. L.'s [Levinas's] work seems to me to have always rendered secondary, derivative, and subordinate, alterity as sexual difference, the trait of sexual difference, to the alterity of a sexually non-marked wholly other. It is not woman or the feminine that he has rendered secondary, derivative, or subordinate, but sexual difference. Once sexual difference is subordinated, it is always the case that the wholly other, who is *not yet marked* is *already* found to be marked by masculinity . . . (Derrida 1991: 40)

Vasseleu and Derrida both identify the problem with Levinas's formulation of ethics in relation to his neutralisation of the participants in the ethical relation. And they both suggest that this neutralisation inevitably results in an insinuation of man into the human involved in the face-to-face relation. This implies that the problem would not be resolved by neutralising the sexual difference evident in Levinas's description of the sexual relation but rather by interrogating the sexual *indifference* evident in the ethical relation.

Rather than assert an equivalence in the erotic relation it may be more useful to trace the articulation of the erotic relation with the ethical relation and so to identify the sexual difference that Levinas's account of the ethical relation has occluded. While Levinas insists that the Agape of the ethical relation is distinct from the Eros of the erotic relation nevertheless both are constituted through the possibility of love and it is perhaps the movement between ethics and Eros that will reveal the place of femininity in ethics.

ENTWINING CARNALITY, ALTERITY AND RESPONSIBILITY

Tina Chanter provides a clue here: in his earlier work Levinas had identified the feminine as the epitome of alterity. It is this alterity who will later become the wholly other of the ethical relation and become the one for whom, as most high and most destitute, we are always responsible.

In *Time and the Other* Levinas insists that it is the feminine, encountered in the erotic relation, who represents absolute otherness. For Levinas: 'the absolutely contrary contrary . . . the contrariety that permits its terms to remain absolutely other, is the feminine' (Levinas 1987: 85). Levinas proposes that the erotic relation, and the relation to the other more generally, fails if it is understood as fusion or as possession, for this would destroy the alterity of the other. Summarising,

Levinas writes: 'If one could possess, grasp, and know the other, it would not be other. Possessing, knowing and grasping are synonyms of power' (ibid.: 90).

This model of alterity returns in *Totality and Infinity* though as Chanter, Derrida and Vasseleu, among others have indicated, in this later manifestation she has been de-sexed and appears as neuter and this neuter is all too easily interpreted as male. Nevertheless, it is apparent that this erotic feminine alterity is the prototype for the wholly other encountered in the ethical relation. But it also turns out that the self who gives to the other and who takes responsibility for the other in the ethical relation is also constituted in relation to models of femininity.

Catherine Chalier suggests that the subject Levinas describes in his account of 'living from . . .' the elements and materials of the world is a virile subject. However, 'Levinas puts in question the virility of being' (Chalier 1991: 119) suggesting that it requires the gentle welcome of the feminine of the home to introduce ethical life. Chalier explains that in the ethical relation: 'Man has to care for his neighbor and the universe before looking after himself, which is contrary to the virility of being' (ibid.: 124). While Chalier admits that this feminine being of the home is not herself accorded the status of the ethical being she nonetheless facilitates the transformation of virility into the gentleness required for ethical giving. Moreover, Chalier also argues that in *Otherwise than Being* maternity becomes the metaphor, and 'not only a metaphor' (ibid.: 127) for the ethical relation. The maternal body is, Chalier explains: 'devoted to the Other before being devoted to itself' and 'answers for the Other and makes room for him or her inside itself' (ibid.: 126). Disturbed, though, by the Levinas's restriction of a feminine enactment of ethics to the role of the mother Chalier goes on to insist that the woman in general can enact and can represent ethical giving. She repeats the biblical story of Rebecca who provides hospitality to the other, offering food and drink to others before herself partaking, as an example of feminine ethical giving and she concludes by suggesting that it is the feminine who disrupts egoistic virility in order to achieve love of the other:

> If there is a universal mission to interrupt the self-satisfaction of those beings who think that they are self-sufficient and reasonable, and . . . to put an end to this everlasting oversight of the Other . . . in order to see peace occur, a peace that will be a life for the others, a peace that will be as concernful as love; then we have to understand the meaning of this disruption of being by goodness. Is this not the meaning of the feminine in the human being? (ibid.: 128)

The feminine provides for Levinas a model for both the alterity of the other, and for the ethical actions of the self toward the other. While this is occluded in *Totality and Infinity* where the masculine-universal is used in discussing ethics and alterity, and where femininity is associated only with the home and the erotic, nevertheless a broader reading of Levinas's work reveals the significance of the feminine behind this masculinisation of the ethical.

The concernful love involved in the ethical relation is not only inextricably associated with femininity but is interwoven with erotic love, with maternal love, and with carnality or embodiment more generally. While Levinas insists that Agape is distinct from, and prior to Eros, it has become evident that the feminine other of the erotic relation (in *Time and the Other*) provides a model or a prototype for the alterity of the other of the ethical relation (in *Totality and Infinity*). Moreover, the maternal figure and the maternal body, metaphorically and literally, represents what is involved in taking responsibility for the other and giving to the other before the self. Interestingly, each of these figures of femininity refers to the feminine in her most intimate carnality, either as an erotic body or as a maternal body. This seems to suggest that the ethical relation, the relation that requires generous, selfless love, is not a disembodied affair but is lived and experienced through the body. The other is not a bloodless, faceless, anonymous being but is the embodied, living, breathing person we encounter each day on the street, in the home, in prisons, hospitals, refugee camps, detention centres, in war and in peace. And the self who faces this embodied and needful other is herself embodied: has a body, a place, a refuge, a home, food and drink, care, gentleness and love to give.

5

Colonial Love in Fanon and Moffatt

❧

While love has been represented variously in Western cultures, it has received a predominantly positive press. Unrequited love and love gone wrong may cause pain, and early-stage love may mimic a certain delirium or perform a particular madness, but, in general, love in all its forms is perceived as a good associated with intimacy, romance, family and friendship, and ultimately with fulfilment and happiness. Yet, as Simone de Beauvoir suggests in *The Second Sex*, inequality can create distortions that destroy the benefits of love, turning women into slaves and tyrants desperately seeking the recognition and love of men. Men, for their part, seek an impossible object who retains her allure and mystery by maintaining an aloof distance and independence yet also and paradoxically succumbs to his every desire, acquiesces to his views, and satisfies all his needs. Beauvoir nevertheless asserts the possibility of an authentic and reciprocal love between equals in which each would recognise, fulfil and sustain the other.

The French Antillean psychoanalyst, philosopher and Algerian anti-colonialist revolutionary, Frantz Fanon, expresses a similar disquiet in relation to interracial love. In the colonial context the black woman and man, Fanon writes, desires the economically, socially and politically privileged subjectivity of the white. Black men may desire white women, as only they are able to confer, through recognition, a human subjectivity. Black women may desire white men for the economic security and racial privileges they can bestow. In colonised societies where only whiteness is recognised, rewarded, and respected, it is unsurprising that whiteness may be sought and desired. These forms of love though socially induced are also, for Fanon, troubling as they accept the racist assumption of white superiority.

Like Beauvoir, Fanon uses a phenomenological approach in his book *Black Skin, White Mask* (first published in French in 1952 and translated into English in 1967), to describe the situation of the black, though he also draws on psychoanalysis to further elaborate the subjectivities and the neuroses that arise in colonial contexts. As a result of the destruction of their cultures, colonised peoples develop a so-called 'inferiority' complex that appears to be ameliorated by renouncing the original culture and emulating the new colonial culture (Fanon 1967: 18). Yet, this is a precarious strategy for only the white culture can determine and provide acceptance into its culture and this is always, inevitably contingent. The humanist, colonial culture may assert its well-meaning intentions to 'up-lift' and 'civilise' the colonised, but this will not, Fanon insists, free the colonised – and not only because assimilation into colonial culture destroys the existing culture but also because the colonised must create and produce their own subjectivity and freedom which cannot be given them by the colonisers, no matter how well-intentioned (ibid.: 30).

While Fanon remains oriented mainly toward the experience of black love of whiteness, Australian Aboriginal artist, Tracey Moffatt, elaborates this story tracing the consequences of black–white colonial love. Implicitly referencing the 1950s' Australian film *Jedda*, which portrays the attempted and failed assimilation of the 'adopted' Aboriginal daughter into a white colonial family, Moffatt's short experimental film *Night Cries* explores the dangers and devastation that lie in wait for the assimilated daughter resentfully and dutifully obliged to care for the aged and dying white mother fifty years on. This colonial humanist love traps the Aboriginal daughter and she forever remains ambivalently subordinated to her white mother, family, society and culture. This white love is a tool of the civilising mission of colonialism that secures compliance and procures allegiance to the rising power that is the colonial culture. Love, may be more effective than violence in producing docile subjects, though as Moffatt's film suggests this compliance is always ambivalent and subterranean resistance lurks beneath and mingles with love's subjectifying strategies.

It is, then, not only inequality between the sexes that troubles love but racial subordination also distorts passionate and affectionate relations. While Beauvoir hoped that these perversions of love might be overcome through attaining equality between loving subjects, Fanon's and Moffatt's analyses might lead to a greater pessimism. For it is not just love between individuals that is put in question but also the more generalised love associated with humanist 'civilising' colonialism. While benevolent love of humanity as a whole may seem an indisputable good, this love and this ethics may also be utilised in association with, and in order to justify, a murderous violence and a cultural annihilation in the performance of colonial benevolence, charity and love. Fanon's and Moffatt's representations and discussions not only upset our romancing of individual inter-racial love stories but also put humanist, benevolent love, used in the service of colonial conquest, in question thereby further perplexing our veneration of love.

RECOGNITION OR SELF-CREATION

Fanon begins *Black Skin, White Mask* with the rather disconcerting claim that 'the black is not a man' (Fanon 1967: 10). This is not a claim that black peoples and cultures are less than human. Rather Fanon is proposing that due to colonialism and to racial subordination more generally black people's humanity is not acknowledged by whites and that this leads to an undermining of subjectivity. Fanon explains this process of dislocation through an anecdote. On a train a child cries to his mother 'Look, a Negro! . . . Mama, see the Negro! I'm frightened!' (ibid.: 112). Fanon describes the destruction of bodily schema and of subjecthood that follows:

> I was responsible at the same time for my body, for my race, for my ances-tors . . . I was battered down by tom-toms, cannibalism, intellectual defi-ciency, fetishism, racial defects, slave-ships . . . I took myself far off from my own presence, far indeed, and made myself an object. What else could it be for me but an amputation, an excision, a hemorrhage . . . (ibid.: 112)

The white world refuses to recognise the subjectivity of the black con-juring instead the horrifying and primitive. The black is not perceived as human so that, as Fanon writes: 'My body was given back to me sprawled out, distorted, recolored, clad in mourning in that white winter day . . . While I . . . want[ed] only to love, my message was flung back in my face like a slap' (ibid.: 113–14). But Fanon also insists that this state of subjective annihilation that he calls 'a zone of nonbeing' provides the basis for a resistance that may enable liberation from this colonised consciousness. For Fanon: 'There is a zone of nonbeing, an extraordinary sterile and arid region, an utterly naked declivity, where an authentic upheaval can be born' (ibid.: 10).

Fanon, like Simone de Beauvoir, conceives of humanity as a reaching beyond basic animal needs through a creative and transformative engagement with the world. Humanity is not simply trapped in imma-nence, in negation, but has the possibility of affirmatively projecting toward the future (ibid.: 10). This possibility though is thwarted for black subjectivity, as it is for women in Beauvoir's analysis, so that transcendence becomes a problem and a struggle. Colonialism destroys the artefacts, products, perspectives and truths of colonised cultures undermining the possibility of projecting a coherent individual subjectivity onto the world. Destabilised by colonialism, black being or subjectivity, confined and constrained, is unable to escape the binds of imperialist domination:

> Uprooted, pursued, baffled, doomed to watch the dissolution of the truths that he has worked out for himself one after another, he has to give up projecting onto the world an antinomy that coexists with him. The black is a black man; that is, as a result of a series of aberrations of affect, he is rooted at the core of a universe from which he must be extricated. (Fanon 1967: 10)

For Fanon, transcendence is central to human subjectivity, but this transcendence cannot be given but must be grasped by each individual for herself and by each group for themselves. In Fanon's perspective, the problem is not simply the liberation of black culture from colonial domination but the liberation of black consciousness. Having internalised the negations and subordinations associated with colonialism, black subjectivity is distorted, trapped in immanence, and this restriction must first be overcome for transcendence to be possible. Fanon's project then is: 'nothing short of the liberation of the man of color from himself' (ibid.: 10).

While Fanon insists that the problem of colonialism is first of all economic, he also argues that this economic exploitation and subordination also has psychological consequences. Black people develop an 'inferiority' complex created by the internalisation or the 'epidermalization' of the social and economic inferiority imposed by colonial structures (ibid.: 13). (As we will see later, Fanon ultimately questions the idea of an inferiority complex suggesting that this formulation accepts the racist hierarchy of white superiority and black inferiority.) One possible expression of this 'inferiority' complex is a desire to become white that may be pursued or sought via association with white society. To be loved by a white person provides the recognition as a human being that is required to overcome the apparent 'inferiority' complex that is itself created by non-recognition. Fanon devotes two chapters to his analysis of interracial love and while there are differences in the way he describes the woman of colour's love of the white man and the man of colour's love of white woman, nonetheless the attempt to overcome or to compensate for inferiority is apparent in each case.

However, as will become evident, Fanon does not believe that the bestowal of white love and recognition can overcome the 'inferiority' complex nor can they necessarily enhance transcendence. While it may appear at first that love must provide a basis for and assist the project of transcendence Fanon, from the outset, insists on the problems of love, arguing that 'transcendence is haunted by the problems of love and understanding' (Fanon 1967: 10). Throughout his analysis Fanon refers to various philosophers and psychoanalysts but perhaps the most significant in relation to the problem of love and recognition is Hegel. In the *Phenomenology of Spirit* Hegel describes the journey of consciousness toward a fully human subjectivity. A significant moment in this journey is the metaphorical battle between consciousnesses that is provoked by the need of each to gain recognition by the other. This battle risks death though each combatant ultimately survives creating a hierarchical relation in which one dominates while the other is enslaved. The victor has been willing to fight to the death while the vanquished, fearing death, surrenders to rule by the victor. While it may at first appear that it is the victor who, by winning, gains recognition Hegel asserts that the slave has a greater humanity. The slave works, transforming the world, producing goods for the master, while the master merely passively consumes. Moreover, the slave, positioned as inferior, is unable to provide the recognition the master seeks and requires in order to gain human subjectivity (Hegel 1977: S178–96).

Fanon modifies Hegel's master–slave relation (as I will discuss later). On the one hand, he acknowledges the significance of recognition suggesting that the race-based 'inferiority' complex arises from the refusal of the dominant race to recognise or to acknowledge the subordinate culture. Negated, annihilated, dehumanised by this non-recognition, people of colour seek recognition by the white other. On the other hand Fanon also rejects the logic of recognition, arguing instead that black peoples and cultures will only find freedom through an assertion of their own value independent of the evaluations of the white. Yet, despite the inadequacies of this approach, recognition is still often sought. Twisting Hegel a little, adapting his master–slave dialectic, Fanon suggests that the black seeks recognition through loving relations with a white partner. For the black man a loving relation with a white woman offers the potential to heal the negation of racism. Fanon describes this attitude characteristic of the black man afflicted by a race-based inferiority neurosis:

> I wish to be acknowledged not as *black* but as *white*. Now – and this is a form of recognition that Hegel had not envisaged – who but a white woman can do this for me? By loving me she proves that I am worthy of white love. I am loved like a white man. (Fanon 1967: 63)

Analysing fictional accounts of inter-racial love, and augmenting these with observations of his contemporaries, Fanon explains both the desire for white love and also the risks and distortions of this enterprise. And these, it turns out, are convoluted, dangerous and finally debilitating. Even if the black man receives white love it is only on the basis that he 'passes' as white or at least performs or enacts a white subjectivity. Love of a white woman is only given on the basis that the black man is an exception. The white accepts the black man as his sister's lover only on the condition that he has 'nothing in common with real Negroes' (ibid.: 69). The white man construes the black here not as a Negro but as an 'extremely Brown' European. But this can only further destroy subjectivity for it requires that the black man metaphorically pass as white, denying his original or his earlier black identity. Performing whiteness, then, only results in further marginalisation. Never fully one or the other the black European remains stranded in-between in a no-man's land in-excluded from both cultures. Quoting from René Maran, Fanon explains:

> . . . this Negro 'who has raised himself through his own intelligence and his assiduous labors to the level of thought and the culture of Europe,' is incapable of escaping his race . . . '. . . the white race would not accept him as one of their own and the black virtually repudiated him'. (ibid.: 67)

The black man may achieve the love of a white woman but this only condemns him to a further space of 'nonbeing' – neither fully white nor any longer black he is ostracised from both communities. Moreover, this original colonial marginalisation and further secondary exclusion (neither black nor white but 'extremely brown') may create further ambivalent feelings – revenge, mastery, guilt, aggression – that taint the love relation. Fanon quotes the fictional protagonist of Maran's novel musing over his motivation for desiring a white woman to illustrate this complex problem:

> . . . enraged by this degrading ostracism, mulattoes and Negroes have only one thought from the moment they land in Europe: to gratify their appetite for white women . . . to marry in Europe not so much out of love as for the satisfaction of being the master of a European woman; and a certain tang of proud revenge enters into this. (Maran quoted in Fanon 1967: 69)

And the protagonist continues:

> And so I wonder whether in my case there is any difference from theirs; whether, by marrying you, who are European, I may not be making a show of contempt for the women of my own race and . . . attempting to revenge myself on a European woman for everything that her ancestors had inflicted on mine throughout the centuries. (ibid.: 69–70)

Yet Fanon argues that this fictional character's dilemmas regarding love, his inability to accept the love offered him by a white woman, and his race-based rationalisation of this, is in the end not so much a matter of race but a non-racial neurosis arising from early separation from his mother that has lead to an abandonment neurosis. Fanon writes that: 'Jean Veneuse [the fictional character] represents not an example of black–white relations, but a certain mode of behaviour in a neurotic who by coincidence is black' (Fanon 1967: 79). René Maran's novel is, Fanon insists, 'a sham' for it attempts to explain Jean Veneuse's behaviour on the basis of race – and indeed even on 'an attempt to make the relations between the two races dependent on an organic unhealthiness' (ibid.: 80) – rather than recognising that Jean Veneuse is a neurotic who uses race difference and racial antagonism to explain or to justify his behaviour: 'Jean Veneuse is a neurotic, and his color is only an attempt to explain his psychic structure. If this objective difference had not existed, he would have manufactured it out of nothing' (ibid.: 78–9).

Having traced the dilemmas that arise in interracial love Fanon stresses that these are not 'organic,' not biological, and ultimately he refuses the myth of 'the quest for white flesh' (ibid.: 81). Maran's fictional character should not be equated with black experience in general, and, Fanon writes: 'The sexual myth – the quest for white flesh – perpetuated by alienated psyches, must no longer be allowed to impede active understanding' (ibid.: 81).

While Fanon concedes that in colonial contexts colonised people relegated to the bottom of the hierarchy may seek 'redemption' (Sharpley-Whiting 1999: 65) through identification and inter-racial love this finally accepts the domination and the beliefs imposed by colonialism. René Maran has assimilated the prejudices of European culture and his writing expresses this internalised hatred:

> René Maran who has lived in France and breathed and eaten the myths and prejudices of racist Europe, and assimilated the collective unconscious of that Europe, will be able, if he stands outside himself to express only his hatred of the Negro. (Fanon 1967: 188)

Instead of the so-called 'inferiority' complex and the 'the quest for white flesh,' instead of the search for recognition and for identificatory love, Fanon insists that what is required is a radical restructuring that would change the world:

> In no way should my color be regarded as a flaw. From the moment the Negro accepts the separation imposed by the European he has no further respite, and 'is it not understandable that henceforward he will try to elevate himself to

the white man's level? . . .' . . . another solution is possible. It implies a restructuring of the world. (ibid.: 81–2)

But though Fanon advocates restructuring the world rather than 'the quest for white flesh' he also recognises, in the chapter on 'The Woman of Color and the White Man' that authentic love is possible explaining that it is because he believes 'in the possibility of love' that he 'endeavour[s] to trace its imperfections, its perversions' (ibid.: 42). Just as he criticises Maran's novel in the chapter on 'The Man of Color and the White Woman', here Fanon analyses the problematics of Mayotte Capécia's autobiographical novel *Je suis Martiniquaise* describing it as 'cut-rate merchandise, a sermon in praise of corruption' (ibid.: 42).

Capécia describes her desire not only for a white man but also for white economic security, for a whitened race – 'lactification' – and for magical transformation into a white self (Fanon 1967: 42–7). This desire for whiteness not only debases the black woman who turns her white partner into a god – 'He is her lord. She asks nothing, demands nothing, except a bit of whiteness in her life' (ibid.: 42) – but destroys love by transforming it into a whiteness obsession so that 'love is beyond the reach of the Mayotte Capécias of all nations' (ibid.: 44). Instead of love the black woman exhibits an exaggerated affectivity, and an inferiority neurosis, fed by the impossible desire to associate with, to internalise, and thus to become, white (ibid.: 59–60). Fanon's analysis finally suggests that subjectivity and transcendence cannot be attained by a loving recognition bestowed by the other of whatever race or culture. Rather subjecthood can only be attained through the action, struggle and resistances of the self.

Elaborating this claim, while contesting Hegel's theory of recognition, Fanon argues that if black cultures are given freedom (from slavery) by white cultures they do not attain an authentic freedom but merely replace one form of subservient life for another. In order to attain freedom and subjecthood each person and each culture needs to assert itself, to act, to fight for freedom from oppression: 'human reality in-itself-for-itself can be achieved only through conflict and through the risk that conflict implies' (Fanon 1967: 218). Fanon points out that the relation between Hegel's master and slave differ from that of whites and blacks in colonialism: insofar as the colonial master merely wants work and not recognition from the colonial slave, and the slave cannot find subjectivity through working with objects but also wants to be like the master (ibid.: 220–1, fn 8). For Fanon we attain self-consciousness not so much through recognition by others but through self-creation and action. Transcendence and subjectivity cannot simply be given, like a gift, by the other but must be claimed and attained by asserting the value of one's own identity and culture.

Kelly Oliver draws on Fanon's analysis in explaining the problem with recognition. Lack of recognition results from the dehumanisation of the minority by the majority. Demanding recognition only reinforces the hierarchical relation created by this lack (Oliver 2001a: 26). Fanon, Oliver suggests, understands that the relation of recognition is integral to colonialism and so proposes instead a self-valorisation that is not reliant on the oppressor for recognition. Oliver writes:

> What Fanon realises is that the logic of recognition that is part and parcel of colonialism and oppression makes those in power the active agents of recognition and those without power the passive recipients. This is why rather than embrace a recognition model of identity and self-worth, or unproblematically endorse the struggle for recognition of oppressed people, Fanon suggests that active meaning making and self-creation are necessary to fight oppression and overcome the psychic damage of colonization. (ibid.: 2–9)

While Fanon rejects identificatory love between black and white cultures – because it is 'another self-deluding resource of emancipation from blackness' (Sharpley-Whiting 1999: 60) – and rejects too a loving recognition that is bestowed rather than attained through struggle and action, he doesn't for all that occlude the possibility of a positive inter-racial love and recognition. Love is possible but only where each asserts her or his freedom, and humanity, and each mutually acknowledges the like freedom and humanity of the other. Fanon argues that we have the right to 'demand . . . human behaviour from the other' and a duty to 'not renounce . . . my freedom through my choices' (Fanon 1967: 229). In concluding he also speaks again of love: 'I, the man of color, want only this: . . . That it be possible for me to discover and to love man, wherever he may be' (ibid.: 231). Fanon is not valorising all and every love here. Rather, for him, only a love based on freedom would count as a love worth achieving. Moreover, Fanon is speaking not so much about individual love relations but about an ethics and politics of love. Love, for Fanon, may restore the destroyed subjectivity and agency of oppressed groups. Through love liberation then becomes possible. As Oliver writes: 'this ethical commitment to love is necessarily part of a politics of liberation . . . The transformative power of love is social and political power' (Oliver 2001a: 42–3).

Fanon exposes the racist basis for the 'inferiority' complex and problematises the politics of recognition. Rather than seeking a recognition that has already been denied by the dominating racial group, Fanon advocates a politics of self-creation and self-valorisation. Yet, this formulation also has difficulties as it seems to suggest a separation into autonomous, disconnected, races and cultures. Homi Bhabha, analysing Fanon's articulation of black subjectivity acknowledges the significance of his exploration of 'the ambivalence of colonial inscription and identification' (Bhabha 1994: 60). Yet, he also expresses some misgivings about Fanon's tendency to shore up the identities of the self and the other, the black and the white. Undermining Fanon's own insights into the complexity and ambiguity of subjectivity, Bhabha contends that Fanon, at times, occludes his own most significant insights:

> Fanon's sociodiagnostic psychiatry tends to explain away the ambivalent turns and returns of the subject of colonial desire . . . It is as if Fanon is fearful of his most radical insights: that the politics of race will not be entirely contained within the humanist myth of man or economic necessity or historical progress, for its psychic affects question such forms of determinism; that social sovereignty and human subjectivity are only realizable in the order of otherness. (Bhabha 1994: 61)

Homi Bhabha's contention is that Fanon undermines the radicalism of his own position by obscuring the importance of the other in the construction of both individual subjectivity and cultural identity. For Bhabha each subject and each culture comes into being in and through its interrelation with others. There is no isolated individual, nor is there pure culture. Rather, each is created through an engagement, interaction, identification and separation with and from others. Cultures only have meaning if they can be compared with other cultures and cultures only come into existence through their exchanges with other cultures: 'Cultures are never unitary in themselves, nor simply dualistic in the relation of Self and Other . . . hierarchical claims to the inherent originality or "purity" of cultures are untenable, even before we resort to empirical historical instances that demonstrate their hybridity' (ibid.: 35–7). Exchanges between cultures produce what Bhabha calls 'hybridity', indicating that all cultures are constantly in a process of transformation, part of which entails the absorption of elements from other cultures while at the same time preserving aspects of longer cultural traditions. This produces a 'hybridity' of exchange and interrelation between cultures that is the process of cultural formation.

While Bhabha is concerned that Fanon obscures this aspect of cultural and subjective identity, he also recognises that Fanon lays a basis for the development of this later theoretical approach. Bhabha appreciates the radical potential especially of Fanon's insight into the instability and constantly changing nature of cultural and subjective identity. It is this aspect of Fanon's theory that Bhabha believes enables recognition of the hybridity, or the in-between, or the interaction and interrelation of cultures. This, Bhabha writes, 'open[s] the way to a conceptualising of *interna-tional cultures, based not on the exoticism or multi-culturalism of the *diversity* of cultures, but on the inscription and articulation of culture's *hybridity*' (Bhabha 1994: 38).

MISCEGENATION AND MISOGYNY

While Bhabha focuses on the problems and potentials of Fanon's conceptions of subjectivity and culture, feminist theorists have concentrated on the differing ways in which Fanon represents women and men in his writings on love. Some feminist theorists have been critical of Fanon's analysis of black women's desires and sexuality (Chow 1999) – though others have defended his views pointing to his similar antagonism toward black men's desire for white love (Sharpley-Whiting 1999 and 1996). Rey Chow reveals the anxieties about postcolonial community that haunt and distort Fanon's analysis. Troubled by Fanon's more strident critique of the desires of the black woman than of the black man for white love, Chow interrogates the positioning of woman in postcolonial community that Fanon envisages. Chow argues that Fanon is more sympathetic in his portrayal of the black man – he, like the black woman, seeks white love but he is a 'helpless victim of his cultural environment' (Chow 1999: 421) filled with ambivalence and angst about his situation and desires. The black woman on the other hand is represented as 'a knowledgeable, calculating perpetrator of interracial sexual intercourses' and as 'potentially if not always a whore, a sell-out, and hence a traitor to her own ethnic community' (ibid.: 42). Moreover, Chow argues that Fanon represents both black women and white women as masochists who fantasise about rape so that Fanon writes: 'it is the woman who rapes herself' (Fanon 1967: 179). For Chow, the disturbing implication of this claim is that 'there is no such thing as a man hurting a woman; there is no such thing as rape'. This explains, Chow continues, why Fanon 'has not attempted/bothered to deal with the prominent issue of the rape of women of color by white men' (Chow 1999: 44).

The different tone adopted in Fanon's reading of black women's and men's desires indicates, Chow suggests, a greater uneasiness about relations between black women and white men. 'Whereas the women of color,' Chow writes 'are required to stay completely within boundaries, the black man is allowed to waver between psychic states and ethnic communities, to be "borderline"' (ibid.: 45). Chow speculates that this sexualised difference in Fanon's analysis ultimately relates to his conception of postcolonial community. She points out that the etymology of the word community associates it with commonality and consensus. The implication of this is that community also involves the exclusion of difference or of those who do not share the commonality of community. As a result the issue of admittance is central to community and here Chow refers to three types of admittance: a physical entering or letting in; a validation, acknowledgement or recognition, and; confession, such as admittance of a crime, which involves repentance and reconciliation with the rule of community (ibid.: 35).

Chow also suggests that racial intermixing and miscegenation may be interpreted as a threat to the concept of postcolonial national community that attempts to empower the colonised subject. She writes:

> If the creation of a postcolonial national community is at least in part about the empowerment of the formerly colonised through the systematic preservation of their racial and ethnic specificities, then such an empowerment could easily be imagined to be threatened by miscegenation, the sexual intermixing among the races. Such sexual intermixing leads to a kind of reproduction that is racially impure, and thus to a hybridisation of the elements of the community concerned. (Chow 1999: 46)

However, Chow argues that Fanon's anxiety about black women's sexuality is not in the end that it threatens the racial purity of the postcolonial community but rather that it enacts, or materialises, the theory of hybridity that he espouses and thus positions women as active agents in that community formation. In Chow's view Fanon hopes to dismantle community based on racial purity, which excludes the racial other, and to replace it with a community of hybridity that mixes 'blood, skin colour, or ethnicity' (ibid.: 47). But if women are the active agents who produce this community through miscegenation then they are abandoning their traditional role as passive victim and usurping man's position as intellectual or revolutionary progenitor of family, community, and nation. This produces a double transgression – a transgression of patriarchal as well as of racial boundaries:

> . . . the crossing of patriarchal sexual boundaries crosses another crossing, the crossing of racial boundaries. The women of color are, accordingly, the site of supplementary danger . . . adding to the injustice of race the revolt of sex (and vice versa), and substituting /transforming the meaning of both at once . . . The fact that the women are equal, indeed avant garde, partners in the production of a future community – is this not *the* confusion, the most

contagious of forces, that is the most difficult to *admit*, to permit to enter, to acknowledge, and to confess? (Chow 1999: 47–8)

Chow's argument is that while Fanon may champion cultural hybridity and racial miscegenation, he is threatened by the further transgressive crossing of boundaries implied by women becoming active agents in this postcolonial community formation. Women as revolutionary and intellectual agents undermine the patriarchal conception of sexual difference which positions women as passive victims and men as active agents. Chow suggests that women's reproductive miscegenation threatens this distinction so that Fanon is not able to admit women, let in or recognise women, within anti-racist, anti-colonial struggles. And it is this that explains Fanon's antagonism to black women's desire for white love revealed in his more strident critique and less sympathetic portrayal of black women's white-love.

However, not all feminist theorists are critical of Fanon's work and some defend Fanon against these kinds of critiques. While she does not respond directly to Chow, T. Denean Sharpley-Whiting argues that other feminist commentators have misrepresented Fanon, failing to see his equal antipathy to the neurotic love of the black man for the white woman and misunderstanding the basis of his condemnation of the black woman's love of the white man. Sharpley-Whiting argues that Fanon's unsympathetic reading of Capécia's semi-autobiographical novel must be read in the context of the reception the novel received at the time. Capécia's novel won the *Grand Prix Littéraire des Antilles* and appealed to a white French readership as it reflected their racist notions of white superiority. As Sharpley-Whiting notes: 'Fanon's scathing condemnation of the novel and writer were rooted initially in the novel's commercial success, literary kudos, and appeal to French audiences, an appeal undeniably linked to Capécia's seemingly effortless adeptness at acting as a mirror for the French, reflecting back their idealised conceptions of themselves' (Sharpley-Whiting 1999: 62). Moreover, she points out that Fanon is equally critical of Maran's depiction of the black man's search for white love calling it a 'sham' (ibid.: 71). Sharpley-Whiting also defends Fanon against the accusation that he obliterates rape and ignores the issue of white abuse of black women pointing out that Fanon does recognise the prevalence of white sexploitation of black women (ibid.: 156) – though it is true that Fanon merely alludes to this in passing (Fanon 1967: 46, fn 5).

While Sharpley-Whiting usefully reminds us of Fanon's similar disquiet regarding the valorisation of whiteness evident in neurotic desire of both black women and men for the white other, Chow has also identified a difference in his treatment of women and men that does seem to be important. Fanon's commentary on black women's whiteness obsession is from the outset unremittingly negative and critical. In relation to the black man's obsession his tone is more ambivalent and while he does finally dismiss male white-philic love he initially represents this desire in a more sympathetic light. Chow's concerns then should be acknowledged but this ought not require a rejection of Fanon's work in total. While his representation of women may be troubling, as Chow insists, Fanon nevertheless provides a significant contribution to philosophical understandings and cultural experiences of love. Love, in a colonial and postcolonial context, Fanon reveals, is intertwined with issues of race. Conceptions of race and attitudes to race imbue our choices, our experiences, our pleasures and anxieties contributing to the complexities and ambiguities and also to the fascination and intrigue of love.

While Fanon focuses on black love of the racial other, the issue of white love in colonial and postcolonial contexts is equally important and here the work of postcolonial theorist Gayatri Spivak and Australian Aboriginal filmmaker, Tracey Moffatt, each provide insight into the dynamics of racial difference and love.

COLONISED LOVE

While the operation of love is not the central issue in Gayatri Spivak's *A Critique of Postcolonial Reason*, she does nevertheless reflect on the effects of the operation of white humanist benevolent love in the colonial context. Beginning with an analysis of Immanuel Kant's ethical framework Spivak identifies a relation between Kantian ethics and the Christian civilising mission – though it is a link based on a 'travesty'. Kantian ethics requires that we treat others not merely as a means to achieve our own projects and desires but as an end in themselves with their own needs and ambitions. This, Kant insists, 'resonates well' with the biblical commandment to 'Love God above all and thy neighbor as thyself' (Kant quoted in Spivak 1999: 123). In the colonial context though, Spivak suggests, the requirement to love and to respect others is used to justify the imposition of Western conceptions of humanity and civilisation onto other cultures. Spivak argues that this ethical framework can be distorted 'in the service of the state' and to 'justify the imperialist project'. This is achieved by the production of a formula that is a travesty of these ethical principles. This formula, Spivak writes, is to: 'make the heathen into a human so that he can be treated as an end in himself; in the interest of admitting the raw man into the noumenon [the realm of freedom and moral law]; yesterday's imperialism, today's "Development" ' (ibid.: 123).

Moreover, this act of 'civilizing' the other is conceived as a benevolent gesture and as a gift to the colonised (Davis 2002: 153–4). Yet this 'gift' has an occluded or disguised coercive effect, as the colonised are required to return the 'gift' through service or contributions to the state, religion, society and economy of the coloniser. Conforming with traditional models of gift giving in which gifts circulate in an economy of exchange rather than being free and unreciprocated (Derrida 1993), the colonial gift of benevolent love and of civilising education puts the colonised recipient under an obligation or debt to be repaid through allegiance, gratitude and especially through labour for the coloniser.

Spivak makes clear the central role of European women in this enactment of colonial love. In particular colonial women performed colonial love through child-rearing and soul-making (Spivak 1999: 116). In the Australian context for example, this has involved not just modelling an ideology of domestic familial organisation but also 'adopting' Aboriginal children, or taking them into white households as domestic servants, facilitating their incorporation into white culture.

Charles Chauvel's 1955 classic Australian film *Jedda* stages this assimilationist civilising quest through the figures of the white 'adoptive' mother Sarah (Betty Suttor) and Aboriginal daughter Jedda (Ngarla Kunoth). In a conversation with husband Doug (George Simpson-Little), Sarah insists that it is her duty to civilise Jedda and Doug, claiming that it is impossible to 'tame' Aboriginals, warns Sarah that Jedda has 'got into your hair':

Doug: Still trying to turn that wild little magpie into a tame canary? . . . They don't tame. Only on the surface . . .

Sarah: That's the old cry, Doug . . . I'm not going to let that child slip back. I've done so much with her . . . I still think it's our duty to try and do something with them. Bring them closer to our way of living. Doug, I really believe I can make something of Jedda.

Doug: . . . You can't wipe out the tribal instincts and desires of a thousand years in one small life . . .

Sarah: I think it's my duty to try.

Doug: . . . don't kid yourself about that duty stuff. That kid's really got into your hair. You've grown fond of her. (*Jedda* 1955)

While *Jedda* was the first Australian film to feature and give top billing to Aboriginal actors, and to raise the controversial issue of assimilation and its effects, it nevertheless cleanses the disturbing history of forced removal of Aboriginal children from their families that was later to be recognised by the National Inquiry into the Separation of Aboriginal and

Torres Strait Islander Children from Their Families (Human Rights and Equal Opportunity Commission 1997).

Moreover, the strategies of loving incorporation – childrearing and soul-making – represented in the *Jedda* story also effectively position the colonised other within the economy of the gift which both assimilates and at the same time obligates. Tracey Moffatt's 1989 short film *Night Cries – A Rural Tragedy* brings into focus some of the consequences of colonial benevolent love for the colonised subject. Implicitly referencing the 1955 classic, Moffatt maps the evolving relation between an Aboriginal daughter and 'adoptive' white mother revealing the ambivalence and anguish of this familial love relation. The fragmented narrative, conveyed in part through flashback is continually interrupted by the repeating image of Aboriginal singer Jimmy Little performing his one chart-making 1960s pop song 'Royal Telephone'. Playing guitar and crooning the religious lyrics ('Made by god the father, for his very own. You may talk to Jesus on this royal telephone'), Little initially appears to epitomise the assimilated Aboriginal. Suit-dressed, slick-haired, and combining white chart-topping pop with Christian sentiments, Little seems to represent the white success that may be gained by adopting white culture. Yet, as an Australian audience would also be aware Little's celebrity was short-lived returning, after his one token success, into an obscurity from which he only recovered in the 1990s – following his appearance in Moffatt's film.

More significantly, Moffatt's filmic rendition of Little introduces an uncanny disquiet with each reappearance, with the sound sometimes muted and with close-up used to focus attention on seeming trivia such as the fluttering gesture of a hand movement or the adjustment of collar and guitar strap in preparation for performance. This deconstructed representation, hauntingly, at once suggests his short-lived white valorisation, his fall from white grace and his ambiguous racialisation – Aboriginal, Europeanised, black, and as Fanon might say 'extremely brown' all at once. His hybridity – both black and white – is perhaps the enduring image that emerges and resonates from this startling and unsettling representation. Larleen Jayamanne, also argues that *Night Cries* explores the intercultural space of hybridity which draws on and brings together, while also preserving, aspects of both cultures (Jayamanne 1993; see also Mellencamp 1995). Jayamanne suggests that Little represents a reworking of white culture that transforms it through its articulation with Aboriginality:

Through the performance of Jimmy Little, Moffatt both explores the violence and the fluent aspects of cultural hybridisation/assimilation and taps into an Aboriginal cultural history which is neither pristinely indigenous nor completely other . . . Here the notion of assimilation may suggest the mimicry involved in camouflage, the point of which is for others not to be able to tell if you are there or not . . . Ambivalent, unsettling perception becomes necessary: the performer is working in a tradition which is not his but which he sings as his own. (ibid.: 76 and 78)

While Little is explicitly depicted in the film another celebrated Aboriginal artist, painter Albert Namatjira, is also implicitly evoked through the use of painterly stylised stage backdrops that replicate Namatjira's distinctive style. While Namatjira is now recognised as an important Australian artist, he was, during his lifetime in the early 1900s, understood merely as producing work for the popular or tourist market (Megaw and Megaw 2000: 655–6). Namatjira used watercolour and developed a 'European' style and was considered till recently 'inauthentic' lacking the symbolism and techniques such as dot painting now often associated with Aboriginal desert art. Yet Namatjira's work was innovative in ways that are now being recognised – especially in terms of the depiction of landscapes that created new meanings and significances via European art practices (Burn and Stephen, 1986). Namatjira's work, like that of Little, may be read as emblematic of assimilation as each adopts significant aspects of European artistic styles and content. Yet each may also be read as developing innovative hybrid art forms and in the context of Moffatt's film their representation highlights the ambiguities and ambivalences of intercultural art production and subjectivity.

Within this context the fragmented and continually interrupted depiction of Aboriginal daughter and white mother becomes richly multi-layered and complexly equivocal. Performed by the distinguished Aboriginal theorist, Marcia Langton, the daughter cares for her now aging and dying mother (Agnes Hardwick) with both tenderness and brusque frustrated annoyance. Each sequence is replete with paradox: the daughter's tender washing of her mother's feet as they hum together the Christian call to arms 'Onward Christian soldiers marching as to war', is juxtaposed with a flashback to the young mother brushing the daughter's hair and to scenes of waves crashing round rocks while the daughter as a child, at first laughs and plays with the mother and with two young boys, and then, alone, sobs silently. The adult daughter's frustrated caring for the dying mother is intercut with scenes of despair – the daughter writing and posting a letter to some unknown other, cracking a whip while the mother flinches and moans – and with flash-backs to an equally unsettling and enigmatic childhood of tenderness and terror. Complex and paradoxical affects are thus at play throughout this short film: fear and terror; grief and mourning; exploitation and duty; pleasure and pain. Each vignette of mother and daughter communicates the complexity revealing the love and the hate; the tender care and the resentful duty; the connection and the alienation. The daughter reads a tourist brochure about South Molle Island resort; a train is heard in the distance – and each image suggests an outside, a possibility of escape, another life desired but unavailable to the daughter. Unavailable because she is bound by the exchange economy of reciprocal colonial love to care for the white mother who has, in 'adopting' her, taken her from this other life that lies outside the frame of the film.

Spivak's analysis of dutiful reciprocal colonial love which traps the colonial subject in an economy of exchange seems to speak through this film indicated by the Aboriginal daughter's frustrated bond with her white mother. Yet the film gestures also toward a more complex account of culture in which the colonised are not simply assimilated but are rather active agents in the creation of a hybrid community. A hybrid community that involves transformation as well as preservation and involves love as well as frustration, disagreement and despair. At the end of the film the daughter lies, foetal-like and weeping, by the side of her now dead mother. Yet the tragedy announced in the title of the film and evoked here is not just a mourning for the dead but is also the grief for a life, a culture, foregone for the sake of the white mother and the white life. While Jimmy Little sings the Christian 'Royal Telephone' at each end of the film, at its centre he also sings – though silently, the sound having been cut – 'Love Me Tender' (Love me true, never let me go). Love is central to this film but it is a love haunted by colonial affects and hybrid ambiguities – a jarring, muted, paradoxical love that reflects the perplexities, dilemmas and contingencies of postcolonial cultures and intersubjective relations.

CONCLUSION

The ambiguities and the paradoxes, the dangers and the destructive poten-tial, of love become evident in the fraught engagements of colonial and postcolonial relations. Yet, this is not to suggest that love always involves exploitation and oppression. Nor does this suggest that intercultural love is impossible. Rather, these distortions of love indicate that a complacent and romanticised view of love may be a trap that disguises the troubles, difficulties and complexities of the formulations and enactments of love.

6

Irigaray: Re-directing the Gift of Love

∽

Virgina Woolf's novelistic homage to her lover, Vita Sackville-West, traces the adventures of the ever-young *Orlando* who, defying convention – and biology – lives for 400-plus years, changing sex from man to woman in the course of a turbulent and varied existence. The novel charts his, and later her, travails in the pursuit of love, in the worlds of politics, society, and the law, and in the experiences of death and birth. Starting life male, Orlando becomes female, though she continues to switch identities with a change of costume, and to consort with ladies and archdukes, professors, poets and prostitutes. Constructing this fantastical scenario, Woolf conjures the atmosphere of each historical age, alluding to the complex and changing articulations of class, race, sex and nation and revealing the inequalities between women and men and the differing destinies that befall each sex.

In her film adaptation, director Sally Potter supplements the text with opulent visions of the ornate costumes, and complex rituals and customs of past times. Segmenting the film into 'chapters' introduced by a date and a single word descriptor – Death, Love, Poetry, Politics, Society, Sex, Birth – the film traces the adventures of Orlando as he, and then she, partakes of courtly life, politics, the search for love, legal entanglements, war, death and birth. Both the novel and the film comment, with wry humour but also affection, on the rituals, customs and beliefs of English life.

A scene of love is staged early and reprised midway through the film: Orlando (Tilda Swinton) declares his impassioned love for Princess Sasha (Charlotte Valandrey), the daughter of a visiting Russian ambassador, and following her rebuttal insists that she is his:

Orlando: But we're linked. Our destinies are linked. You're mine.
Sasha: Why?
Orlando: Because I adore you. (*Orlando* 1992)

This insistence on ownership of the beloved – 'You're mine' – returns when Archduke Harry (John Wood) declares his love of the now female Orlando:

Archduke Harry:	. . . I'm offering you my hand.
Orlando:	Oh Archduke. That's very kind of you. Yes. I cannot accept.
Archduke Harry:	But I am England. And you are mine.
Orlando:	I see. On what grounds?
Archduke Harry:	That I adore you.
Orlando:	And this means that I belong to you? (ibid.)

The male Orlando and the Archduke Harry each assume a right to whatever they desire. They are each perplexed. Orlando, in the first instance, turns to the camera and comments 'The treachery of women'. In the second the Archduke responds by berating Orlando: 'With your history, quite frankly, who else would have you . . . This is your last chance of respectability . . . You will die a spinster . . . Dispossessed and alone' (ibid.).

This commonplace assumption of ownership and control of the object of desire, evoked in these love scenes, underlies, in part, Luce Irigaray's exploration of different ways of loving in her *I Love To You*. A contemporary French philosopher and psychoanalyst, Irigaray, interrogates the relation between woman and man frequently focusing on the work of earlier philosophers and psychoanalysts and arguing that all too commonly woman is represented as the opposite, the complement, or the lacking and diminutive reflection of the main representative of humanity – man. Analysing love relations, Irigaray repudiates the conventional experience of merging, identification and union with the other, seeking instead to maintain a distance between the lovers so that they may love each other as other and not as a reflection or reproduction of the self. Irigaray imagines a love based on maintaining difference between the self and the other, between the beloved and the lover, and this she suggests requires mediation rather than immediacy, indirection rather than direct connection.

In this chapter, Irigaray's vision of love is juxtaposed with and against Sally Potter's and Virginia Woolf's differing representations of love in *Orlando*, to create a dialogue about alternatives to traditional conceptions of love. While Woolf, Potter and Irigaray all resist the conventional discourses of love each formulates the problematics of love differently and each develops alternate visions of loving otherwise.

DIFFERENCE

Midway through the film, Orlando, waking after extended sleep, discards his eighteenth-century courtly wig revealing flowing feminine strawberry-blonde hair. Orlando splashes saffron-coloured water over her face and hair as the surrounding room slowly transforms from deep black shadow to a glowing amber light. This mystical golden light continues as Orlando turns to the mirror, and the camera, taking up Orlando's point of view, reveals the reflected naked body: the breasts, curvaceous hips, and pubic hair announcing an indisputably feminine form. Orlando ruminates, speaking first to the mirror and then turning to speak directly to the camera: 'Same person. No difference at all. Just a different sex' (*Orlando* 1992).

The contradiction in her introspective musing – claiming no difference but also positing sexual difference – neatly captures the difficulty involved in describing the relation between the sexes. Throughout the twentieth century, when gaining equality between women and men was the main objective of feminist campaigns and theories, 'no difference at all' was the prevailing dictum. Gaining equality seemed to require a claim that women were, in all relevant respects, the same as men – same mental abilities and very similar physical abilities. Women should, therefore, have the right to vote, access to education and work, and equal wages for equivalent work.

But in the later 1900s this emphasis on sameness – 'no difference at all' – began to disintegrate as it became clear that women needed different rights, protections, services and supports. Women, not men, needed access to safe abortion as well as the right to bear and to keep their children; as the carers of children they required access to affordable childcare so that they could participate equally in the workforce; they demanded guaranteed maternity leave; and they sought anti-discrimination and affirmative action programmes that would ensure full participation in all aspects of life. So, differences between women and men began to be more clearly acknowledged. Joan Scott's analysis of the complex relation between equality and difference makes clear the need to distinguish between equal treatment and equal outcomes: in order to achieve equality, difference may need to be recognised and different treatment provided to ensure an equal outcome. Scott also discusses the effects of a deconstructive differing and deferring produced through the play of words in language that create difference in representations (Scott 1990). Leaving this latter form of difference aside, differences between the sexes were generally construed as socially constructed, resulting from women's assigned responsibility for children, and from the social, economic and legal disadvantages that women had endured due to a history of discrimination and marginalisation. The physical differences between women and men were still largely ignored or overlooked.

Luce Irigaray, however, extends this focus on difference suggesting that the embodied differences between women and men are also significant. Irigaray rejects the claim that there is 'no difference at all' insisting instead on the acknowledgement of a 'different sex'. For Irigaray, egalitarianism would only neutralise sexual difference risking the complete destruction or obliteration of sexed identity. 'Demanding equality, as women', she writes: 'seems to me to be an erroneous expression of a real issue. Demanding to be equal presupposes a term of comparison. Equal to what? What do women want to be equal to? Men? A wage? A public position? Equal to what? Why not to themselves?' (Irigaray 1996: 32).

Irigaray argues that Western culture has always been a one-sex society insofar as men are the only recognised and valued sex and women are seen as merely the opposite or complement of men. This situation cannot be overcome through equality campaigns that risk exacerbating this one-sex construction by turning women into replicas of men. Rather, this monosexual culture needs to be augmented and extended by recognising woman as a different sex or a different genre, so as to reconstitute social relations as founded on two. In *This Sex Which Is Not One* Irigaray critiques existing social and sexual relations and dreams an alternate social architectonics and way of life based on recognition and valorisation of woman and man as different beings.

This Sex Which Is Not One uncovers a tradition of disguised occlusion of feminine sexuality. It argues that the female sex is not a sex, in that it is not recognised as a sex independent of men:

> Female sexuality has always been conceptualised on the basis of masculine parameters . . . women's erogenous zones never amount to anything but a clitoris-sex that is not comparable to the noble phallic organ, or a hole-envelope that serves to sheathe and massage the penis in intercourse: a non-sex, or a masculine organ turned back upon itself . . . (Irigaray 1985a: 23)

The title *This Sex Which Is Not One* implies, however, a further meaning: not just that she is not a (recognised) sex but, in addition, that her sex (organs) cannot be limited to one. Human sexuality is oriented around the one sexual organ of the male – the penis – and women's sexual organs are seen as either a diminutive copy of, or as a sheath for, the male sexual organ. But Irigaray seeks to rewrite women's sexuality speculating that we could understand or interpret women's sexuality and sexual organs differently. Women's erogenous zones are not one but plural:

> Her sexuality, always at least double, goes even further: it is *plural* . . . woman's pleasure does not have to choose between clitoral activity and vaginal passivity . . . Fondling the breasts, touching the vulva, spreading the

lips, stroking the posterior wall of the vagina, brushing against the mouth of the uterus, and so on . . . *woman has sex organs more or less everywhere.* (ibid.: 28)

Rather than conform to a male standard, or emulate masculine endeavours, Irigaray proposes that woman's embodied specificity be rediscovered and embraced so as to create a society founded on two sexes and not just the one (masculine) sex. Importantly though, Irigaray is not advocating a return to the discourse of biological sexual difference frequently associated with a theory of biological determinism that has insisted on women's 'natural' role as mothers and on their inferiority in physical strength and intellect. Rather Irigaray is venturing beyond the biological-determinism versus social-construction debate and proposing an understanding of the body that sees the body itself as 'written' or interpreted by culture. Traditionally, women's bodies have been interpreted in relation to man: as a vehicle for his pleasure and an instrument for his reproduction. She has been imagined as a lacking man, or as the mirror reflection of man. But Irigaray argues that these are not the only ways to conceive of woman: instead we may see her in her own terms, having a sexuality and multiple pleasures beyond those required for servicing masculine desire. This feminist theory of embodiment understands the body not as a biologically determined entity but as a materiality that is interpreted by culture in different ways so that woman may have been seen as a non-sex, as the second sex, as the other sex, but may also instead be construed as the polymorphic sex who is never simply one. Sexual difference needs both to be recognised (insofar as there is a pre-existing material difference between the sexes) and invented (insofar as this difference is open to multiple interpretations and enactments).

MEDIATION

Chasing behind the voluminous, crinolined and bustled figure of Orlando, the camera pursues her through a maze and across fields, shrouded in mist, as she races to escape the law with its suit to disinherit her now that she is a woman. She falls to the ground muttering 'Nature, nature. I am your bride. Take me' (*Orlando* 1992). The ironic histrionics of the scene is augmented by the theatrical appearance of a galloping horse that, rearing up, dislodges its rider who falls head to head with Orlando. Thus enters Shelmerdine (Billy Zane) – Orlando's metaphorical and paradoxical knight in shining armour – who immediately disabuses her, and us, of our expectation that he is her prince come to the rescue.

He asks 'Are you hurt? Can I help?' She replies 'I'm dead' and he, introducing a jocular element observes 'That's serious.' Undeterred she continues the parody of rescue, asking 'Will you marry me?' and he, queering the rescue fantasy, proclaims 'Ma'am, I would but I fear that my ankle is twisted' (ibid.). Nevertheless, a love story follows – albeit one that reframes our expectations of love. Shelmerdine does not offer to rescue Orlando through marriage but does offer love: 'You don't really want a husband . . . You want a lover', he says.

Introducing her book on love, Irigaray tells an anecdote about her encounter with Renzo Imbeni, the Mayor of Bologna, to whom she dedicates her book and who was at that time standing for the European Parliament. The anecdote illustrates what she will then, in the body of the book, theorise as an alternate model of love founded on indirection. She explains that she was speaking at a public meeting that was part of his election campaign. And that night she and he, along with others at this public forum, talked: 'We talked; we talked to each other: he and I, his citizens and my insurgents. Between us, each and every woman and man, there were truths, questions, passions, fidelities, works' (Irigaray 1996: 7).

Despite their differences, or because of them, a real communication occurred and one that revealed him to be a trustworthy, clear-thinking, fair and honourable man. A man of integrity and intelligence who demonstrated a sense of equity as well as attentiveness to the other (ibid.: 8–9). His behaviour made like-behaviour possible for others and for her – although Irigaray also emphasises that while mutual respect and reciprocal recognition developed between them they did not for all that become one, united by their shared views. Rather they remained two who expressed their differing views and knowledges informed by their divergent positions and histories: 'We were two: a man and a woman speaking in accordance with our identity, our conscience, our cultural heritage, and even our sensibility' (ibid.: 9).

Irigaray writes of Imbeni in a way that suggests a passionate love:

So alive, faces light up around him . . . Alive, he is daring and unsubmissive, but he does have respect, both for nature and for others . . . He is prudent and daring. He only makes promises he can keep. It is possible to have faith in him. One can take from him without renouncing one's self. (ibid.: 15)

Though she also warns against this interpretation saying:

You are probably thinking that I must be blinded by some sort of passion for him, some projection onto him? I can only say that these praises are commonplace in all the squares, restaurants or public places in his city. (ibid.: 16)

Whether this is an example of passionate love or of friendship love – and after all, the two may be confused and our desires unclear, even to ourselves – it demonstrates aspects of Irigaray's alternate love, a love that she describes as based in indirection or mediation. For Irigaray this is an example of mediated love because it preserves the difference of the two, avoiding collapsing into unity and thus becoming one. Irigaray invents the phrase 'I love to you' as an alternative to 'I love you' because she fears that the direct address 'I love you' implies an ownership or control of the beloved and risks turning the beloved into the *object* of my affections:

> I love you, I desire you, I take you, I seduce you, I order you, I instruct you, and so on, always risks annihilating the alterity of the other, of transforming him/her into my property, my object, of reducing him/her to what is mine, into mine . . . (Irigaray 1996: 110)

The male Orlando and the Archduke Harry are perplexed, even affronted, when their objects of desire don't reciprocate their adoration – as though they had assumed that 'I adore you' and 'I love you' inaugurated and necessitated an echoed response. 'I love you', they seem to presuppose, makes the beloved my property by turning her or him into the object of my adoration. This obliterates difference by imposing my wishes on you, by imposing my self on you. Shelmerdine, in contrast, deflects the fantasy of union and the possession it implies by offering himself not as a husband who would rescue and so possess but as a lover maintaining a certain separation between the one and the other.

Irigaray theorises this difference between imposing love and offering a more open form of love. 'I love to you' redirects the expression of love so that the beloved is only indirectly addressed creating space and air, preserving distance and difference, between the two. Inserting 'to' into 'I love you', Irigaray hopes to overcome the construction of the beloved as an object and as the property of the lover: 'The "to" is an attempt to avoid falling back into the horizon of the reduction of the subject to the object, to an item of property', she writes (ibid.: 111).

'I love to you' operates a little like 'I speak to you, I ask of you, I give to you'. Thus it is not I speak for you, or speak of you, or speak you in the sense of make you. Instead it involves speaking *to* you, or loving *to* you. 'The "to"', Irigaray writes, 'is the guarantor of indirection' (ibid.: 109).

Irigaray's objective then is to imagine a model of love, and a form of loving address, that undermines the ownership and control implied in conventional relations between lover and beloved. Love as it has generally been experienced already activates this relation of control and ownership. Even the words 'lover' and 'beloved' already evoke a hierarchical relation, for the lover is conceived as the active pursuer and possessor while the beloved is passive and is possessed. Moreover, the lover is generally conceived as male and the beloved as female. With this division Irigaray observes: 'we no longer have two subjects in a loving relationship' (ibid.: 111).

Undoubtedly, the insertion of the word 'to' cannot, on its own, transform relations of ownership into relations of love. Rather the 'to' signifies the preservation of a distance that enables the alterity of each to be sustained. It interrupts the immediacy of love, the merging and unification involved in love, allowing each their singularity and difference so that each is able to recognise the other as other, and respect this alterity of the other. It bequeaths a space between so that the one cannot be consumed or incorporated by the other.

Irigaray's narration of her encounter with Renzo Imbeni functions allegorically, within her book, to illustrate this indirection of affection. To proclaim her love (whether friendly or erotic) directly would constitute him as the object of love. Instead, Irigaray sketches an ethics of love directed to her readers so that an indirection in relation to Imbeni can be maintained. She does not declare her (friendly or erotic) love to Imbeni. Rather she speaks to her readers about love, redirecting her affection via her manuscript and her re-conceptualisations of love. Thus her book actualises her demand for indirection expressed in the phrase 'I love to you'.

PROXIMITY

Shelmerdine does not rescue Orlando but the two do become lovers. They talk, revealing both differences and similarities between them. She says: 'If I were a man . . . I might choose not to risk my life for an uncertain cause . . .' and Shelmerdine, divining her meaning, ends her speculation by suggesting: 'You might choose not to be a real man at all.' He continues: 'If I were a woman . . . I might choose not to sacrifice my life caring for my children . . . Would I then be . . .' and she concludes: 'a real woman?' (*Orlando* 1992).

This scene re-articulates the sexual difference question. Each sex in fulfilling conventional roles and obligations risks or sacrifices life for others – men through political causes; women through family duty. Each questions the other's adherence to this conventional expectation and, in so doing, asserts her or his difference. But, in addition, a certain sameness also emerges in this scene. Neither would accept the assigned role of the other, but each also acknowledges the restrictions on the other sex.

While they express disagreement – neither wanting to fulfil the position of the other – they also express mutual comprehension as each finishes the thought of the other. The editing and cinematography augment this movement from difference to identity. As the conversation begins the image cuts from one face to the other clearly demarcating one from the other. But as the conversation deepens the camera pans back and forth from one to the other, from listener to speaker, creating connection and conveying a sense of merger or conflation of the two.

Orlando and Shelmerdine finish each other's sentences and converge through the panning movement of the camera undermining difference by producing identity. Moreover, though they each question the role of the other sex, this rejection is expressed as a mirroring opposition. Her sentiments are a mirror reverse image of his so that each is not so much different from the other but a reversed reflection of the other. The sexes here are depicted not as different, but as opposite and complement of each other, and this mirroring quickly collapses into a merger or a union that may once again reinstate a monosexual sociality.

Irigaray attempts, in *I Love To You*, to thwart the possibility of merger evident in conventional love conceived as the union of two souls. She does this partly by insisting on an indirection in the expression of love that preserves the differences between the lovers. Wishing to avoid a cannibal love (Irigaray 1996: 110) that would consume the other, making her a part of the self, or the same as the self, Irigaray insists on the necessity of difference. Yet she doesn't, for all that, want difference to be a form of excommunication or exclusion between the self and the other. She seeks instead an encounter, an engagement, and an exchange in the relation between the two. In order to counteract the risk that difference might contract back into sameness, Irigaray also envisages proximity between the self and other and between woman and man. Proximity is not a relation of exclusion or disconnection; but neither is it a relation of union and synthesis. Moving beyond the opposition of difference and sameness, proximity is a relation of vicinity and tangency that refuses the alternatives of segregation on the one hand and conflation on the other.

In *I Love To You*, Irigaray insists on both proximity and difference. Sexual difference provides a means to identify a limit to my experience and subjectivity so that I can avoid imposing myself, projecting myself, onto others and the world as though my experience were universal. Challenging Hegel's conception of the 'labour of the negative' Irigaray proposes that sexual difference functions as the negative or limit that undermines a universalising moment that conflates the other into the same. Irigaray argues that in Hegel's formulation the negative or limit is incorporated within the self, creating a synthesis that destroys the difference of the other. The other (who represents the limit or boundary of the self, or the negation of the self) is subsumed within the self so that the self believes itself to express universal being or experience. Irigaray resists this assimilation that destroys difference; and she also proposes that sexual differences epitomise the limit that thwarts this incorporating and universalising tendency (Oliver 2001b: 63–5; Joy 2000: 117–23). Irigaray writes:

> Sexual identity rules out all forms of totality as well as the self-substituting subject . . . The *mine* of the subject is always already marked by a disappropriation: gender. Being a man or being a woman already means not being the whole of the subject or of the community or of spirit . . . Therefore, I am not the whole: I am man or woman . . . I am objectively limited by this belonging. (Irigaray 1996: 106)

Sexual difference is central for Irigaray because it indicates definitively the boundaries and limits of my experience, challenging universalising gestures that assume all others are like me. Feminist and postcolonial theorists have been especially concerned about theories and philosophies that make universal claims based on a particular position that obscures the distinct experiences of the other, and that thereby obliterates this otherness. For Irigaray, recognising sexual difference and seeing the other sex as a limit or negative of my experience overcomes this conflation of all into one. She writes:

> Hegel knew nothing of a negative like that. His negative is still the mastery of consciousness (historically male), over nature and human kind. The negative of sexual difference means an acceptance of the limits of my gender and recognition of the irreducibility of the other. (ibid.: 13)

Yet, if Irigaray insists on difference she is also aware of the risks of this strategy. As the history of philosophy amply demonstrates, difference is all too easily subsumed into the same – Hegel's sublation being only one example. In *Speculum of the Other Woman* Irigaray warns that domination tends to destroy difference by a fusion into unity:

> For Being's domination requires that whatever has been defined – *within the domain of sameness* – as "more" (true, right, clear, reasonable, intelligible, paternal, masculine . . .) should progressively win out over its "other," its "different" – its differing – and, when it comes right down to it, over its negative, its "less" (fantastic, harmful, obscure, "mad," sensible, maternal, feminine . . .) . . . fission . . . is eliminated in the *unity of the concept*. (Irigaray 1985b: 275)

Commenting on Irigaray's concern about the tendency for difference to be subsumed within the same, Krzysztof Ziarek argues that Irigaray's work has consistently traced a movement from difference to proximity (Ziarek 2000: 45). In order to subvert the congealing union of difference into sameness Irigaray identifies the significance of space between, the mediation between, and proximity of self and other. This nearness or contiguity deflects incorporation into sameness, there being no need to overcome or dominate the distance and opposition of the other. The proximity of the other erases the threat of the other, deflecting the movement of domination. Throughout her work Irigaray employs metaphors that express this idea of mediation or proximity. The recurring images of the lips, of mucous, angels, love, sensible transcendental, and so on reflect the concepts of mediation and proximity in Irigaray's writings.

For Ziarek, Irigaray's image of the lips illustrates this relation of proximity and also the erasure of the threat of difference. While there are at least two lips, they are not divisible into one(s). In constant contact, the lips create autoerotic pleasure but also defy division into one and other, or sameness and difference (Irigaray 1985a: 24). Always touching, their proximity defies separation and also union. Ziarek comments:

> . . . the two lips indicate an interplay which refuses the terms of difference and identity. The lips, both sexual organs and the organs of language, cannot be understood as either two distinct and separate lips or as parts of a unified, "same," structure. What defines the specificity of the lips is their nearness or proximity . . . (Ziarek 2000: 147)

Yet for all that Irigaray does not, as Ziarek notes, relinquish the significance of difference, and especially the irreducibility of sexual difference (ibid.: 145). Her strategy involves rather a movement back and forth between, or a simultaneous insistence on, proximity and difference: the two lips are, for example, both a sign of sexual difference and an image of proximity.

In *I Love To You* this dual strategy of staging difference and proximity is deployed through the re-articulation of love. In her engagement with Plato Irigaray already emphasises the intermediary character of love. As we saw in Chapter 1, Irigaray, agreeing with Diotima-Socrates, conceives love not as fulfilment but as movement between. In *I Love To You* the dynamics of the love relation are further elaborated. Rephrasing the conventional declaration of love – transforming 'I love you' into 'I love to you' – Irigaray obviates the imposition, mastery, assimilation and unity performed by the direct address. The indirection gives love not as a gift that would require a reciprocal return of love – not, then, as a gift within an economy of exchange (Derrida 1995) – but as a free gift imposing no obligation on the other. Indirection removes the debt incurred by a direct giving of love, removing the mastery and possession of the giver and the debt and obligation of the receiver. 'I love you' makes you the object of my loving action. 'I love to you' introduces indirection creating a space, a little room to move and play between the two. It creates a mediation, a tangency, that approaches and touches but does not subsume. It thereby preserves difference while also creating engagement and nearness. Irigaray's strategy of indirection then is double: preserving difference it also facilitates proximity enabling and expressing amorous exchanges. In this framework, Ewa Ziarek suggests: 'The other who is loved is not a hostile freedom opposed to my own, but the very source of my becoming . . .' (Ziarek 1998: 71).

At the end of her book Irigaray writes of approaching and retreating, passing by and moving toward. The retreat of the other separates, creating a limit that defines the self and reveals the difference. The approach toward creates a connection. Indirection maintains the movement between of love. Addressing her readers, including perhaps Imbeni, Irigaray concludes: 'Without a doubt, we approached, maybe even passed by, one another. Your retreat reveals my existence, as my withdrawal is dedicated to you. May we come to recognise the intention here as a pathway leading indirectly to us' (Irigaray 1996: 150).

HYBRIDITY

The film closes with Orlando gazing skyward as she sits beneath an ancient oak. Between the branches floats an angel (Jimmy Somerville), who, in an ethereal falsetto voice, sings of a freedom found by traversing the passage between self and other, between woman and man: 'I am coming . . . across the divide to you . . . Neither a woman nor a man. We are joined, we are one with a human face . . . At last I am free' (*Orlando* 1992). In Potter's construction, sexual difference is replaced by merger so that no longer either a woman or a man we may become simply 'one with a human face'. Difference again is reduced to sameness represented by this shared face. This process of merger, that risks obliterating the specificity of difference and especially of once again subsuming the feminine within a masculine human, is the ever-imminent danger that Irigaray hopes to counteract through her insistence on an irreducible sexual difference.

Yet, Irigaray risks another process of effacement and exclusion as a result of her privileging of sexual over other forms of difference. To the extent that she posits sexual difference not just as one example, but as the definitive form of difference, Irigaray implicitly marginalises other forms of difference – racial, cultural, class, generational and so on. She also overtly repudiates same-sex relations, which she contends lack the limit or the negative that facilitates differentiation and becoming.

For Irigaray:

> The natural . . . is at least two: male and female. This division is not secondary or unique to human kind. It cuts across all realms of living which, without it, would not exist. Without sexual difference, there would be no life or earth. (Irigaray 1996: 37)

In her earlier formulations, Irigaray has argued that sexual difference has not yet been realised, as woman is subordinated within a solo-sex culture, and so has to be invented or fabricated by the creation of new forms of femininity. While there is an underlying material difference onto which this invented difference is 'written' this underlying materiality is not determining, as it is open to multiple interpretations and expression. In *I Love To You*, however, Irigaray appears to suggest that there is already a fixed 'natural' sexual difference upon which rests the 'labour of the negative' or limit that would enable positive differential subjectivities to be achieved. This is still a rather complex conception of difference for Irigaray insists that this biological raw material still needs to be transformed into a subjectivity through the work of the negative – that is, sexual difference needs to be simultaneously recognised (as preexisting) and created. Distinguishing her own position from that of Beauvoir, she writes: 'It's not as Simone de Beauvoir said: one is not born, but rather becomes, a woman (through culture), but rather: I am born a woman, but I must still become this woman that I am by nature' (Irigaray 1996: 107).

By simultaneously insisting on the materiality of the sexed body and on the processes of becoming that 'writes' or creates or transforms this body into various subjectivities and meanings Irigaray hopes to move beyond the biology versus culture debate. Yet, in *I Love To You* Irigaray risks re-emphasising a natural or pre-existing difference in positing this as the originary basis for differentiation. Moreover, she exacerbates this problem by specifically identifying same-sex relations as a failure of difference.

Irigaray writes that the same-sex relation: 'is paradoxically less straightforward [than the relation to the other sex] due to the risk of objectivity dissipating into sameness' (ibid.: 145). She argues that: 'engaging with a person of my own gender is threatened with superficiality, dissolution, with an unethical sensibility as long as there are no just institutions appropriate to it' (ibid.: 146). While for Irigaray the marriage between woman and man 'realises the reign of spirit' (ibid.: 147), same-sex love is unethical because it fails to allow differentiation as 'remaining within affectivity in relations among women . . . risks ensnaring their freedom in an attraction that exiles them from a return to themselves and distances them from the construction of a specific will and history'. The 'immediate sensible love' of same-sex love is, for Irigaray, 'delusive, alienating, and utopian' (ibid.: 5).

Irigaray's formulations are quite careful – for example, the same-sex relation only risks sameness and dissolution while 'there are no just institutions appropriate to it'. Nevertheless, the overall tenor of her argument clearly privileges hetero-sociality and heterosexuality as the site of difference over homo-sociality and homosexuality as dissipation into sameness.

Penelope Deutscher interrogates the slippage from sexual difference as a future possibility that we may create or invent to sexual difference as an already determined foundation. She suggests that the latter formulation indicates that Irigaray imposes an impermeable boundary between the self and the other and ignores the complex internalisations of others that are necessary to form the ego or subjectivity of the self. Tracing Derrida's theories of impossible mourning and cannibalistic internalisation of others, Deutscher explains that 'cannibalizing the other is both inevitable and impossible' (Deutscher 2002: 133). Internalising others is necessary for the constitution of the subject. Yet the other resists this assimilation, always preserving an excess or difference beyond the appropriations by the self. The question is not whether to 'eat' others (as this is in any case inevitable) but how to eat ethically so as to respect the others' difference (ibid.: 130–6). Elaborating this conception of necessary ingestion, Deutscher illustrates describing the necessary exchanges between cultures. She suggests that: 'Cultures always contain aspects of other cultures' (Deutscher 2002: 136). There is no pure culture unaffected by exchanges with other cultures through which elements of each infiltrate the other creating new formations while also preserving aspects of older traditions (Bhabha 1994). This concept of cultural hybridity may be equated with a hybridity of the subject formed through its relations, its internalisations, of other subjects. Hybridity need not be understood as the destruction of difference but as a movement of exchange and connection, and also of distinction and separation, between the one and the other.

While Irigaray has, as Deutscher carefully demonstrates, elaborated similar conceptions of intersubjectivity in her earlier work in *I Love To You*, she represents the relation between self and other, and specifically between man and woman, as an absolute limit or as the boundary that delimits the identity of each. The reverse side of this foundational difference is a similarly rigid image of same-sex relations as inevitable merger. Deutscher comments: 'There is a significant difference between wishing to write alternative possibilities . . . represented by heterosexuality and taking heterosexuality as the privileged emblem of . . . difference' (Deutscher 2002: 127). She suggests also that: 'Difference does not lie between two identities, the male and the female' but is something we 'imagine' and create (ibid.: 121). It is not a pre-existing determined identity but is instead a way of relating to others. This will involve ingestion of the other that reveals the limit or difference of the other. It is not an absolute separation but an exchange between self and other that transforms while also respecting the alterity of each.

Irigaray's theory of difference and proximity attempts to thwart the merger that is evident in Potter's vision of the sexual relation. Orlando's angel forgets difference by describing a unity of man and woman expressed in their shared human face. In addition, as the film closes Orlando is transformed into an androgynous figure clad in breeches and jacket striding through her former estate. No longer a woman or a man she is now a conflation of the two in one: a congealed image of unity. Irigaray challenges this representation of a unified human because it tends to subsume the feminine into a human understood within masculine parameters. However, to the extent that she relies on a fixed and resolved difference and prioritises sexual difference over other differences she risks, in turn, marginalising and abjecting other differences – racial, cultural and so on, but also the difference that homoerotics represents in the context of a dominant heterosexual culture.

Potter's articulation of the sexual relation may be interpreted as an expression of an equality feminism that hopes to overcome women's subordination by emphasising the similarities between women and men. The risk is an inadvertent reinstating of masculine frameworks by turning women into androgynous pseudo-men. Irigaray attempts to deflect this outcome through a feminist politics of sexual difference. The danger of her strategy lies in the refusal to recognise the multiplicity of differences including the difference that exists between each and any other through their differing histories, relationships, productions and ambitions. Nevertheless, Irigaray provides a valuable re-articulation of both femininity and love. No longer restricted to the role of a complementing helpmate or pleasuring instrument of man, Irigaray's feminine seeks her own pleasures and projects. In addition, Irigaray's rejection of the possessive and unifying demands of love enables a reinvention of love that, through indirection, creates exchanges between and across the proximities of lovers. More than this, indirection also signals the never completed, never resolved, movement of love. It avoids the finality of the fulfilment that would be the end of love, extending the mediation, the movement between lack and fulfilment that is the ceaseless trajectory of love.

Virginia Woolf's depiction of Orlando in her novel might be read as a more radical extension of Irigaray's conceptions of loving indirection and difference. The novel may be interpreted as Orlando's extended search for more beyond the confines of conventional life. He and she pursue various projects, engage with diverse groups and cultures and classes, and express multiple desires and obsessions, attempting always to augment and extend the experiences not only of erotic love but also of love of life more broadly. Orlando does not restrict herself to one sexual identity or to one form of sexual desire but creates a hybridity of sexualities, subjectivities and erotics. She plays between and experiences all the pleasures available within multiple expressions of love:

> . . . she found it convenient at this time to change frequently from one set of clothes to another. Thus she often occurs in contemporary memoirs as 'Lord' So-and-so, who was in fact her cousin; her bounty is ascribed to him, and it is he who is said to have written the poems that were really hers. She had, it seems, no difficulty in sustaining the different parts, for her sex changed far more frequently than those who have worn only one set of clothing can conceive; nor can there be any doubt that she reaped a twofold harvest by this device; the pleasures of life were increased and its experiences multiplied. For the probity of breeches she exchanged the seductiveness of petticoats and enjoyed the love of both sexes equally. (Woolf 2004: 141–2)

Radically refiguring difference, Woolf also refigures the modes and possibilities of the amorous encounter. While Potter's lovers – Shelmerdine and Orlando – do not marry, Woolf's lovers do exchange vows and commitments. However, this marriage is not a unifying of two into one, or a happy-ever-after merger that ends the story. Rather, the marriage signals Shelmerdine's departure and Orlando's continuing pursuit of life as a writer. This marriage is not resolution, conclusion or closure, and nor does it end the relation, for Orlando and Shelmerdine's relationship continues in its own idiosyncratic way. Instead, this marriage is a radical indirection that extends the detours, divergences and deviations of love, making of it not completion and closure but a permanently circuitous reaching for more and openness to the future:

> Together they ran through the woods, the wind plastering them with leaves as they ran, to the great court and through it and the little courts, frightened

servants leaving their brooms and their saucepans to follow after till they reached the Chapel . . . some sang aloud and others prayed, and now a bird was dashed against the pane, and now there was a clap of thunder, so that no one heard the word Obey spoken or saw, except as a golden flash, the ring pass from hand to hand . . . the Lady Orlando . . . held the swinging stirrup . . . for her husband to mount . . . and the horse leapt forward and Orlando, standing there, cried out Marmaduke Bonthrop Shelmerdine! And he answered her Orlando! . . . Orlando went indoors . . . There was the ink pot: there was the pen . . . And she plunged her pen neck deep in the ink . . . (Woolf 2004: 170–3)

Irigaray's *I Love To You* facilitates an indirection that thwarts possession and closure and enables an openness to the otherness of the other for 'It is the surprise, the unknowability, the otherness of the other that open and maintain the transformative and futural vector of relationality' (Ziarek 2000: 153). Woolf's Orlando takes this further extending the indirection of love not as a project or goal, unity or closure, but as an amorous encounter between ever-transforming alterities.

7

Barthes: A Lover's (Internet) Discourses

☙

Waiting to meet for the first time her anonymous email friend, *You've Got Mail*'s heroine Kathleen places on the café table the objects that will identify her to him – a single red rose and the Jane Austen novel *Pride and Prejudice*. Kathleen's rose is more than a natural object, undisturbed by cultural connotations – it also signifies, of course, romance and passion. As Roland Barthes (Barthes 2000: 113) explains, red roses are the emblem of love and within cultures that associate roses with love it is impossible to ignore this inherent message. Kathleen's rose is also, though, a passport – a means of identification intended to facilitate her entry into a face-to-face romantic relation.

Kathleen's other identificatory object also connotes on various levels – not simply a novel she happens to be reading, nor just a means of identification, *Pride and Prejudice* is the quintessential love story, whose title conjoins Austen's articulation of pride and prejudice with those in Kathleen's own very modern, or perhaps postmodern, tale of love.

While *You've Got Mail* reprises many of the orthodox codes of the romance genre – finding, losing and re-finding love; the obstacle that thwarts, temporarily, the fulfilment of love; the transformation of antipathy or even hatred into love – it re-contextualises this familiar story situating it within a scenario of anonymous emailing often associated with internet dating and sex services. Yet, *You've Got Mail* normalises and romanticises internet cruising, dating and chat services, allaying the cultural anxiety arising from recent changes to courting rituals and sexual encounters, and dispelling the threat, danger and titillation allied with net-dating.

Zygmunt Bauman worries that online chat is replacing relationship with the endless circulation of messages, and that this undermines commitment, longevity and trustworthiness (Bauman 2003: xlii, 34–7). While online relations appear smart and modern, Bauman is concerned that they transform the other into a deletable object. He cites a research participant interviewed in relation to computer dating who explained the 'one decisive advantage of electronic relations: "you can always press 'delete' " ' (ibid.: xii).

This chapter engages with these representations of online love, along the way employing several Barthesian strategies to demystify and decode on-line romance. Barthes' work moves from an early structuralist to a later poststructuralist approach. Employing in his early work the methods of structuralist linguistics and semiotics, Barthes reveals the myths inherent in texts (including visual texts) and decodes the cultural assumptions embedded in them. Later, adopting a more poststructural posture, he playfully questions, reverses and transgresses the oppositional structures of language and cultural belief by, for example, valorising the romantic and the sentimental – a genre that, though ubiquitous, is often derided as superficial and illusory. While this shift in Barthes' work illustrates the movement from structuralist to poststructuralist analyses, it also reveals a continuity, suggesting that the 'post' here does not connote a complete rejection or reversal of the earlier framework but rather a development.

This chapter identifies the transitions and continuities between structuralism and its 'post', utilising three Barthesian texts: *Mythologies*, *S/Z*, and *A Lover's Discourse*. It applies the framework evident in each text to a reading of contemporary debates about representations of cyber-love. While Nora Ephron's *You've Got Mail* employs online connections as a central plot device it also reprises many of the classic features of the conventional romance genre. Representing the new courtship rituals and technologies associated with cyber-love, as well as the old formulas of romantic narrative, *Mail* employs multiple discourses that may be analysed via Barthes' articulation of the mythologies and codes of the text.

MYTH

In 'Myth Today' Barthes draws on Saussure's distinction between the signifier, signified and sign in order to explain the workings of language. He illustrates the meaning and relation of these terms using the rose. The rose may operate as a signifier that is used to convey a signified, which is passion, and the two together (the signifier and signified) create the sign: 'passionified' rose (Barthes 2000: 113). Another example may help clarify. Take the word woman. The word, 'woman', just the sound of the word, without any content or attached meaning, is the signifier. The signified, however, is not the female person to whom I might point before me. Rather, the signified is the concept or idea of woman that I imagine. It is the image of woman – an image that, in Western culture, includes within it a range of associated characteristics such as being more emotional, less rational, more nurturing and so on (when compared with man). The sign is the coming together of the empty word with the meaningful concept creating a sign in which woman already contains culturally invented associations.

Taking this analysis further Barthes explains how this structure is elaborated in the construction of myth. Myth operates, Barthes suggests, by adding another layer of relation onto the first layer of meaning created by the signifier-signified-sign system. In myth, the sign from the first layer of meaning becomes a signifier on the second layer, which then has its own associated signified, and sign. The second layer of meaning is described by Barthes as a meta-language: it is, he says, a second language 'in which one speaks about the first' (ibid.: 115). Illustrating this creation of a mythological meta-language Barthes analyses a *Paris-Match* cover photo. The photo is of a black man dressed in French military uniform saluting presumably the French flag (though this latter is cropped out of the image). This is the first layer of meaning. But beyond this Barthes identifies a second mythical meaning:

> . . . that France is a great Empire, that all her sons, without colour discrimination, faithfully serve under her flag, and that there is no better answer to the detractors of an alleged colonialism than the zeal shown by this Negro in serving his so-called oppressors. (ibid.: 116)

Here, the first layer of meaning produces a sign – a black French soldier saluting. On the second level of meaning the sign becomes a signifier which produces further mythical connotations: the myths of equality between black and white, the myth of the colonised welcoming and even patriotically saluting and serving the colonisers. The photo is not just a photo of a particular man, captured at a particular moment, but in addition it surreptitiously signifies (without having to explicitly spell out) the concept or idea of racial equality and colonial allegiance. This furtive and hidden meaning is a mystification – a kind of smoke screen – that enables a mythology to camouflage and at the same time to valorise French imperialism.

You've Got Mail, like the Hollywood romance genre more generally, carries with it its own mythologies. The particular story of love, the narrative, is the first layer of meaning. In this narrative Kathleen (Meg Ryan) and Joe (Tom Hanks), using pseudonyms, are chatting on line. Offline they are business rivals who meet and form an instant antipathy. Once their 'true', online identities are revealed, the blinkers and obstacles are removed and they fall into offline love. At the end of the film they embrace, suggesting a happy-ever-after conclusion foreshadowed by Joe's earlier romantic proposal: 'how about some coffee, or drinks, or dinner, or a movie . . . for as long as we both shall live' (*You've Got Mail* 1998).

The second, meta, mythical level arises not only from this single narrative but from its participation in a broader genre whose formula is echoed in *Mail*: boy meets girl; the initial attraction thwarted at first they hate, fight and bicker; but the obstacle finally removed allows a final embrace signifying undying devotion. This story surreptitiously (or not so surreptitiously) conveys the myths of love conquering all, of happy endings and everlasting love, and perhaps also, given the lengths taken to overcome the obstacles, that we each have only one true love.

Mail iterates not only the general formula of the Hollywood romance genre but reinforces this by remaking and frequently referencing the classic and much praised 1940 romance *The Shop Around the Corner*. This twofold repetition – of the genre in general and of a particular earlier film – redoubles the mythic messages of the film bringing the implicit connotations closer to the surface and half-revealing these myths of romance. This creates a dual and paradoxical pleasure in watching the film – the pleasure of being seduced by and identifying with these reassuring romantic myths and at the same time the pleasure of deciphering the myths themselves.

Yet *You've Got Mail* does not just replicate *The Shop Around the Corner*. Although it borrows the central premise of unrecognised love it updates the methods, technologies and contexts of that metaphorical blindness (Schor 1999: 96–100). The central device of each film is a correspondence between anonymous 'friends' who, while falling in love by mail, feel nothing but antipathy in their real-life relation. The *Shop* lovers are lonely-hearts penpals corresponding by letter, while the *Mail* lovers are internet chat-room emailers. This updating manoeuvre – from letter to email and from lonely-hearts column to internet chat room – creates further mythical meanings in Ephron's film.

Internet love, sex and dating have been reviled and extolled. For some, cyber-relating destroys intimacy and commitment and transforms the other into a disposable commodity. Zygmunt Bauman, writing of the frailty of human bonds more generally, despairingly reflects on a range of innovations in love relations from net-dating, to 'top-pocket-relationships', to 'semi-detached-couples', to de facto relationships all of which he contends undermine deep and lasting love. For Bauman:

> Loose and eminently revocable partnerships have replaced the model of a 'till death us do part' personal union . . . An unprecedented fluidity, fragility and

in-built transience (the famed 'flexibility') mark all sorts of social bonds which
but a few years ago combined into a durable, reliable framework inside which
a web of human interaction could be securely woven. (Bauman 2003: 90–1)

Bauman warns that quantity has replaced quality in love: while there is
an illusion of learning more about love with each new experience, in fact
all that is acquired is a skill in quick endings and new beginnings which
amounts to a '*de-learning* of love; a "trained incapacity" for loving'
(ibid.: 5). In a culture obsessed with commodities and investments love
that fails to provide a profit – here profit means security and nurturing –
is quickly reinvested elsewhere (thereby undermining the possibility of
the sought security), and like a disposable commodity is replaced with
the latest model (ibid.: 12–15).

Net-dating, net-working and net-surfing epitomise this troublingly
'liquid love'. Net communication, Bauman suggests, has no (meaningful or
significant) content. The point is the constant circulation of messages,
staying in the loop, permanently connected, rather than deep communication (ibid.: 34–5). Like mobile phones and texting, emailing and messaging
create connections irrespective of location, proximity and circumstances. A
multiplicity of superficiality replaces deeper communication, caring and
commitment; and replaces, too, face-to-face interrelation, the phone and
the net having priority over those physically present (ibid.: 58–61). Virtual
proximities, for Bauman, replace physical connection with material bodies,
and destroy the skill of human communication (ibid.: 64–5). This has consequences for dating in particular. As texting replaces talking, the social
skills required to meet and engage with others is eroded. Moreover, the rules
of courtship are also transformed as email connections are easily made and
broken. Internet dating, in Bauman's view, is a form of 'shopping for partners': 'Just like browsing through the pages of a mail-order catalogue with
a "no obligation to buy" promise and a "return to the shop if dissatisfied"
guarantee on the front page' (ibid.: 65).

You've Got Mail could be read as a direct refutation of Bauman's concerns. The messages Kathleen and Joe send each other are intimate and
intense revealing more than each express to their respective offline partners. Indeed, Kathleen and Joe's email relation is depicted as more
rewarding, meaningful and mutually supportive than their rather superficial and selfish offline relationships.

However, both these depictions of cyber-love produce or contribute to
existing mythologies about offline relationships. Bauman nostalgically
remembers an earlier age of more authentic and committed genuine
'till death us do part' relationship – but this image is itself mythic. As

Beauvoir's analysis of love, discussed in Chapter 3, demonstrates, inequality between the sexes reduces the love relation to servitude and tyranny with each partner trapped in their respective roles of dependency and mastery. Bauman's belief in a more authentic relation, now under threat by technology, obscures the inequality that creates inauthentic, destructive and even violent relationships. In addition, some theorists suggest that cyber-relating facilitates engagements that resemble those stereotypically associated with feminine desire including a focus on getting to know the person rather than on superficial appearance, and a great deal of talk, which frequently involves self-disclosure and intimacy (Ben-Ze'ev 2004). Bauman's critique of the role of the new communication technologies in transforming love relations, relies on a mythical image of a halcyon age of genuine committed relationship and an equally mythic conception of the superficiality of the present.

Interestingly, though *You've Got Mail* appears to present an opposite view, by valorising cyber-love against Bauman's alarmed detraction, it also perpetuates the same myths. While Kathleen and Joe communicate by email, the film constantly references the traditional values evident in *The Shop Around the Corner*. Kathleen and Joe envisage, seek, and in the end commit to a meaningful and everlasting relationship, replicating not just *The Shop Around the Corner* but the romance genre more generally. Moreover, the superficiality of modern love that Bauman abhors is also disparagingly represented here through the figure of Joe's father (Dabney Coleman) with his serial failed marriages that appear to be founded on greed and status – the trophy wife, the alimony settlement – and on the disposable commodity circulation that Bauman identifies. *Mail* valorises cyber-love but only by representing it as a return of the golden age of committed love of which Bauman dreams, replacing the modern liquid love represented here by the father.

Beyond the literal narrative level of *Mail* we may decipher a meta-level of meaning which valorises the traditional values of commitment and security, and of truth and authenticity embedded within the romantic mythology of everlasting and true love. Similarly, Bauman's text may be interpreted through a Barthesian frame revealing, beyond his concerns about the transience and frailty of modern love, a meta-theory that is committed to a conventional ideal that sanctions marriage, monogamy, durability and security. Identifying this meta (mythical) theory does not require a rejection of Bauman's concern about the frailty of human bonds. Rather it reveals the unquestioning assumption that human bonds were once upon a time more secure and that traditional institutions such as conventional marriage and family structures guarantee this security.

Barthes' 'Myth Today' enables a reading beyond the explicit meaning or narrative level revealing a meta-language or meta-narrative hidden in both the filmic and the theoretical texts. However, the analysis rests on an assumption that there is something behind the text: a hidden meaning, an overarching broader structure or genre, that provides the key to the further meanings or messages contained within the text. In *S/Z* Barthes undertakes a self-critique in which he questions the hierarchical structure that this approach entails.

CODES

In *S/Z* Barthes implicitly critiques, though he doesn't entirely reject, his own earlier theory. Barthes had identified two levels of meaning in signs and utterances. The first is the literal meaning (or what Barthes later calls denotation) – in the earlier example this was the black soldier saluting the French flag. The second is the mythic meaning (later called connotation) – the myths of equality and colonial allegiance connoted by the photographic image. Barthes acknowledges that this structure involves a hierarchy in which the first level is privileged as the primary and original meaning – the objective and incontestable meaning – while the second level is derivative and reliant on the first level of meaning. As Barthes acknowledges this structuring is problematic as it implies an originary, stable, foundation that can guarantee a determinable truthful or authentic meaning. Barthes explains:

> . . . the endeavor of this hierarchy is a serious one: it is to return to the closure of Western discourse (scientific, critical, or philosophical), to its centralised organization, to arrange all the meanings of a text in a circle around the hearth of denotation (the hearth: centre, guardian, refuge, light of truth). (Barthes 2002: 7)

Yet Barthes also defends this approach pointing out that connotation indicates that texts can have multiple meanings, and also that these meanings do not simply emerge from the text but also externally from the social and literary-theoretical context of the text. The plural meanings or polysemy of the text arises, in part, from its relation to other texts implicitly invoked in the text – it is the texts 'power to relate itself to anterior, ulterior, or exterior mentions, to other sites of the text (or of another text)' (Barthes 2002: 8). The relation between the text and its entire context determines the mythic or connotative meaning so that the myths of equality and colonial allegiance can only be associated with the photo of the black soldier in the context of a cultural and political valorisation of equality and of imperial conquest. Moreover, following Barthes' theory this image could acquire quite another meaning if it were placed in other contexts. The photo of a black French soldier saluting may acquire additional connotations if it were found on a website for uniform fetishists, for example, or in a documentary about army regulations and rituals, or a book on non-verbal gestures of communication.

Further, Barthes argues that denotation should not be understood as the originary, truthful, meaning but as an illusion of a literal foundational meaning. The denotation is only another level of connotation – the level of connotation that innocently masquerades as the most basic and incontestable meaning of the image or text. For Barthes: 'denotation is not the first meaning, but pretends to be so; under this illusion, it is ultimately no more than the last of the connotations (the one which seems both to establish and to close the reading), the superior myth by which the text pretends to return to the nature of language, to language as nature' (Barthes 2002: 9). Following this elaboration the 'originary' meaning of the saluting soldier is called into question. Not only does the image conjure myths of French empire and of racial equality but in addition the image of the saluting soldier evokes homage of and defence of national interests, rights and freedoms. These terms in turn conjure further meanings: propriety, morality, and nation, to name a few. Just as the sign 'woman' evokes culturally invented associations so too does 'soldier' and 'salute'. The 'originary' denotation reveals an ever unfolding chain of connotations.

Barthes begins to move here from a structuralist to a poststructuralist approach while also demonstrating a certain connection between them. Barthes' interest in the structuralist project of the scientific study of sign systems, and his attempts to classify and to explain systematic relations that create signs and myths, evolves into a poststructuralist recognition of a plurality of meanings and of a complex inter-relation between texts.

Barthes advances the project further in *S/Z*, a book in which he analyses Balzac's short story 'Sarrasine', by elaborating a reading method involving breaking the text down into very short sections, or lexia, and interpreting these through five codes which organise textual meanings. The five codes are the hermeneutic, proairetic, symbolic, semic and referential. The hermeneutic code refers to the aspects of a narrative or text that contain an enigma and its solution, a question and the movement toward the answer, the mystery and suspense in a story. In *You've Got Mail* the enigma revolves around the anonymity of the emailing friends and the question of how their online friendship will be affected by their offline enmity. The suspense element of the film is sustained by tracking the two parallel relationships between Joe and

Kathleen – their offline antagonism created by business rivalry between their respective bookshops (one a mega-chain, the other a family-owned children's book store called The Shop Around the Corner) and their online infatuated friendship.

The proairetic code refers to the series of actions and their effects that together make up a recognisable element of the plot. Barthes provides examples such as 'stroll, murder, rendezvous' (Barthes 2002: 19) to illustrate but we could add other common action codes such as rituals of courtship or friendship or of business rivalry. Jonathan Culler explains: 'because we have stereotyped models of "falling in love", or "kidnapping", or "undertaking a perilous mission," we can tentatively place and organise the details we encounter as we read' (Culler 1990: 84). This code of actions affects our reading of Kathleen and Joe's romance. Knowing already the patterns and devices of the conventional love story we interpret this particular romance through this broader frame. Kathleen and Joe's offline antagonism for example is already a sign of its opposite – love – for the romance plot frequently uses this delaying device.

This opposition between love and antipathy is also related to the symbolic code, which for Barthes is 'the province of the antithesis . . . linking . . . two adversative terms (A/B)' (Barthes 2002: 17–18). Barthes elaborates writing: 'this is the place for multivalence and for reversibility' (Barthes 2002: 19) and Culler clarifies writing that: 'the symbolic code guides the extrapolation from textual details to symbolic interpretations' (Culler 1990: 84). So, not only does hate already herald, through the proairetic code, a future love but in addition this dichotomy is associated through the symbolic code with various other oppositions between Joe and Kathleen. They come from different worlds – Joe from the world of entrepreneurial mega-corporations and private yachts, and Kathleen from the world of small business, eccentric friends and small pleasures. The film implicitly debates the viability of love between opposites with the Joe and Kathleen couple replacing Kathleen's earlier coupling with Frank (Greg Kinnear) who is represented as having common values and a shared lifestyle with Kathleen. The film thus reflects and validates the 'opposites attract' cliché and it does this by amassing a detailed account of the differences and the antipathy between the protagonists and then transforming difference into a basis for love rather than hate.

The semic code refers to the construction of the characters through stereotyped and therefore recognisable signs and attributes. Joe's character connotes first of all wealth, privilege and conservative attitudes – the yacht, the mega-corporation, the palatial office with a view, the suits.

This though is quickly augmented with more whimsical and endearing qualities – his love of children, his love of animals, his pleasure in spring sunshine and in playful conversations – traits that correlate with Kathleen's character. So while the symbolic code creates differences between the lovers, the semic code creates an opposing trajectory of similarity. While they come from different worlds they also share a sensibility – one in which family is valued, and ultimately in which genuine love triumphs over status, position and circumstances.

Finally, the referential code or what Barthes also calls the cultural code draws on existing cultural references, on 'a science or a body of knowledge' (Barthes 2002: 20). The referential codes reproduce 'maxims and proverbs about life' which transform cultural constructions into seemingly natural observations. As Barthes observes: ' "Life" . . . in the classic text, becomes a nauseating mixture of common opinions, a smothering layer of received ideas . . .' (Barthes 2002: 206). Here again, Barthes' codes enable yet another layer of meanings and associations to be deciphered in *You've Got Mail*. Kathleen's character references not only *The Shop Around the Corner*'s Klara (Margaret Sullivan) but also a host of other heroines epitomised by an endearing vulnerability combined with a feisty singularity. She is playfully (though never effectively or threateningly) rebellious. When her anonymous email friend advices her to 'go to the mattresses', to fight to the end against her business rival, she comically limbers up by prancing round the shop punching the air like a cartoon boxer. The stereotyped romantic heroine is reprised – playful and fun, charming, endearing, vulnerable, needing advice, support and guidance, and ultimately saccharine and vacuous.

Ultimately Barthes' codes reveal that the meanings in *You've Got Mail* are not primarily created internally within this filmic text but rather adhere to it through the cultural codes and associations that the film, and our reading of it, evoke. In addition, the meanings of this film are potentially endless being created through the multiple articulations with other texts – not just other films, but also the discourses and knowledges produced by literature, art, history, psychology, sociology, philosophy, ethics and so on, more generally.

In addition, the meanings of the film may even be acquired retrospectively as the context of its reception and interpretation alters. Texts do not simply draw on and reiterate existing 'common opinions' and 'received ideas' through the referential code but may also acquire new meanings subsequently attributed to the text by future readers. *You've Got Mail* might, for example, be retrospectively read as a metaphorical representation of the merger between the mega-corporations associated with its production. The Warner Bros studio produced *You've Got Mail* and it features the internet company AOL (America Online) – the company that forwards mail between Joe and Kathleen and announces to each 'You've Got Mail'. The film was released in the USA in December 1998. A little over a year later in January 2000 a merger between Time Warner (parent company to Warner Bros) and AOL was announced. Jerome Christensen reads the narrative, and the other signs used in the film, in relation to this subsequent acquisition of Time Warner by AOL. Christensen argues that the final happy-ever-after embrace between Joe and Kathleen that ends the film signifies not only the 'merger' between these characters and between Fox Books and The Shop Around the Corner (though actually Fox puts The Shop out of business), but also heralds that between AOL and Time Warner. He points out that the film's opening credit sequence involves a desk top-like image with the Warner Bros logo in the top left-hand corner, a column of generic desktop icons on the right-hand side, ending with the AOL logo in the bottom right-hand corner, diagonally opposite the Warner Bros logo. Christensen comments: 'The appearance of the paired logos establishes the identities of corporate characters prior to the appearance of the human characters and forges an allegorical connection' (Christensen 2003: 206). Initially, he suggests, Joe Fox and his mega-corporation represents Warner Bros and Kathleen's Shop the then relatively small internet company, AOL, though as each company's respective stockmarket position subsequently altered these allegorical connections may be reversed. Ultimately, though, what is significant for Christensen is that the film doesn't just depict a particular internet romance but also anticipates and contributes to the later corporate romance between Warner Bros and AOL.

Perhaps it would not be out of keeping with Barthes' intentions to add a sixth code to his list – the retrospective code of endless meaning proliferation. The referential or cultural code appears to refer to a history of existing knowledges and discourses that inhere within the text. The sixth code, the proliferation code, highlights that the meanings are never final or complete but may emerge from the future contexts of textual interpretation. Moreover, the sixth code emphasises that the meanings are not buried already within the text waiting evacuation and unveiling but rather that meanings are also bought to the text from outside the text – these meanings may arise from the past and present but most significantly may also arise from the future contexts of the text.

This proliferation code raises the troubling problem of 'presentism', in which a concept or concern of the present is read into, or imposed on, a prior historical period. Writing about Michel Foucault's genealogical method, Hubert Dreyfus and Paul Rabinow distinguish between Foucault's 'history of the present' and the presentist projection of contemporary meanings onto earlier times (Dreyfus and Rabinow 1983: 118). Like Foucault's history of the present, which diagnoses the current situation in part by examining how and why it arose in the past, the proliferation code does not rewrite the meanings of earlier texts but identifies the emergence of our present in past texts. The merger of AOL and Time Warner is not exactly depicted in *You've Got Mail*: rather the conditions of possibility for this later merger are laid out and perhaps partly facilitated by the internet romance that the film does represent.

LOVER'S DISCOURSE

While in *S/Z* Barthes demonstrates the intertextuality of texts in *A Lover's Discourse* he takes this a step further, enacting (rather than explaining) this inter-textuality. *A Lover's Discourse* is made of fragments, mimicry and repetition. Drawing on literary, philosophical and psychoanalytic texts, on conversations, and on personal experiences Barthes creates a series of figures or gestures of love organised alphabetically around framing words such as 'Absence', 'Declaration', 'Fadeout', 'Monstrous' and 'Gossip'. Without providing detailed referencing, Barthes nevertheless indicates a range of sources – Nietzsche, Plato, Freud, Winnicott, Proust and, recurring most frequently, Goethe's *The Sorrows of Young Werther* – that perhaps quintessential story of tragic unrequited love. *A Lover's Discourse* makes clear that a text can never be absolutely original – it has its inspiration and sources in its heritage and its contemporary contexts. *A Lover's Discourse* suggests that lovers' discourses in particular are saturated by a plethora of textual models and codes. More significantly still, love itself is the performative re-enactment of lover's discourses. Barthes suggests that 'no love is original' arguing that 'love proceeds from others, from language, from books, from friends' (Barthes 1984: 136). This suggests that love is discursively constructed – it is a montage of earlier amorous declarations; it is a mimicry of the representations of love (filmic, literary, visual and textual, poetic, philosophical, psychoanalytic, biological and spiritual); it is an enactment of rituals and conventions. Love in this view may be best understood as a script. A lover's discourse arises from the 'memory of the sites (books, encounters) where such and such a thing had been read, spoken, heard' (ibid.: 9).

A *Lover's Discourse* elaborates this love script identifying the images and texts that weave together to form the script. Imitating this 'repository of cultural conventions' (Raval 2001: 286) lovers identify with earlier lovers – with earlier love models. Discussing Goethe's *Werther* Barthes comments:

> Werther identifies himself with the madman, with the footman [other unrequited lovers]. As a reader, I identify myself with Werther. Historically, thousands of subjects have done so, suffering, killing themselves, dressing, perfuming themselves, writing as if they were Werther . . . A long chain of equivalences links all the lovers in the world. (Barthes 1984: 131)

While we might normally assume that the lover loves the beloved, for Barthes, the lover is in love with love: 'by a specifically amorous perversion, it is love the subject loves, not the object' (ibid.: 31). The lover loves an image (what Barthes calls the image repertoire) ordained by the historical and cultural context rather than the love object itself. Turning again to Werther, Barthes' explains: 'Charlotte [the object of Werther's love] is quite insipid . . . by a kindly decision of this subject [Werther], a colorless object is placed in the centre of the stage and there adored, idolised, taken to task, covered with discourse, with prayers . . .' (ibid.: 31)

And he continues:

> . . . it is my desire I desire, and the loved being is no more than its tool . . . And if the day comes when I must bring myself to renounce the other . . . I weep for the loss of love, not of him or her. (ibid.: 31)

Not only is the experience of love scripted but in addition the being that is loved is itself an image constructed through intertextuality. Love is love for an ideal image rather than of the Other subject. Nevertheless, Barthes continues, the lover attempts to ensure that the beloved participates in and shares the same image-repertoire. The lover constantly searches for indications of a shared discourse and, if needs be, invents signs of reciprocated love:

> Accidentally, Werther's finger touches Charlotte's, their feet under the table, happen to brush each other . . . he creates meaning, always and everywhere, out of nothing, and it is this meaning that thrills him . . . A squeeze of the hand – enormous documentation – a tiny gesture within the palm, a knee which doesn't move away, an arm extended, as if quite naturally, along the back of a sofa and against which the other's head gradually comes to rest – this is the paradisiac realm of subtle and clandestine signs: a kind of festival not of senses but of meaning. (ibid.: 67)

If the touch of a finger, the movement of a head, can be endlessly scrutinised for signs of love, so too can texts including email texts. In their online conversation Kathleen and Joe send messages that convey more than their literal content. The frequency and speed of response, the length of the message, the level of intimacy, the confiding of secret wishes and dreams, the request for advice are all signs that may be deciphered just like those of bodily gesture. The online conversation contains its own intensity created by the proliferation of signs – and by their ambiguity. The unseen online other, like the visible love object, is a blank screen on which the lover projects her idealised image. The online other becomes the tool for the creation of a love that loves love – the perfect object to place centre stage and to lavish with praise, adoration, prayers, fantasies and hopes.

So potent is this idealised image that contrary evidence is eclipsed by the power of the idealised image. Kathleen and Joe's emailing gathers romantic intensity leading to the question 'Shall we meet?' In their parallel offline encounters this couple are locked in business and personal battle. His bookstore chain destroys her tiny speciality shop; his life of greed and status is antithetical to her more bohemian milieu. But this disjunction between their online attraction and offline repulsion is quickly resolved, first for Joe and subsequently for Kathleen, as the online idealised image triumphs over the abjected offline image. Once Joe learns that his online correspondent is Kathleen, he revises his offline judgements and implements a seduction aimed at overcoming Kathleen's antipathy to the man who has destroyed her business. Drawing on the repertoire of love discourses he courts her by offering the conventional signs of love – the gift of flowers (daisies, not roses, as Kathleen had earlier referred to her preference for the simple daisy), the lazy afternoon stroll together, the easy pleasant teasing conversations veering ever so slightly into flirtation. His aim is to transform himself from monster, to friend, to lover and in so doing he borrows from the repertoire of images of the lover and of love. His final success is signalled by the most repeated and clichéd of all love symbols – the embrace among the flowerbeds that slowly dissolves into end-credits signifying the happy-ever-after conclusion.

You've Got Mail is saturated with sentimental platitudes about love – that opposites attract, that true love lasts forever, that love conquers all, that genuine love cares not for fame and fortune, that the active male pursues and persuades the resisting, vulnerable passive female beloved. These common-sense clichéd ideas about love are not invented by the film but are conveyed, passed on, by the film. They are acquired from the plethora of texts, rituals and codes on love and re-enacted reinforcing their hold.

Barthes does not straightforwardly reject the sentimental. *A Lover's Discourse* is not only, and perhaps not primarily, a critique of the iteration of lover's discourses. Instead it is, in part, a defence of amorous, sentimental addresses. Barthes attempts throughout his writings to challenges the doxas, the conventions, of society and of thought. *A Lover's Discourse* challenges antithetical doxas: the orthodox romanticised beliefs about love, but also the denigration of these beliefs as trite, sentimental and delusional. Barthes' book responds to both the valorisation of love and the deprecation of love. He reveals the cultural fabrication of love undermining the mythical naturalisation of love but equally he elaborates and expands love's texts contesting the critique of love and its pleasures.

While love is on the one hand valorised it has also been dismissed as a delusion, a restriction of freedom, and a distraction from more urgent political agendas. Jean-Paul Sartre, for example, dismisses love as a form of escapism that avoids or distracts from the difficult and painful realities of life. For him it also involves an attempt to dominate the other and to limit her or his freedom and this inevitably ends in hatred and cruelty (Sartre 1995: 364–412). Following Freud, love is often perceived as delusional – it involves idealisation such that it is not the beloved who is adored but an ideal phantom. For Freud, all love is either narcissistic or anaclitic: it involves projections onto the other of either the self or of the founding love experienced with either the mother or father. What is loved is not the other but the image of the self or parent imposed upon the other (Ferrell 1996: 47–55). Feminist theorists have also been wary of love, regarding it as a trap that keeps women subservient as they provide care, security and nurturance of family for love rather than for money. Shulamith Firestone, for example, contends that 'Men were thinking, writing, and creating because women were pouring their energy into those men; women are not creating culture because they are preoccupied with love' (Firestone 1971: 142–3) This relentless critique resulted in an antipathy to love conceived as a bourgeois ideology, a sort of opiate, that disguised real oppression and exploitation and distracted from political action. Love came to be seen as personal, sentimental and illusory obviating the need for public concrete politics. As Culler comments: 'sentimentality, "discredited by modern opinion", makes love unfashionable, even "obscene", a topic not to be discussed in polite company – unlike sex, which is accepted as an important subject of current discourse' (Culler 1990: 112).

In this context Barthes attempts a double transgression: a refusal of both the valorisation and the vilification of love. Barthes begins his

Lover's Discourse with an explanation: because love is 'ignored, disparaged . . . derided . . . exiled' his book 'has no recourse but to become the site, however exiguous, of an *affirmation*' (Barthes 1984: 1).

While Barthes enables a disentangling of the language systems and discourses of love he does not therefore reject the sentimentality, romance, passion and obsession of love. Rather, *A Lover's Discourse* is a reflection of the obsessions and anxieties of love which attempts an impossible transgression by valorising the sentimental while at the same time analysing the cultural repetitions and mimicry of passion and revealing the doxas and para-doxas of love talk. For Barthes 'It is no longer the sexual which is indecent, it is the sentimental – censured in the name of what is in fact another morality' (ibid.: 177). He knows that sentimentality leaves the lover 'alone and exposed' (ibid.: 175) and appearing 'stupid' (ibid.: 177). Yet he transgressively attempts a recuperation or affirmation of love despite the impossibility of this project, for:

> Amorous obscenity is extreme: nothing can redeem it, bestow upon it the positive value of a transgression . . . The amorous text (scarcely a text at all) consists of little narcissisms, psychological paltrinesses; it is without grandeur: or its grandeur . . . is to be unable to reach any grandeur, not even that of a 'crass materialism'. (ibid.: 178–9)

Yet, this does not mean that Barthes lapses back into a renewed sentimentality. Rather he also contests the platitudes about love by revealing their contagious textual effects. The result of Barthes' dual transgression against orthodox love and against the antithetical doxa that disparages love, is a transporting or trans-positioning of love – returning us to another different love inflected with the intertextual but also with transgression. *You've Got Mail* does not transgress. Rather it naturalises love representing even cyber-love as a prelude to a white-picket-fence normality. Barthes' intuition would not be to reject the sentimental in *You've Got Mail* but to reveal its reliance on a history of romantic tales and to unravel the discourses that make the rose-coloured outcome appear to be only natural.

8

Butler and Foucault: Que(e)rying Marriage

The debate about same-sex marriage has polarised not only the straight community but also the gay and lesbian community. Same-sex marriage provides the extension of rights available to heterosexual couples to those previously excluded because of discrimination and prejudice and so appears, at first, an unquestionable good from a progressive viewpoint. Yet many radical gays and lesbians reject marriage, arguing that it imposes a heterosexual institution on a queer lifestyle thereby constraining the difference signified by homosexuality. Moreover, they argue, marriage, as an institution that regulates both citizenship and kinship relations, functions as a means of excluding the alien, the other, the foreigner and as a mechanism for normalising family within traditional structures. On the other hand, many gay men and lesbians welcome marriage, rejoicing in the opportunity to publicly declare their love and embracing the legal and economic benefits it bestows – including, depending on the particularities of each nation's legal framework, citizenship rights, access to adoption and fertility services, and tax, inheritance, health and executorial benefits. (While different countries have adopted varying frameworks and terminologies, civil unions, civil partnerships, etc., I use the term same-sex marriage here to refer to the broad concept rather than to the details of these varying legal constructions.)

The debate among queers has been fraught and complex but can perhaps be most succinctly represented as a debate between the right to equality and the right to express queer difference. The USA TV series *Queer as Folk* encapsulates this debate in the representation of Michael and Ben's marriage in Toronto while on an AIDS fundraising 'Liberty' bicycle ride. Following a romantic proposal from his partner Ben (Robert Grant), Michael (Hal Sparks) debates with his friend and ex-lover, bad-boy-with-heart-of-gold Brian (Gale Harold), the pros and cons:

> Brian: We're queer. We don't need marriage. We don't need the sanction of dickless politicians and pederast priests. We fuck who we want to, when we want to. That is our god given right.

Michael: But it's also our god given right to have everything that straight people have. Coz we're every bit as much human as they are.

Brian: You're the writer. Rewrite the story. (*Queer as Folk*, Season 4, Episode 13)

For Brian, marriage represents a restriction of sexual freedom and a conditional acceptance under sufferance by a hypocritical society. For Michael, marriage provides the extension of equal rights and recognition of the full humanity of lesbians and gays.

While these positions convey the two predominant gay and lesbian responses to the recent marriage proposals, restrictions and reforms, the issues behind these dichotomous positionings are complex and significant not only for same-sex, but also for heterosexual, marriage. In this chapter I will examine the debates around kinship, recognition, erotic love and ceremony. I will suggest that marriage offers both liberatory and repressive potentials and that the political effects of marriage are undecidable, variable and ambiguous. Same-sex marriage is a coming out of the closet, but the secrecy of the closet has offered a space for an unconventional Eros to proliferate. Marriage enables a making public of homosexuality. The risk is the loss of a culture of difference that may only flourish in the margins that resist and ignore the strictures of normality.

KINSHIP

Judith Butler finds herself somewhat awkwardly positioned in relation to the same-sex marriage debate. While not wanting to participate in a dichotomously constructed debate, in which one must be either for or against same-sex marriage, she feels obliged to refute the homophobic arguments against same-sex marriage when she is invoked as a representative of the threat supposedly posed by queer life. In the context of the debate in France, Butler writes, she has been named as the representative of 'a certain American strain of queer and gender theory' associated with 'the monstrous future for France were these [same-sex marriage] transformations to occur' (Butler 2002: 24–5). While not necessarily an advocate of same-sex marriage, then, Butler feels constrained to at least respond to these assertions about a 'coming monstrosity' and to do so by revealing the prejudices and contradictions inherent in the homophobic attack on same-sex marriage. In doing this Butler takes on, not the dogmatic assertion that homosexuality is unnatural nor the simplistic claim that same-sex marriage would undermine the institution of marriage, nor the argument that children need a parent of each sex. Instead, she responds to a more sophisticated variant of these assertions.

In France, public intellectuals including philosophers and psychoanalysts became involved in the debate with some contending that it would undermine the 'symbolic order' were lesbians and gays entitled to form families (Butler 2002: 21; Fassin 2001: 215–32). This claim is not founded directly on a belief in a 'natural' family but rather on an assertion about a socially conceived system that regulates family life producing normative subjects. Butler explains:

> The belief is that culture itself requires that a man and a woman produce a child and that the child have this dual point of reference for its own initiation into the symbolic order, where the symbolic order consists of a set of rules that order and support our sense of reality and cultural intelligibility. (Butler 2002: 29)

At base, Butler suggests, this requirement for a mother and a father for each child is founded on an Oedipal construction in which the father disrupts the child's initial love, which is for the mother, so as to ensure a transferral of love onto a more appropriate object in later life and also to facilitate the child's transition into the social and legal order. While those opposed to same-sex marriage may acknowledge that many children lack the two parents required for this structure, they contend that an idea or a story of two opposite-sex parents must exist for the child. What is required, they suggest, is not necessarily two opposite-sex parents both actually involved with the child, but the idea or the 'symbol' of these two parents as an origin for the child.

However, as Butler points out if it is merely a symbolic structure that is required, and not two actual empirical opposite-sex parents, then this is equally available to conventional families, single parent families, and same-sex families as all exist within a heterosexual culture. Butler suggests, then, that behind the argument for a 'symbolic order' there is an assumption about a 'natural order' of sexual difference (ibid.: 31). Moreover, the further implication is that kinship relations more broadly must also be founded on heterosexuality and that non-heterosexual relations would only become legible in this system if they mimicked traditional forms. In other words: 'those who enter kinship terms as nonheterosexual will only make sense if they assume the position of Mother or Father' (ibid.: 34).

Butler suggests that the insistence on a 'founding heterosexuality' is not only a fantasy but also a manifestation of the operation of power (ibid.: 34). She counters the postulation that heterosexuality is required in familial and kinship structures referencing recent anthropological reinterpretations of kinship that perceive it as a process of actions, 'a kind of *doing*' (ibid.: 34), rather than a biological structure. Kinship practices, Butler argues, are formed in response to various forms of dependency 'which may include birth, child-rearing, relations of emotional dependency and support, generational ties, illness, dying, and death (to name a few)' (ibid.: 15). It is not distinct from friendship, community and the state, but imbricated with these structures and its forms may vary in different times and contexts. The enduring legacy of slavery, for example, has produced African-American kinship structures predominantly organised through relations between women where there may or may not be biological connections. Lesbian and gay kinship structures are distinct from biological family ties and differ in form from those family structures (ibid.: 15). Biotechnologies and international adoption regulations have expanded kinship structures revealing the fantasy that kinship and family are necessarily biological. Butler concludes that these transformations and developments challenge the separation of kinship, community, friendship on one hand and the union of family, kinship and biology on the other:

> . . . the relations of kinship arrive at boundaries that call into question the distinguishability of kinship from community, or that call for a different conception of friendship. These constitute a 'breakdown' of traditional kinship that not only displaces the central place of biological and sexual relations from its definition, but gives sexuality a separate domain from that of kinship, allowing as well for the durable tie to be thought outside of the conjugal frame, and opening kinship to a set of community ties that are irreducible to family. (Butler 2002: 37–8)

Returning to the assertion that culture is founded on an Oedipal structure based on a heterosexual family, Butler does not reject the significance of the Oedipus relation but instead questions the assumption that this requires a heterosexual foundation. She describes the Oedipal relation as a triangular structure and asks: 'what forms does that triangularity take? Must it presume heterosexuality? And what happens when we begin to understand Oedipus outside of the exchange of women and the presumption of heterosexual exchange?' (ibid.: 38).

While the conservative critics of same-sex marriage have insisted that children need a story of origin which includes a father and mother, Butler speculates about the possibility and viability of alternative stories, asking about the varying stories produced by and for adopted children and children conceived through assisted insemination. She speculates that these stories may be numerous and subject to transformation as they are re-narrated over time and she ponders the possibility that non-normative origin stories may un-couple the 'homology between nature and culture' (ibid.: 39) that conservative opponents of same-sex marriage have assumed.

Butler concludes that the aim ought not be to assert the normality of same-sex families, as this acquiesces to the dominant frameworks that define and delimit the normal. Nor would a defiant valorisation of the 'pathological' or 'deviant' succeed in challenging the status quo for it leaves the opposition between normal and pathological, the inside and the outside, the acceptable and the abject, in place. Rather Butler advocates a double-edged thinking' (ibid.: 40) which refuses the terms of the current debate – refuses to answer either yes or no to marriage – and instead advocates a more radical politics that contests the assumption of a necessary relation between family and kinship, and the linking of sexuality and marriage.

Butler's main objective in this article is to uncouple the articulation of marriage, family and kinship and to insist on a sexuality that exceeds the confines of marriage. For Butler, kinship is an 'enacted practice' through which dependents are nurtured and cared for. As the AIDS crisis demonstrates, this care is not necessarily provided by biological family members or by partners but is often provided by the gay community, friends and lovers and it is this that creates kinship relations. Butler also refuses the restriction of legitimate sexuality to marriage relations. While marriage may ratify and justify certain relations, at the same moment it further marginalises others so that multiple and temporary liaisons become illegitimate or legally and socially invisible. While Butler critiques the homophobic fear of same-sex marriage she neither supports or rejects the legal recognition of lesbian and gay partnerships. What she does rather is refuse the fantasy that kinship and family are founded in biology and the illusion that a legitimate sexuality is expressed only in marriage.

RECOGNITION

Lesbian and gay rights theorists have advocated for same-sex marriage on various grounds – that it provides economic and legal benefits, that it provides a framework that supports long-term committed relationships, that it provides equality for lesbian and gay couples. Yet, perhaps the most compelling argument is that it provides recognition by legitimising relationships that have been variously criminalised, pathologised, rendered illegitimate or invisible. Andrew Sullivan argues that marriage is crucial, even the 'centrepiece', of lesbian and gay politics because it involves public state sanction of homosexual relationships and recognition of homosexual identity. He writes:

> This is a question of formal public discrimination, since only the state can grant and recognise marriage. If the military ban deals with the heart of what it means to be a citizen, marriage does even more so, since, in peace and war, it affects everyone. Marriage is not simply a private contract; it is a social and public recognition of a private commitment. As such, it is the highest public recognition of personal integrity. Denying it to homosexuals is the most public affront possible to their public equality. (Sullivan 2004: 205)

Yet recognition may not be as straightforwardly beneficial as Sullivan assumes. Michael Warner responds to Sullivan, suggesting that the recognition bestowed through same-sex marriage in effect imposes the norms of heterosexual culture upon the lesbian and gay community, conferring respectability on those who marry while denying it to others (including those who are single, have multiple partners, or more transient relationships), and thereby regulating and restricting other forms of sexual relation (Warner 2000: 88–9). While Judith Butler acknowledges the pragmatic benefits of state legitimation (Butler 2002: 25) she also develops Warner's critique of recognition asking why the right to provide (or withhold) recognition should be assigned to the state. To grant the power of recognition to the state undermines other possible forms of validation and reproduces the hegemonic and hierarchical control of the state. Butler suggests that relying on state-based recognition both extends state power and acquiesces to norms of identity and sexuality determined by the state. She adds: 'in making a bid to the state for recognition, we effectively restrict the domain of what will become recognizable as legitimate sexual arrangements, thus fortifying the state as the source for norms of recognition and eclipsing other possibilities within civil society and cultural life' (ibid.: 26–7).

Alexander Düttmann further challenges the call for recognition by dissecting and revealing the paradoxical nature of recognition. The act of recognition necessarily involves a moment of incorporation, or of normalisation, in absorbing the minority (who call for recognition) into the terrain of the majority (who provide recognition). Recognition, in this moment, is a re-cognising or an identification that, through cognition, categorises and defines. This re-cognising involves a normalising tendency that absorbs and neutralises the other, thereby destroying their difference. Düttmann writes: 'the struggle for recognition disappears in a reformism which admits differences only to the extent that they can be considered as valid differences, that is, differences justified by their relation to a unity' (Düttmann 2000: 105). Re-cognising is achieved by identifying a commonality – 'we're every bit as human as they as' as Michael, in *Queer as Folk*, asserts – and ignoring the differences and incommensurability between groups. This re-cognition tolerates the minority but only on the basis that they relinquish their difference and conform to the standards and behaviours, morality and lifestyles of the majority. Immigrants are expected to assimilate and to learn the language of the new nation. Working women are expected to conform to corporate objectives and workplace regulations, setting aside family responsibilities. Queers may be recognised on the condition that they create conventional monogamous pairings and traditional two-parent families. In this context, Düttmann describes Sullivan's *Virtually Normal*, in which he argues that homosexuals are in essence normal, as an 'apologetic pamphlet' that 'enables normality to affirm itself even more forcefully and relentlessly' (ibid. 2000: 115–16).

Yet Düttmann identifies a paradoxical effect also inherent within recognition. Recognition both confirms an identity *and* establishes an identity. It is both constative and performative; that is it both makes a statement confirming an existing identity *and* simultaneously produces or establishes or creates an identity. For Düttmann: 'Recognition does not leave the presupposed identity of the one who is recognised untouched' (ibid.: 4). Rather the act of recognition involves a transformation. Even more significantly, it is not just the group seeking recognition that is transformed but also those who bestow recognition. The majority are constructed within the relation of recognising as the potential bestowers of recognition and so seek confirmation or recognition as this identity – as bestowers of recognition, as the majority who hold the power to bestow recognition. Those seeking recognition have already conferred an identity upon themselves in order to be in a position to solicit recognition – in order to demand recognition of same-sex marriage, for example, those making the demand already identify as homosexuals, gays or lesbians, and as same-sex couples. But in seeking recognition the minority can determine whether to allow the majority the identity of those who bestow recognition. Judith Butler, for example, as we have seen, questions whether queers ought to ascribe to the state the role or the task of providing recognition. Düttmann, explaining this paradox within recognition writes:

Whoever demands recognition has already arrived at his destination, is already where he still has to get to; he does not require the recognition he demands. His polemical presumptuousness consists in the fact that he, the one who wishes to be recognised, transforms the others, the ones who are meant to recognise him, into those who have to be recognised. Thus the roles, functions and positions become involved in an uninterrupted and uncontrolled exchange. Ultimately one cannot decide who it is that is supposed to be recognized here and now, and who it is that is recognizing the other here and now. (2000: 111)

Recognition for Düttmann is a complex and uncontrolled process that has the potential to endlessly invert the roles – those who recognise are themselves recognised, while the recognised also recognise the recogniser. This does not however create balance or a harmonious reconciliation but rather results in unceasing disturbance that puts in question identity by interrupting any stable settled identity (ibid.: 27).

For Düttmann then, recognition has a double potential. It may function through assimilation, normalising the other and destroying difference. Or, it may trouble identity creating new subjectivities not only for the minority calling for recognition but also for the majority who may or may not be in turn recognised by the minority. Same-sex marriage appears at first to be limited to the first aspect of the paradox of recognition in that it requires gays and lesbians to conform to the strictures of a quintessentially heteronormative institution. Yet, same-sex marriage may also simultaneously queers this very institution and the structures of kinship and citizenship it supports. By producing families founded on care and commitment, rather than biology, queer families challenge the orthodox understanding of family and kinship created through biological linkages. And by producing future citizens outside of heterosexual structures queer families may challenge the image of the ideal normative citizen.

More significantly still, the same-sex marriage debate may also transform our current understandings of gay and lesbian identity, furthering rather than dismantling the queer project by acknowledging the significance of love and friendship in queer life and articulating these with queer erotics.

EROTIC LOVE

The claim that marriage is about love and offers recognition of gay and lesbian love is also central to the pro-same-sex marriage position. Barbara Cox, writing of her non-legal ceremony, expresses this viewpoint:

When my partner and I decided to have a commitment ceremony, we did so to express the love and caring that we feel for one another, to celebrate that love with our friends and family, and to express that love openly and with pride . . . My ceremony was an expression of the incredible love and respect I have found with my partner. My ceremony came from a need to speak of that love and respect openly to those who participate in my world. (Cox 2004: 112)

However, the argument that marriage recognises love and ought therefore be available to gays and lesbians has also been resisted. Michael Warner argues that this position – that it is just about love – ignores the effects on those who remain unmarried, on the continuing marginalisation of non-normative sexual practices and relationships, and on the normalisation of queer life that marriage portends (Warner 2000: 98). Moreover, he continues, marriage does not require love and, on the other hand, many unsanctioned relationships are founded on love. For Warner, the love argument facilitates an occlusion of the state and its regulatory role that create 'invidious distinction[s]' and 'harmful consequence[s]' for those who are excluded from marriage. Warner writes: 'Even though people think that marriage gives them validation, legitimacy, and recognition, they somehow think that it does so without invalidating, delegitimating, or stigmatising other relations, needs, and desires' (ibid.: 99).

The love argument is for Warner 'based on . . . a sentimental rhetoric of privacy' and is 'a false idealization of love and coupling' (ibid.: 100). Warner's critique is founded, in part, on a concern about the risk of normalisation that marriage represents and on the further stigmatisation of non-normative relationships, but it also exhibits a discomfort with the sentimental and the romantic associated with lover's discourses. Warner quotes Hannah Arendt to support his argument that love is anti-political and therefore, in his view, a threat not only to queer theory but also to queer life. Arendt writes: 'Love, by its very nature, is unworldly, and it is for this reason rather than its rarity that it is not only apolitical but antipolitical, perhaps the most powerful of all antipolitical forces' (Arendt, quoted in Warner 2000: 139). Warner comments that 'in the name of love . . . the world-making project of queer life' is obliterated (ibid.: 139).

As we saw in the previous chapter, however, some theorists have questioned that dismissal of love as sentimental, as a form of false consciousness or misplaced idealisation, as apolitical or anti-political. Michel Foucault, perhaps rather unexpectedly, given his positioning as a leading queer theorist, also affirms the importance of affectionate relations. As is by now well understood, Foucault is critical of a liberation politics that implies a repressive power that denies our desires and represses our identities and subjectivities. Instead, Foucault argues that power is not restricted to the state and is not a top-down repressive force but is distributed across society and is inherent in all relationships. Power is a relation in which 'one person tries to control the conduct of the other' but importantly it is 'mobile, reversible and unstable' (Foucault 2000: 292). Resistance is inherent within power relations and it is only through freedom that power is able to operate – each uses their freedom to resist, contest and even to reverse the power relation. Foucault carefully distinguishes states of domination from relations of power. In the former, he argues, 'power relations are fixed in such a way that they are permanently asymmetrical and allow an extremely limited margin of freedom' (ibid.: 292). In contrast, power relations are not only reversible but are also productive, creating new identities and possibilities through their unpredictable fluctuations. Foucault famously illustrates this through the figure of the homosexual who, though criminalised and pathologised in legal and medical discourses, is also produced or created through these discourses. Where previously there were only stigmatised sexual practices, these discourses invented the category or the identity labelled the homosexual. This enabled a resistant discourse to evolve which challenged the negative representations of this identity (Foucault 1980: 101).

This rejection of the 'repressive hypothesis' also suggested that sex and sexuality are not repressed but actively produced through the operation of power. Foucault is unconvinced by a politics of liberation as he argues that we do not need to be liberated from a repressive force. He asks in relation to this issue: 'does it make any sense to say, "Let's liberate our sexuality"?' And he speculates:

> Isn't the problem rather that of defining the practices of freedom by which one could define what is sexual pleasure and erotic, amorous and passionate relationships with others? This ethical problem of the definition of practices of freedom, it seems to me, is much more important than the rather repetitive affirmation that sexuality or desire must be liberated. (Foucault 2000: 283)

In a late interview, Foucault develops this critique further. While gay and lesbian politics have often focused on issues relating to freedom of sexual expression and the right to engage in non-normative sexual practices, Foucault suggests that it is friendship and love between men, rather than sex between men, that the dominant culture finds disturbing. He writes: 'To imagine a sexual act that doesn't conform to the law or nature is not what disturbs people. But that individuals are beginning to love one another – there's the problem', (ibid.: 136–7).

While Foucault does not in any way champion the institution of marriage as a means to express affectionate relations he does suggest that loving relations between men need to be acknowledged.

He suggests that the question of identity and even of desire is beside the point. Instead he proposes that inventing a way of life and a multiplicity of relationships would be more productive. Relationship, not simply sex, is central for Foucault:

> As far back as I can remember, to want guys was to want relations with guys . . . Not necessarily in the form of the couple but as a matter of existence: how is it possible for men to live together? To live together, to share their time, their meals, their room, their leisure, their grief, their knowledge, their confidences? What is it to be 'naked' among men, outside of institutional relations, family, profession, and obligatory camaraderie? (ibid.: 136)

Foucault rejects the image of homosexuality as predominantly the expression of a certain desire but he also rejects the idea of a conventional coupling: 'We must escape and help others to escape the two readymade formulas of the pure sexual encounter and the lover's fusion of identities' writes Foucault (ibid.: 137). Yet, while he is not advocating conventional institutions such as marriage he is insisting on the importance of 'affection, tenderness, friendship, fidelity, camaraderie, and companionship' (ibid.: 136).

Foucault's insistence on the significance of love, friendship and affection explains perhaps why same-sex marriage has become so central to lesbian and gay politics. While lesbian and gay communities have developed a range of alternate intimate relations these have not been highly visible or widely acknowledged. Indeed, Foucault suggests that while friendship between men was important in antiquity it was later discouraged as it threatened to undermine the emerging bureaucratic, administrative, educational and military structures (ibid.: 170–1). Yet, intimate relations proliferated in lesbian and gay communities. This intimacy was not only, and perhaps not primarily, located within monogamous couple relationships but often within a complex and intertwining network of erotic-friendship relations often involving ex-partners, casual sexual partners, friendships that become erotic and erotic relations that become friendships (Weeks 1997: 324). These diverse and continually transforming networks provide intimacy, connection, erotic pleasures, care and nurturing undermining the strict rules and boundaries that regulate and determine the limits and relations between family and kinship on the one hand, and public institutions on the other. The USA TV series *The L Word* demonstrates not only the significance of friendship in lesbian communities but also the interrelation and frequent exchanges between friendship and erotic relations. Alice (Leisha Hailey), a central character in the series, overtly maps, in diagrammatic form, the multiplicity of sexual connections, demonstrating that through this network there is a series of ambiguous and multilayered connections between the friends and lovers constituting her community (*The L Word*, Series 1, Episodes 1, 2 and 3).

While Foucault rejects conventional family institutions he nevertheless acknowledges the importance of loving relations. Despite Foucault's concerns about family institutions, same-sex marriage has the potential not only to acknowledge the love between men that Foucault suggests troubles dominant culture, but also in the process to reinvent the meanings, and significance and practices of marriage. If Foucault is right in suggesting that it is love, not sex, between men that is disturbing, then marriage as a symbol of love may disrupt dominant discourses about male homosexuality. And if Düttmann is correct in suggesting that recognition has the potential to transform both the recognised and the recogniser then same-sex marriage as a mechanism of recognition has the potential to disrupt the hetero–homo binary by redefining both sides of this opposition. Finally, while Foucault focuses mainly on gay men rather than lesbians in his discussion of friendship, his discussion may nevertheless prompt a rethinking of lesbian life. For Foucault, gay male identity has been defined as a sexual identity occluding the man-on-man love that troubles dominant culture. Lesbians have a different history. Sex between women has been denied and occluded, with their relations imagined as non-sexual friendships. In this context marriage as a symbol of erotic love that would recognise both love and sex between women may also have a disruptive potential insisting on the sexual as well as the affectionate aspect of the lesbian relation.

If erotic love has been denied both lesbians and gays – with the former viewed as asexual and the latter as purely sexual – then marriage as the symbol of erotic love may have the potential to overturn these reductive and restrictive formulations. This is not to deny the risks inherent in same-sex marriage – the tendency toward normalisation, the continued stigmatisation of non-normative relations and sexualities, and the assimilation into a restrictive dominant culture. Yet, there is also a possibility that same-sex marriage may disrupt and transform not only heterosexual culture, but also homosexual culture, in unpredictable and possibly productive ways.

QUE(E)RYING MARRIAGE

Same-sex marriage does not simply replicate heterosexual marriage. In imitating or mimicking opposite-sex marriage, same-sex marriage also introduces difference that has the potential to transform, albeit in unpredictable ways, not only the institutions of marriage, family, kinship and citizenship but also the identities and practices of hetero-sexuality and homosexuality. Various theorists have discussed, in dif-fering contexts, the unstable relation between identity and difference, pointing out that repetition introduces change undermining the stabil-ity of an identity, opening it to the possibility of difference. Discussing the functioning of language, for example, Derrida suggests that the meanings of utterances change with each iteration creating a prolifer-ation or a dissemination of meanings. Derrida writes that: 'The iteration structuring it [the utterance] a priori introduces into it a dehiscence and a cleft which are essential' (Derrida 1988: 18). This gap or this diver-gence introduces the possibility of transformation creating new and dif-fering nuances or significances in the meaning. Roland Barthes, too, as we saw in the previous chapter, points to the multiplicity and variabil-ity of meaning in texts. Not only are there meta or mythi[...] within texts, but also these meanings may change with ea[...] repetition that places the text in new contexts or in new [...] other texts. Just as meanings of utterances and texts may tr[...] each iteration, so too, ceremonies and rituals may also tra[...] repeated enactments which over time introduce differences[...]

The changes in the marriage ceremony over recent decad[...] partly through the influence of feminism, are already ev[...] now, the bride no longer promises obedience and she may n[...] be given away by her father to her husband. Often now ther[...] exchange of rings and the vows are equivalent. Same-sex [...] likely to create its own differences and transformations and [...] cations of these are already evident.

Jill Johnston describes her wedding in Denmark in [...] partner, Ingrid Nyeboe, explaining that after a brief legal c[...] wedding party became a Fluxus art performance organised [...] Hendricks. The wedding procession walked from the city hall to a nearby gallery exhibiting Hendricks's work led by a great dane and accompan-ied by the overture to Lohengrin and the story of Bambi in Danish played simultaneously on two boom boxes. A thirty-person blue wedding dress, designed by Eric Anderson, also formed part of the procession, clothing various members of the wedding group. At the gallery a ritual of sepa-ration and union was enacted by cutting in two the Wedding Chair – a small red-painted wooden child's chair – that was then reversed and lashed together with cloth. Johnston comments that onlookers were heard to remark: 'It's a crazy wedding' and 'It was the wedding of the future' (Johnston 1995: 218).

Mary Conway, analysing this event, argues that the same-sex marriage debate has generally overlooked the significance of the symbolism of ritual and ceremony and how this may contribute to altering the meanings of marriage and subjectivity. She discusses the Fluxus art movement, which resists commodification through its ephemeral and often unscripted fleeting performances and describes the strategy of 'goofing off' that suspends serious judgements about meaning and gestures toward the ineffable and uncontainable mystery of existence. Conway writes:

> Fluxus works criticise Western ideals, especially capitalism and utility. The emphasis on purposelessness is evident in the way many works that present 'goofing off', or the ability to not take one's self seriously as an artist: suspending participation in the earnest production of meaning, art and politics – while, paradoxically, making art. Goofing off may also reinvest the familiar world with mystery: in suspending evaluation or production of meaning, the illusory aspects of the world are made more palpable. (Conway 2004: 177)

Conway reads the Fluxus wedding chair ritual as a resistance to the symbolic conjoining of two individuals into one often associated with marriage, and sometimes represented by the bride and groom simultaneously lighting a single candle from their two separate candles and then extinguishing the separate candles indicating that the two are now one. The red wedding chair reveals the fabrication and the contingency of this union:

> . . . at the Fluxus wedding, a single unified object is torn apart, then lashed back together. While two become one in the candle ceremony, here one is revealed as a construction easily disintegrated. The chair emphasizes that there is nothing natural about either the one (chair) or the couple (lashed together): a fabricated one becomes two, then one again. This re-union, however, is marked as a fabricated joining. (ibid.: 180)

The blue wedding dress is also significant for Conway – it is not simply an oppositional gesture in which case it may have been a black, opposing the traditional white, dress. It holds thirty people, challenging the exclusive coupling of marriage, but it also exceeds the more conventional alternatives of the *ménage à trois* threesome and the couple swapping foursome (ibid.: 183). Most importantly for Conway the dress symbolises a threatening monstrous breakdown of individuality and separation that is achieved in part by putting clothing between self and other. The thirty-person dress challenges these boundaries engulfing the wedding party within its folds undermining the autonomy of the self (Conway 2004: 183).

The thirty-person wedding dress also rewrites the relation between the couple and the guests at the wedding. It incorporates the guests into the ceremony transforming them from passive observers into active participants and integrating them into the wedding event. The demarcation between the couple and their broader network of family and friends is subtly shifted challenging the boundaries that marriage traditionally produces. The web-like network of extended intimate connections is intimated through the dress suggesting their ongoing importance and their permeation of coupling.

This acknowledgement of a queer erotic network and its interconnection with the marrying couple is even more evident in the Seven Years of Love as Art performance that is traced on www.loveartlab.org. This seven-year art collaboration between porn star performance artist, Annie Sprinkle, and her multimedia artist partner, Elizabeth Stephens, incorporates a range of events – The Weddings, Xtreme Kiss, Cuddle, Breast Cancer Ballet, Post Porn Love – and is a satellite project to Linda Montano's Seven Years of Living Art project. Having been denied a legal marriage, Sprinkle and Stephens propose to hold a wedding ceremony each year for seven years. The ritual is a protest against war – they 'propose love as an alternative vision to the war' – and also against anti-gay marriage amendments in the USA which they describe as 'a thinly disguised and hateful proposition intended to discriminate against Americans seeking alternative family structures' (www.loveartlab.org).

Each wedding is related to a body chakra and has a corresponding colour and theme. Wedding One with a red security theme was officiated by Fluxus artist Geoffrey Hendricks and involved friends and artists performing, singing, playing, reading, and assisting with red food, make-up, costumes, bouquets, red rice, decorations, photography, video, webcasting and thereby co-creating the ceremony. An anti-marriage lap-dancing fairy participated ensuring that all viewpoints were included. Yet, this was not just art but also an expression of a serious commitment. Writing of the art project Katrina Fox explains, quoting Sprinkle:

> The pair are also trying to generate more love in the world. 'We're lovers, not fighters,' Sprinkle says. 'Well, we are fighters but we fight with love. We're love warriors. We got rings and took the wedding seriously and made a commitment to love, honour and cherish each other as girlfriends, life partners and also as love art collaborators.' (Fox 2005: 26)

The love art laboratory wedding transforms marriage by emphasising the ongoing process or becoming of a marriage overturning the more conventional image of being married. The repeated yearly ritual emphasises the developing and changing nature of relationship challenging the settled static state of being rather than becoming married. Sprinkle and Stephens use the chakras and their related colours and themes to trace these transformations from security in the first red year to sexuality and creativity in the orange year to courage, love, communication, bliss and wisdom in the following yellow, green, blue, purple and white years.

While Sprinkle and Stephens make a commitment to be a monogamous couple the ongoing marriage and the related love art laboratory events demonstrate the networks of relations within which and into which they relate. Their artwork is an offshoot of another project and it involves a multitude of collaborators. This is not a union of two into one but an exploration of interrelating on multiple levels between the two and beyond the two. The Cuddle Project invites visitors to cuddle with Annie and Elizabeth in their gallery/performance space bed extending the expression of love to all who visit. Another artwork, iPatch, is a collection of designer eye patches made for a 'beloved family member' who developed an eye problem. Breast Cancer Ballet transformed Annie Sprinkle's treatment for breast cancer from a purely medical procedure into an art event described by Sprinkle as 'an adventure, a whole new world and we're meeting new people and learning new things.' (quoted in Fox 2005: 27).

The Fluxus and Love Art Laboratory weddings challenge the static nature of traditional weddings, the reduction of two to one, and the exclusion of the intimate friend/family network from marriage. They queer marriage while also querying marriage, creating an aesthetics and a politics that troubles the normal and, through an unpredictable playful adventuring, enables new becomings of subjectivity and of marriage.

Amorous Politics: Between Derrida and Nancy

಄

Lars von Trier's film *Dogville* (2003) stages the paradoxical possibilities and impossibilities of hospitality and forgiveness. A young woman, fleeing gangsters, seeks refuge in a small town. Concerned about the risks involved, the townsfolk reluctantly agree to offer her refuge or hospitality. A time limit is set and she offsets the risk by giving something in return: her initial 'helping out' turns into arduous labour and finally sexual exploitation as the town places increasing conditions on their welcome.

Jacques Derrida, elaborating Emmanuel Levinas's theory of the feminine hospitable welcome of the home, traces the relation between a conditional welcome that in the end would be no welcome at all and an unconditional hospitality that has no limits. Extending Levinas's ethics of the face-to-face relation and his image of the welcome of the home (both founded on love, as we saw in Chapter 4), Derrida investigates the limitations of the hospitality offered to the guest, the refugee, the migrant, and the guest worker. While love is implicit here it is bought closer to the surface in Derrida's articulation of friendship and democracy. Rejecting the idea of fraternal friendship as the foundation of the democratic relation, Derrida nonetheless formulates a non-fraternal friendship that would include the sister and the cousin – the woman and the racial other – within democratic politics.

While Derrida's politics recognises ethical and friendship love, his friend and colleague, French philosopher Jean-Luc Nancy more explicitly identifies the significance of love in the formation of subjectivity, community and culture. Also influenced by Levinas, Nancy proposes that subjects (or what he terms 'singularities') only come into being through the effects of the 'touch' of love. Love, for Nancy, cuts or marks the heart, inaugurating the becoming of the singular being. That is, it is through affectionate and passionate relations with the other – through plurality – that singularity is constituted. Community and culture, too, are formed through love: through a melee of engagements and resistance, sharing, disagreement and connection that are all always passionate.

Jacques Derrida may be the most controversial philosopher of the twentieth century. Contributing to the development of poststructuralism, and famously inventing neologisms such as deconstruction and *différance*, Derrida has been criticised as impenetrable and illogical. Yet, Derrida's often difficult work is precisely an attempt to disrupt the unquestioning belief in reason and logic and to dissect the claims to truth of scientific and humanist discourses. While his formulations may be complicated, Derrida nevertheless offers insights into the complexities and paradoxes of ethics, politics and philosophy that challenge more conventional 'logical' formulations. Jean-Luc Nancy, working within a similar framework also questions orthodox articulations of subjectivity, sociality and ethico-political experience. While their approaches intersect, they also develop differing trajectories, though both reveal or allude to the significance of love in the dynamics of human inter-relation.

The themes, images and concepts of 'shattered love,' hospitable love, democratic friendship, and the cultural melee of Ares and Aphrodite that emerge in their respective works point to the centrality of love. In addition, both insist that love inaugurates philosophy and even that thinking itself is a form of or expression of love.

LOVING WISDOM

Alcibiades loves Socrates: amorous, erotic, ludic, he is 'touched' by this insane, unreasoned, unrequited love. Socrates, however, learns of love not from the mad passion of Alcibiades but from the wisdom – the wise words – of Diotima. As the conversations and speeches in Plato's *Symposium* reveal, philosophy begins with words of love, with addresses and stories of love. The *Symposium* (as we saw in Chapter 1) stages a debate about love among partying friends. Socrates, mouthing the words of Diotima, celebrates love of the beautiful and the good as the highest form of love. Alcibiades, drunkenly crashing the rather sedate party, wildly proclaims his love of Socrates and tells the story of his failed attempts to seduce the philosopher who snubs him, proclaiming that he (Alcibiades) wants to trade bronze for gold; erotic love for love of knowledge.

Derrida acknowledges the centrality of love at the origin of philosophy. He expresses this through the image of the kiss. The kiss may express love, friendship, sometimes erotic desire, but it may also, as Derrida points out, be at the heart of philosophy. Quoting Novalis, Derrida writes:

The first kiss . . . is the principle of philosophy – the origin of a new world – the beginning of an absolute era – the act that accomplishes an alliance with self that grows endlessly. Who would not like a philosophy whose kernel is a first kiss? (Novalis, quoted in Derrida 1993: 140)

Philosophy may forget or repress this first kiss, Derrida suggests, but it nevertheless initiates all sensation and every experience. Not only philosophy, not only sensibility, but all touching: 'This latter [the first kiss], as auto-hetero-affection, inaugurates all experience, in particular speech and the declaration of love'. Derrida continues: 'it does not bring closer only lips, my two lips to the two lips and to the tongue of the other, but everything of that body that lets itself be touched in this way by auto-hetero-affection: for example, the eyes' (Derrida 1993: 140–1). In a paper in which he considers the significance of touch in Nancy's philosophy, Derrida reflects on the place of the kiss, the touch, the carnal, erotic and amorous, at the heart, and in the beginning of philosophy.

Love, is central too in Nancy's work, and indeed he proposes in all philosophy. 'Since the *Symposium* [or even before] . . . the general schema of a philosophy of love is at work', Nancy ruminates, 'and it has not ceased to operate even now, determining philosophy as it understands and construes itself, as well as love as we understand it and as we make it' (Nancy 2003a: 249). Since Plato, for Nancy, thinking and love are imbricated: 'This intimate connivance between love and thinking is present in our origins: the word 'philosophy' betrays it . . . [It] means this: love of thinking, since thinking is love' (ibid.: 247). While we may be familiar with the proposition that philosophy means love of thinking, Nancy's reversal of the terms requires us to understand that this is so because 'thinking is love'. This inversion reframes and enriches the idea of philosophy, which is no longer simply love of thought, but a thinking that is love itself.

HEARTBEAT – HEARTBREAK

In 'Shattered Love' Nancy does not just reflect on philosophy as love of thinking but also on the ethics, politics and phenomenology of love. He writes of the fibres of and the beating of the heart, of the broken heart that is also the breaking or rupturing of the self, and of the transcendences and transports of the heart. Against a philosophical tradition that has (for the most part) sceptically rejected love – fearing the unruly effect of the passions on reason and fearing, too, that love always collapses into self-love – Nancy reveals the significance of love not just for human happiness but for the very existence of the human being. Nancy rejects the idea that love is always an egoistic expression of self-love, formulating instead an alliance between, rather than an opposition of, love and self-love. Love overcomes the opposition between love of the other 'in which I lose myself without reserve' and self-love 'in which I recuperate myself' (Nancy 2003a: 260). This overcoming is achieved not by subsuming one within the other, through a dialectical sublation but through the actions and effects of love, actions which transform the subject, who, in love, or through love, is broken into, touched and fractured by love. Love is an opening of the subject to the other so that the subject is from that moment, that is to say from the outset, shattered. Nancy writes in 'Shattered Love': 'he, this subject, was touched, broken into, in his subjectivity, and he *is* from then on, from the time of love, opened by this slice, broken or fractured, even if only slightly . . . From then on, *I* is *constituted broken*' (ibid.: 261). For Nancy, there is no isolated individual. Rather we are all constituted through our relations with other – loving relations that transform us into complexly multiple, un-unified, 'shattered' subjectivities.

This transformation and fracturing of the subject does not just occur in a grand passion, an obsessional, romantic, or lifelong love that might conventionally be thought to change the subject. Rather, the smallest gesture or experience of love performs this transforming and constituting of the subject:

> As soon as there is love, the slightest act of love, the slightest spark, there is this ontological fissure that cuts across and that disconnects the elements of the subject-proper – the fibres of its heart. One hour of love is enough, one kiss alone, provided that it is out of love – and can there in truth be any other kind? (ibid.: 261)

This breaking of the self means that the autonomy, the individual-ness, of the subject is opened by, and opened to, the other. The I is no longer, or rather was not ever, an immanence, closed in upon herself. Rather she is a transcendence; open, exposed, transported or transplanted within and by the other. Love is always a form of heartbreak because all love – even the most joyous love – breaks the I so that 'the immanence of the subject . . . is opened up, broken into . . . Love is the act of transcendence (of a transport, of a transgression, of a transparency . . .)' (ibid.: 261). This transcendence is not a surpassing of either the self or the other; it is the breaking open of the self, not as wounding but as the exposure to and experience of the outside. 'Transcendence will thus', Nancy proposes, 'be better named the crossing of love' (ibid.: 262). Love in this perspective is a cutting across the heart. This crossing exposes and reveals the heart. This crossing is a beating, a pulsation, a coming-and-going that reveals finitude at the heart of love and of being. Nancy proposes that: 'What love cuts across, and what is revealed by its crossing, is what is exposed to the crossing, to the coming-and-going – and this is nothing other than finitude' (ibid.: 262).

The vacillations of the beating heart – its coming and going – is not quite a dialectical movement between opposing terms through which one is subsumed by the other. The law of the dialectic – the oscillating movement of the dialectic – might appear similar to the pulsations of love. However, for Nancy, the resolution of the thesis and antithesis in the sublation (or sublimation) of the synthesis is never final: 'the resolution of a contradiction that remains a contradiction' (ibid.: 251), the fluctuations of the dialectic are infinite. The heart of being is an e-motion, a quasi-dialectical throbbing producing 'being-nothingness-becoming, as an infinite pulsation' (ibid.: 252). Yet this throbbing dialectical ontology is not quite the heartbeat of love. Nancy proposes both that love is at the heart of being: 'the essence of being is something like the heart: that which alone is capable of love' (ibid.: 252), and that love is not being: 'Love remains absent from the heart of being' (ibid.: 252). This paradoxical formulation indicates that while love provides the model for the endless dialectics of being-nothingness-becoming, it does not itself partake of the dialectic. Rather love 'shatters' the dialectic and lives through exposition. Love does not appropriate the other, it gives to the other: 'If the dialectic is the process of that which must appropriate its own becoming in order to be, exposition, on the other hand, is the condition of that whose essence or destination consists in being present: given over, offered to the outside, to others, and even to the self' (ibid.: 253).

In Nancy's formulation, love does not appropriate the other or subsume the other. Rather, love gives. This is to be understood not as a giving of materials, objects and possessions. It involves a giving which is an exposure of the self: 'The heart exposes the subject' (ibid.: 254). Nancy describes the experience of love explaining that the subject is constituted through the touch and the effects of love. Love opens the subject to the other and is broken into by the other so that the subject is never an autonomous existent but is always in relation with others. Love shatters the atomistic being introducing alterity into the heart of being.

ENTWINING EROS AND AGAPE

Nancy does not only reflect on the phenomenological and ontological operations of love. He also investigates the ethics of love and here he is indebted to Levinas – a debt, a gift, a legacy that Nancy announces through an exposition of Levinas and an exposure of his own thought to that of Levinas. His engagement with Levinas is both a critique and a further elaboration; a redirection and re-signification of Levinasian ethics. Levinas, Nancy says, was the first to understand the centrality of being-with-others, and he 'cleared the path toward what one can call' Nancy writes 'in the language of *Totality and Infinity*, a metaphysics of love' (Nancy 2003a: 269). Nevertheless, love creates a perplexity for Levinas as, in his framework, love involves a return to self-love that undermines the priority of the other: 'To love,' writes Levinas, 'is also to love oneself within love and thus to return to the self' (Levinas, quoted in Nancy 2003a: 259). While the love of the ethical face-to-face relation preserves love of other, erotic love involves egotism. This reduction to self-love is transcended through fecundity and fraternity but erotic love is a carnality that occludes the face. For Nancy, Levinas hierarchises love creating a dialectical teleology or progression commencing with ethical love in the face-to-face relation and moving through an erotic self-centred swooning that is finally sublated in paternal and fraternal love in which the face returns once more (ibid.: 270). While Levinas insists that 'Love is originary' (Levinas 1998b: 108) he also bisects love, separating Agape from Eros. Agape, experienced in the face-to-face, preserves ethics and responsibility; in Eros love becomes egoistic enjoyment (ibid.: 113).

Nancy disturbs and displaces this opposition and dialectical movement implicit in Levinas's formulation, suggesting that love shatters this dialectic and shatters the heart, and that this is the event that constitutes the self. Nancy, like Levinas, makes solicitude toward the other central, but in his conception this concern, experienced in all forms of love, cuts us and exposes us, forming us in relation with the other (Nancy 2003a: 271). While Nancy acknowledges the significance of Levinas's ethics he rejects the relegation of Eros to the realm of egoistic pleasure and the elevation of Agape as the epitome of ethical love. For Nancy all forms of love facilitate the ethical relation of responsibility as all expose us to the sociality of existence.

HOSPITABLE LOVE

Just as Nancy endorses but then also extends Levinas's ethics, Derrida also engages with and develops further the Levinasian account of the ethical relation. While Levinasian ethical responsibility is reformulated as love in Nancy, in Derrida it returns as hospitality.

Derrida admits the word hospitality does not occur frequently in *Totality and Infinity* but he nevertheless reads Levinas's book as 'an immense treatise *of hospitality*', suggesting that 'hospitality becomes the very name for what opens itself to the face' (Derrida 1999a: 21).

The welcome afforded by the feminine other of the home is the emblem of this hospitality. Levinas writes that: 'the other whose presence is discreetly an absence, with which is accomplished the hospitable welcome which describes the field of intimacy, is the Woman' (Levinas 1969: 155). This welcoming feminine other, while lacking the 'height' of the face nevertheless partakes of the human, Derrida contends (Derrida 1999a: 37). Moreover, the hospitality she offers is not just one example among others but is the epitome of welcome: she is the 'hospitable welcome,' 'the welcoming one par excellence;' she is 'welcome in itself' (Levinas 1969: 155 and 157). Even though Levinas confines this welcoming hospitality to the pre-ethical privacy of the home, Derrida extends the space of hospitality tracing its effects within ethics and politics more broadly. However, Derrida, like Levinas, distinguishes hospitality from erotic love. The feminine other of the home becomes a model for ethical relating but this is not to be confused with the feminine erotic other. While there is a relation between familial love and hospitality, the transcendence experienced in Eros is to be distinguished from that of Agape. Levinas writes:

> The metaphysical event of transcendence – the welcome of the Other, hospitality – Desire and language – is not accomplished as love. But the transcendence of discourse is bound to love. We shall show how in love transcendence goes both further and less far than language. (Levinas 1969: 254)

Comments Derrida: 'Levinas must begin by distinguishing . . . between hospitality and love, since the latter does not accomplish the former . . . What goes further than language, namely, love, also goes "less far" than it' (Derrida 1999a: 41).

Derrida's reiteration of Levinas reveals the operation of welcome and hospitality within Levinasian ethics. In this gesture he also reveals the centrality of feminine hospitality to ethical thought. Nevertheless, like Levinas, Derrida continues to demarcate erotic love from the hospitable love of the face-to-face relation. For Nancy, as we saw earlier this would risk a continuation of the hierarchy, which constructs erotics as secondary, and would finally sublate them both within the dialectical return of the face-to-face in the paternal relation. While Nancy does not seek to conflate all forms of love – 'charity and pleasure, emotion and pornography, the neighbor and the infant, the love of lovers and the love of God, fraternal love and love of art, the kiss, passion, friendship' (Nancy 2003a: 246) – he does attempt to discern the cut that touches and creates being-with-others evident in all of these possibilities of love.

Yet Derrida is sensitive to and concerned about the issues of sexual difference and feminine alterity. Elaborating the implications of an ethics of hospitality Derrida distinguishes between conditional and unconditional hospitality. Conditional hospitality limits the gift and assumes the return of the gift of hospitality, while unconditional hospitality is without limit. Conditional hospitality does not disturb or threaten the mastery of the host for: 'The host remains the master in the house, the country, the nation, he controls the threshold, he controls the borders, and when he welcomes the guest he wants to keep the mastery' (Derrida 1999b: 69). Conditional hospitality sets limits so that the guest – whether in the home or nation – must conform to the law or culture of the host. In addition, the guest must reciprocate through exchange or gratitude respecting the authority and the territory of the host. Immigrants and refugees may only enter on certain conditions and often this may include providing an economic return by filling skill shortages or labour needs.

Unconditional hospitality on the other hand welcomes without controlling or identifying the foreigner or stranger. This, Derrida warns involves risks and perils for unconditional hospitality demands: 'that you give up mastery of your space, your home, your nation. It is unbearable. If, however, there is pure hospitality it should be pushed to this extreme' (ibid.: 70). Hospitality without condition would involve giving all and risking all, as the other may take over the home or nation, unseating the mastery of the host. Derrida's discussion of conditional and unconditional hospitality reveals that conditional hospitality is, in the end, no hospitality at all for the generosity must be reciprocated or the host lauded for this minimal act of welcome. Real hospitality would be unconditional and would not require acknowledgement or exchange but this puts at risk the control exercised by the host.

In discussing this paradox, Derrida points out that the costs may be especially significant for woman. In Levinas's formulation it is the woman who provides the unconditional hospitality of the home. But even when the host is a man, Derrida suggests, woman is put at risk by unconditional hospitality. Citing biblical examples Derrida describes Lot's sacrifice of his daughters in order to protect and to provide unlimited hospitality for his guests. The people of Sodom demand that Lot give up his foreign guests so that they can abuse them. Lot, refusing, offers instead his daughters (Derrida 2000: 149–55). Unconditional hospitality, then, Derrida suggests, may conflict with ethical responsibility to the family and especially to the daughters.

Lars von Trier's allegorical film reframes this dilemma within hospitality. Grace (Nicole Kidman) is offered, by the people of Dogville, only a limited hospitality. She is exploited and abused though this is justified or disguised by the representation of hospitality as a gift – one that she must acknowledge by giving back. While Dogville offers hospitality only on condition that this generosity be repaid, Grace responds to her violation and maltreatment (at least until the final scenes) with unlimited forgiveness. This may be read as a form of unconditional hospitality: she allows others to use her labour and her body unconditionally (Atkins 2005). She provides unlimited hospitality to the people of Dogville in return for their limited hospitality. Von Trier's film reveals the risks of both limited and unlimited hospitality: in each case violence and suffering are unleashed.

Here again the consequences for woman – of both forms of hospitality – are revealed. Derrida does not propose that our currently violent forms of limited hospitality be exchanged for an equally dangerous unconditional welcoming. Rather he seeks to expose the failures and the lack of generosity evident in the current enactments of welcome offered to the visitor, the refugee, the migrant and the guest worker. While political hospitality may also need to be answerable to the voice of justice (to ensure that the rights of all are preserved within hospitality) nevertheless it also needs to be guided by a love that moves beyond the self to respond to, take responsibility for, and provide real hospitality for the other.

Derrida compels an acknowledgement of the complexity of issues of ethics, responsibility and hospitality, insisting that the functioning of and consequences for sexual difference continue to be central in any articulation of the relation of self and other.

DEMOCRATIC FRIENDSHIP

Struggling to think this complexity further, Derrida attempts in *Politics of Friendship* to articulate and disarticulate the relationship between friendship, democracy and fraternity. Carole Pateman had already pointed to the transition from patriarchal monarchy to fraternal democracy, drawing on the Freudian account of brothers overthrowing the father so as to gain both political power and sexual access to women (Pateman 1995). She elaborates this metaphorical story to demonstrate that the democratic fraternal social contract not only excludes women but also establishes the basis for men's sexual access to women through marriage and prostitution. While Pateman already reveals and critiques the fraternal nature of democracy, Derrida demonstrating a similar concern about the exclusion of the feminine follows another trajectory: rather than an Oedipal overthrow of the father by the sons, Derrida traces the ideal of friendship that underlies democracy and reveals the brotherly love associated with ideal friendship. Analysing the history of philosophical accounts of friendship, Derrida reveals the connecting of brotherhood with friendship and with democracy. But he also unravels these associations opening the possibility for a non-fraternal friendship and democracy to come (Derrida 1997a).

Derrida deconstructs Friedrich Nietzsche's accounts of friendship, for example, revealing the complexity and instability of friendship's fraternal commitments. If Nietzsche insists that 'woman is not yet capable of friendship' (Nietzsche 1986: 85) this is because, Derrida cautions, friendship is only possible in a context of freedom and women have not attained this status (Derrida 1997a: 282). While women can, according to Nietzsche experience love (since love, for Nietzsche, involves a hierarchical relation) they do not participate in the freedom required for friendship. Yet, as we saw in Chapter 2, Nietzsche also questions man's capacity for friendship for man is not yet sufficiently generous for friendship: 'But tell me, you men, which of you is yet capable of friendship? Oh your poverty, you men, and your avarice of soul! As much as you give to your friend I will give even to my enemy, and will not have grown poorer in doing so' (Nietzsche 1986: 84).

Not only does Nietzsche require an 'infinite gift' (Derrida 1997a: 283) be proffered in friendship but he also proposes that friendship requires love of the most distant and futural (Nietzsche 1986: 86–8). Rejecting love of the neighbour as an emblem of friendship Nietzsche, in Derrida's reading, proposes a love of the most distant, an unrequited generosity, and a boundless and giving love as the sign of friendship. Derrida reconceptualises friendship, rupturing its foundation in freedom, equality and fraternity by foregrounding the endless responsibility owed to the friend. Derrida then asks: 'Without sharing and without reciprocity, could one still speak of equality and fraternity?' (Derrida 1997a: 296). Moreover, Derrida questions the association between friendship and community suggesting that community founded on being-in-common reintroduces the brother. Against this fraternal, communal model Derrida proposes that it is friendship with the stranger that constitutes 'star friendship' (Derrida 1997a: 296–9). Instead of community, then, Derrida calls for an 'indefinitely perfectible' democracy 'to come' that exceeds fraternal exclusions of the sister and cousin, the feminine and racial/cultural other. This democracy 'to come' is not only an indication that democracy is yet to be achieved. It is also an indication that democracy should be conceived as a promise of justice, respect, and freedom. Derrida explains:

When I speak of a 'democracy to come', I don't mean a future democracy, a new state, a new organization of nation-states (though this is to be hoped for) . . . The idea of promise is inscribed in the idea of democracy: equality, freedom, freedom of speech, freedom of the press – all these things are inscribed as promises within democracy. (Derrida 1997b)

Derrida thus reconceptualises a relation between friendship and democracy, eliminating the commonality so often assumed in each relation, and hospitably welcomes the stranger, the woman and the racial other, within this democracy 'to come'. He thereby radically alters the structures of friendship and of democracy; not founded on fraternity but on responsibility to the other and on love of the stranger this friendly democracy would exceed the calculations and evaluations of reciprocal exchange and the homogenizing imperatives of fraternal similarity.

Nancy, concerned too to rethink political relations, nevertheless elaborates another path toward a sociality beyond the fraternity of our contemporary democracies. While Derrida follows a path linking friendship to democracy, Nancy explores the possibility of a sociality marked by love and expressed through the melee, the turmoil and chaos, of community.

MELEE OF APHRODITE AND ARES

Rejecting both racial purity and a 'melting pot' homogenising multiculturalism, Nancy conceives of community as melee, as disturbance, disagreement and agitation. Even the well-meaning talk of unity within diversity oversimplifies and misleads. What is needed, Nancy speculates, is not a mixture of race, sex and other differences as this implies that there is a pre-existing purity that can be combined. Moreover, mixture becomes either a fusion that homogenises differences, or an entropic disorder that is resistant to engagement, sharing and connection (Nancy 2003b: 281). Instead, Nancy conceives of community as a melee understood as 'an action rather than a substance' (ibid.: 281). Melee suggests first combat, confrontation and disagreement though Nancy also points beyond the melee of Ares (that of combat) to the melee of Aphrodite (that of love). Both these forms of melee (of combat and of love) require the other: an 'appeal to the other as an always other other' (ibid.: 281). Even the melee of Ares, which is not the modern warfare of absolute obliteration but rather a 'hand-to-hand' combat (ibid.: 282), an engagement, a joust or a skirmish with the other.

Nancy defines melee very specifically as 'crossing, weaving, exchange, sharing' and he adds: 'in a melee there is countervalence and encounter, there's resemblance and distancing, contact and contraction, concentration and dissemination, identification and alteration' (ibid.: 282).

Every culture is, from the outset, this melange and medley. Even and especially 'the West,' priding itself on its 'Greek' origins which is already a cosmopolitan melee of 'Egypt, Mesopotamia . . . Asian Minor . . . Syrian-Lebanese . . . Crete . . . Mycenae' and also 'the near East and the Aegean – Cretans, Mycenaean's, Palestinians, Nubians, Canaanites . . .' (Serres, quoted in Nancy 2003b: 282–3). Culture is always and already melee, undermining cultural and racial purity: culture does not exist outside this 'confrontation, transformation, deviation, development, recomposition, combination, cobbling together' (ibid.: 283).

Nancy concedes nevertheless that there are distinct peoples, nations and civilisations but these distinct cultures, these singularities, produce their specificity through the melee of differences jousting and exposed to each other within culture. Nancy explains:

> It is a melee that, within any given 'culture,' brings out a style or a tone; equally, however, it brings out the various voices or vocal ranges that are needed in order for this tone to be interpreted. There is a French culture. But this culture has many voices and is nowhere present 'in person' as it were. (ibid.: 283)

In his essay 'In Praise of Melee' Nancy speaks of cultures rather than communities. Yet his elaboration of culture as melee is already discernable in his earlier work *The Inoperative Community*. Opposing any nostalgic conception of a harmonious, unified communal community, conceived either as already destroyed by the alienation of modernity or as a utopia achievable in the future, Nancy conceives of community as the interrelation exposed through the experiences of finitude and passion. Community can never be an entity, a hypostasis or a completion: it is a passage, an incompletion constituted through the ever-transforming relations of finite being-together. Living and dying structures this being together creating an exposure of each to other that touches and cuts the heart of each bringing us all into being as singularities that share:

> Sharing comes down to this: what community reveals to me, in presenting to me my birth and my death, is my existence outside myself . . . A singular being appears, as finitude itself: at the end (or at the beginning), with the contact of the skin (or the heart) of another singular being . . . Community means, consequently, that there is no singular being without another singular being, and that there is, therefore . . . an originary or ontological 'sociality' . . . (Nancy 1991: 26–8)

Nancy proposes that community always already exists and continues to exist through the passionate engagements of being-with-others. Each and every encounter touches you and me, each encounter exposes us to others, each inaugurates us as singularities, touched and constituted through this plurality. The melee of passion then is the life of community:

> The singular being, because it is singular, is in the passion – the passivity, the suffering, and the excess – of sharing its singularity. The presence of the other does not constitute a boundary that would limit the unleashing of 'my' passions: on the contrary, only exposition to the other unleashes my passions. (Nancy 1991: 32)

For Nancy then there is no pure identity or culture as all are already touched by others; this is not accidental or contingent, rather we can only constitute our singularities through the touch, the melee, or plurality. The melee of love and of disagreement, of Aphrodite and Ares, involves us in 'blows and embraces, assaults and truces, rivalry and desire, supplication and defiance, dialogue and dispute, fear and pity, and laughter as well' (Nancy 2003b: 287) and this is the making and the unmaking of cultures and communities.

Derrida, like Levinas, rejects erotic love in favour of friendship and community in favour of democracy. This risks reinstating reason and order rather than exposing sociality to the collective, to the emotive and volatile, and even to the feminine attributes that haunt the erotic body politic. Nancy, however, risks the problematics posed by both love and community reaching beyond the relative security and conventionality of democratic friendship. Nevertheless, Derrida's conception of friendship (and perhaps also of democracy) is itself touched by passion. Derrida turns away from Nancy's conception of community as the love and melee of shattered singularity. He nevertheless, in touching and embracing Nancy and his philosophy, acknowledges the significance of love and the kiss at the beginning of philosophy and in the constitution of the shattered subject. Derrida reveals the significance of love for his thought and his life most explicitly when he speaks of his friendship for Nancy. Returning to this personal account of friendship recalls the significance of love not just as a political and ethical issue but also as a personal and passionate experience.

WHEN OUR EYES TOUCH . . .

Inventing an anecdote to introduce his essay on Nancy's thinking on touch Derrida writes: 'I thought at one point about inventing a story: as improbable as it may seem, I read this anonymous inscription on a wall in Paris ("When our eyes touch, is it day or is it night")' (Derrida

1993: 123). Drawing the essay to a close he again adopts an anecdotal style, confessing his dream of kissing Nancy on the mouth – a dream that occurred shortly after Nancy's (actual) heart transplant when, Derrida reveals, he had embraced his friend for the first time, never having done so before because of the 'reserve or modesty of old friends' Derrida writes:

> One day, and I don't believe I have ever told this to him himself, but to Helene Nancy over the telephone, I dreamed that I kissed him, on the mouth; it was not long after the transplant of his new heart, when I had just seen him and did embrace him in fact, on the cheeks, for the first time . . . The truth is I would have liked to be capable of recounting what was and remains, for my old heart, striking it itself, the ordeal of his other heart that Jean-Luc Nancy was nevertheless alone in undergoing at the bottom of his heart, his, the only one, the same. (ibid.: 148)

Building on the chiastic self-touching of Merleau-Ponty's insight that 'To touch is to touch oneself' (Merleau-Ponty, quoted in Derrida 1993: 136), Derrida traces the centrality of the touch in Nancy's work. Moving from eyes to lips, from sight to touch, from the optic to the haptic, Derrida reveals how Nancy introduces alterity into this theory of touch. In Nancy's reformulation the I and the you embrace in the concept of the 'self-touching-you' disrupting monadic self-presence. Derrida writes: 'You, metronome of my heteronomy, you will always resist that which, in my "self-touching," could dream of the reflexive or specular auton-omy of self-presence . . .' (ibid.: 139).

The caress, the kiss, the touch interrupts the monadic, autonomous, isolated subject. Kissing the eyes, the meeting of looks, or eyes touching is an example of this self-touching-you. This look 'if desire or love passed through [it]' (ibid.: 139) invokes the tactility of the touch of the other that cuts or marks and thereby inaugurates the self. Touching eyes or kissing eyes do not, as do lips, bring skin in contact with skin – except perhaps when one kisses the eyes of the sleeping and the dead. Kissing eyes touch through the gaze, the meeting of glances, the returning of a look. The kissing gaze nevertheless touches, caresses, and like love may cut and cross the heart.

Nancy elaborates a conception of love that connects and disconnects, weaves and unravels, through the touch that marks, crosses and creates the heart of community. Derrida, following another path, traces the rela-tion between friendship and democracy indicating along the way the sig-nificance of hospitality to the other (the stranger, the sister, the cousin) in this trajectory. Yet Derrida acknowledges Nancy's thought on touch and love anticipating the elaboration that Nancy himself later publishes. Derrida writes:

> I said a moment ago that philosophy has spoken little about the kiss, and I was going to do just that. But here again, what is left for me? [Nancy's] *Corpus* does it, as I have just discovered . . . I who planned a year ago, well before *Corpus*, to constitute an index of the concepts and lexicon of 'touch' in the work of Jean-Luc Nancy, here I find *Corpus* will have said it all, anticipating me without warning me. It will have said everything about the kiss, the caress, tact and the intact. (Derrida 1993: 149)

Identifying a 'discrete' thematics of touch in Nancy's early work Derrida plans to write about this theme in Nancy, only to have Nancy pre-empt him by explicitly exploring these ideas himself leaving Derrida with 'nothing to say' except to repeat to Nancy 'in other words, what he has already said very well himself' (ibid.: 148). In a community of touching, sharing, and exposure between each and the other, perhaps there is a contamination so that writers anticipate and pre-empt each other creating a 'self-touching-you' through words. Reflecting on his dream of kissing Nancy's lips, Derrida writes:

> I will speak to him so as to touch him, about what a 'kiss on the eyes' might be [freedom given to see or to 'touch,' perhaps] . . . In the kiss of the eyes, it is not yet day, it is not yet night, but day and night are promised/promise themselves. I'm going to give them to you, says one to the other. At the break of day. (ibid.: 148–9)

'When our eyes touch, is it day or is it night' Derrida says to Nancy and we may decipher within the differing yet intersecting texts of Nancy and Derrida their entwined response: When our I's touch, there is the promise of day and night, the anticipation of life and death, that facilitates friendship and love, and the singular–plural democracy and/or community to come.

Conclusion

◅

From the time of the *Symposium* the association between love and philosophy has been evident: philosophy is love of wisdom. Jean-Luc Nancy, acknowledging this association in Plato's work, has elaborated this linkage suggesting not simply that philosophy is love of thinking but that thinking itself is love (Nancy 2003a: 247). This hints at the depth and complexity of the connection: philosophy and thinking are not the attainment of a final wisdom but the movement toward, or the movement back and forth between knowledge and its lack. Philosophy is not wisdom itself – for the attainment of wisdom, if it were possible, would be the end of philosophy – but a fascination, an infatuation, with thinking. Philosophy plays with thought, invents concepts, speculates, ruminates and investigates. It is not closure or completion but unending intrigue.

Love, too, is an incompletion. As Diotima explains to Socrates, and as he subsequently reports to his gathered friends, and as Plato then recounts in the *Symposium*, love is mediation not fulfilment. It is a movement between lack and completion, between Poverty and Plenty, between ignorance and wisdom, between monstrosity and beauty. Love and philosophy, both, live from the deferring and differing movement of indirection, non-arrival, endless delay and detour. They both move toward their object of desire but this object remains forever tantalisingly out of reach. This, at least, is what Sappho says of love and Diotima-Socrates' image of the ladder of learning suggests a similar concept of wisdom as a higher state beyond the capacity of the mere mortal (see Chapter 1).

While Jean-Luc Nancy and Jacques Derrida have both articulated this connection (see Chapter 9) a further association may be discerned in the *Symposium* – a third element that triangulates this coupling of love and philosophy, disrupting their union or fusion, deflecting their conventional partnering. The *Symposium* is structured as a series of stories or speeches about love and philosophy. Philosophy as love, and love as philosophy, are articulated through story. They are communicated, explained and evoked through the images and narratives and mechanisms of stories.

This is not simply a pedagogical device or a contingent or inessential writerly contrivance. This is not a use of fiction as a method that is external to the content or subject matter of love and philosophy. Rather stories and literature, participate in and share with love and philosophy the structure of mediation, deferral, unendingness and even of unworking.

Literature is not structured by logos or reason; it is not an idea or message, a communication or revelation. Literature is not the production or organisation of systems of meaning, nor is it fulfilment and completion. Rather literature is an endless circulation that opens up and disseminates, defying a totalising closure. Literature is an interruption or mediation that endlessly proliferates the story, the work, or the text. Nancy explains:

> It [literature] does not come to an end at the place where the work passes from author to reader, and from this reader to another reader or to another author. It does not come to an end at the place where the work passes on to another work by the same author or at the place where its narrative passes into other narratives, its poem into other poems, its thought into other thoughts, or into the inevitable suspension of the thought or the poem. It is unended and unending – in the active sense – in that it is literature. (Nancy 1991: 65)

This incompletion is the enactment or performance of mediation – between reader and writer, the text and the interpretation, the writer and other writers who rework endlessly the proliferation of stories. Literature participates in mediation, passage, movement and sharing, defying closure or completion. It is, for Nancy, an unworking that unravels a settled completed totalised existence, thought, community or subjectivity. Literature undoes mythic notions of a final knowledge, an idealised hero or body politic, a static or completed fusion or union:

> For the unworking is offered whenever writing does not complete a figure, or a figuration, and consequently does not propose one, or does not impose the content or the exemplary (which means also legendary, hence, mythic) message of the figure. (Nancy 1991: 79)

The *Symposium* identifies a link between love and philosophy suggesting that both are an unending movement between ignorance and knowledge, lack and fulfilment. It does this through the medium of literary stories that are also structured by this incompletion, or unworking. Diotima-Socrates' story of love as mediation and as reaching toward an ineffable and unattainable wisdom is often understood as the final word on love and philosophy – followed by the light comic relief offered by the drunken and debauched story of Alcibiades. But instead Alcibiades' story may be interpreted as an unworking or unravelling of any final word, of any final settled conception of either love or philosophy. While Socrates appears to propose a love that overcomes and moves beyond the embodied erotic passions in its search for wisdom, Alcibiades' story deconstructs or unworks this image recommencing and proliferating the stories of love. Interrupting the Socratic love of wisdom, Alcibiades reintroduces the mediation of love, the passage, movement and incompletion of love – and also of philosophy and the story. The story, like love and philosophy, never reaches a destination. They exist, they live, only through proliferation, deferral and endless circulation.

Love, then, is not just conveyed, described, or theorised by and through philosophy and literature (and here literature stands in for all cultural productions – film, TV, visual and performing arts, websites, ceremonies and rituals). Nor do these accounts of love simply predetermine, influence and shape the subsequent experiences and performances of love. Rather, in addition, love, literature and philosophy are all structured by an incompletion that opens rather than forecloses, that unworks rather than produces, a totalising ending and finality.

This complex articulation of love, literature and philosophy is enacted in Derrida's 'satire of epistolary literature' (Derrida 1987: back cover), 'Envois'. This work, an undecidable melee of genres – philosophy, literature, autobiography and love letter – is, Derrida explains, an attempt to performs the hospitable welcome between philosophy and literature that creates a blurring of boundaries (Derrida 1999b: 73).

Discovering a postcard reproduction of Matthew Paris's 'Plato and Socrates', Derrida experiences an epiphany (Derrida 1987: 9). Reversing the orthodoxy that Plato writes the words of his master Socrates, the postcard depicts the thirteenth-century image of Socrates sitting, writing dictation, under the direction of the gesticulating Plato. Derrida (or a character authored by Derrida in this fictional or perhaps autobiographical series of postcard 'retro love letters' that is 'Envois') writes:

> I stopped dead, with a feeling of hallucination (is he crazy or what? He has the names mixed up!) and of revelation at the same time, an apocalyptic revelation: Socrates writing, writing in front of Plato, I always knew it . . . (Derrida 1987: 9)

Framed as messages sent from lover to beloved and written on an endless series of this same postcard, 'Envois' explores the question of authorial intent and identity and the problem of inheritance and legacy. Who speaks and who writes the *Symposium*, and other Platonic texts? Has Socrates dictated to Plato or is Plato putting words in Socrates' mouth? Who authors? Who inherits? Who begets whom? The 'revelatory catastrophe' uncovers what Derrida always already knew: teleological progression is unravelled by reversals of lineage, by for example the Platonic student dictating to the Socratic master. 'What a couple', Derrida writes, '*Socrates* turns his *back* on plato, who has made him write whatever he wanted while pretending to receive it from him' (ibid.: 12).

This postcard, and Derrida's speculations upon it, put in question the authorship of the Platonic texts. While it appears that Plato wrote the words of Socrates, the reversal of positions in the postcard suggests that Plato may have been dictating to Socrates or to put it another way, putting words into Socrates' mouth. Through this image, Derrida raises the question of the circulation of philosophies and stories, of their origin, and of their acknowledgement. All writing reiterates the history of ideas and texts that precede it – whether acknowledged or not. Writing is necessarily indebted to this legacy. Texts and concepts circulate endlessly and proliferate ambiguously, elaborating the stories of the past. On the other hand, the reading and interpretations of texts already rewrite the text creating additional inflections, meanings and nuances between and in the lines, words and letters of the text. This ambiguity of authorship, raising the question of whose ideas and philosophies are actually communicated in Plato's texts, is not limited to this single example but raises the more general issue of textuality.

Additionally, this image of the circulating and proliferating mediation of texts becomes an emblem for Derrida's exploration of love in 'Envois'. '[T]he overturning and inversion of relations' (Derrida 1987: 22) is not restricted to Socrates and Plato. The 'Envois', like Plato's dialogues, themselves perform the complexity of authorial origin and genre categories. Located indeterminately between a work of philosophy, a reproduction of fragmentary love letters, and an epistolary fiction, these writings apparently authored by Derrida may themselves be 'ghost written'. The lover writes to the beloved:

> I am your old secretary, you burden me with everything, even with my letters . . . But I would like to be your secretary. While you were out I would transcribe your manuscripts of the night before or the tapes on which you improvised, I would make several discreet interventions that you alone would recognise . . . (ibid.: 70)

Enigmatically echoing the reversals of Socrates and Plato, the love letters themselves may be dictated by the beloved who is only apparently the recipient.

The authorial 'ghost writer' affirms this connection with Socrates speculating that: 'Socrates . . . writes under hypnosis' immediately adding: 'Me too ... You speak and I write to you as in a dream everything that you are willing to let me say. You will have resoundingly stifled all my words' (ibid.: 160). The reversal of Socrates and Plato returns, like a revenant, haunting the transpositions of lover and beloved.

The roles of lover and beloved become ambiguously entwined. The conventional opposition between active and passive, pursuer and pursued, is deflected by this questioning of 'authorship'. The letter-writing lover appears to initiate the words and letters of love, but this reversal suggests that the relation is more complex. Love oscillates between, is a movement between, lover and beloved so that the question of 'authorship', of the origin of love, or initiator of love, becomes irresolvable. Love, like writing, circulates and proliferates, resisting any determination of origin or source. Paris's postcard reveals this ambiguity of origin in the Platonic text and Derrida extends this, through comparison, to the experience of love.

This ambiguous circulation of philosophies, stories and love is elaborated further in 'Envois' through the image of letter-writing and postal delivery. Derrida reflects on the operation of a postal principle that he equates with the Freudian conception of the pleasure principle. For Freud, the child comes to terms with the comings and goings of the mother, and with her seemingly permanent departures, by playing games of loss and retrieval. This 'fort:da' (here:there) game, is evident for example when a cotton reel, or other toy or object, is repeatedly thrown and retrieved. This discarding and retrieval represents the loss and return of the mother and involves the child 'mastering' the loss by itself throwing away the mother-object. This oscillating coming and going is, Derrida speculates, re-enacted in Freud's own writing as he moves between and entwines the concepts of the pleasure principle and the death drive, for Derrida writes: 'The death drive is *there*, in the PP [pleasure principle], which is a question of a *fort:da*' (Derrida 1987: 323). The pleasure principle is inflected with loss, departure, death and the recovery of these dispossessions and bereavements. Derrida's concept of the postal principle reproduces this unending movement between lack and fulfilment. The missive is sent, the arrival is delayed and never guaranteed, and even on receipt the intended message may yet be misinterpreted or read otherwise. The responding dispatch may never be sent, or may be delayed, derailed, returned to sender, never arriving at a final destination. Derrida returns often to the issue of a poste restante letter never received, sent to the dead-letter office, and finally returned to sender (Wills 2005: 69–78), signifying the risks of the oscillations of love. The oscillation and indeterminacy of posts mimics the mediating movement of love, and the work (whether literary or philosophical). Throughout the correspondence, the functioning of posts and its relation to love returns and recurs:

> Would like to address myself, in a straight line, directly, without *courrier*, only to you, but I do not arrive, and that is the worst of it. A tragedy, my love, of destination. Everything becomes a post card once more . . . it might always arrive for you, for you too to understand nothing, and therefore for me, and therefore not to arrive, I mean at its destination. (Derrida 1987: 23)

In a subsequent letter, and relating the postal principle to Freud's delayed articulation of the pleasure principle and the death drive, this theme is reiterated: 'And it is the *postal*, the Postal Principle as differential relay, that regularly prevents, delays, endispatches the depositing of the thesis, forbidding rest and ceaselessly causing to run, deposing or deporting the movement of speculation' (ibid.: 54).

The coming and going of the pleasure principle is restaged in the sending and receiving of the lovers' correspondences. While only the letters of the Derridean letter-writer are reproduced here, the beloved's responses haunt and invade the letters. Her or his words, demands, decisions, movements, infiltrate the words and letters and text of the lover. Derrida thus portrays the strange oscillations of the heart signified by and reproduced through the relay-effect of the postal service: 'our telegraphic style, our post card love, our tele-orgasmization, our sublime stenography . . . for finally fort:da is the post, absolute telematics' (ibid.: 43–4).

From Sappho and Plato to Derrida, and returning in differing formulations in the philosophies and stories in between, love resists a closure or completion that would end the mediations and oscillations of love. From Nietzsche's paradoxes and Shelley's monsters, through Beauvoir's ambiguous love and Levinas's ethico-political love, to Moffatt and Fanon's colonial misadventures of love, the deferrals, differings and displacements of love have been multiply articulated. Irigaray's indirection performs this delay; Barthes' proliferating lover's discourses demonstrates the endlessness of love; and Butler and Foucault's refiguring of queer love re-articulates again the story of love. Bringing together philosophies and stories of love, and reading these re-presentations as unworking disseminations and deconstructions, reveals the entwining of love, philosophy and cultural creations. All three unravel finality, stasis, closure and totality, exposing the sharing and the openness or exposure that creates connection between self and the other in sociality.

References

Atkins, Adam (2005), 'On the Nature of Dogs, the Right of Grace, Forgiveness and Hospitality: Derrida, Kant and Lars Von Trier's Dogville', *Senses of Cinema*, 36.

Baker, Geoff (1999), 'The Predication of Violence, the Violence of Prediction: Reconstructing Hiroshima with Duras and Resnais', *Dialectical Anthropology*, 24.

Bal, Meike (2002), *Travelling Concepts in the Humanities: A Rough Guide*, Toronto: University of Toronto.

Barthes, Roland (1984), *A Lover's Discourse: Fragments* (trans. Richard Howard), New York: Hill and Wang.

Barthes, Roland (2000), *Mythologies* (trans. Annette Lavers), London: Vintage.

Barthes, Roland (2002), *S/Z* (trans. Richard Miller), Oxford: Blackwell.

Bauman, Zygmunt (2003), *Liquid Love: On the Frailty of Human Bonds*, Cambridge: Polity.

Beauvoir, Simone de (1994), *The Ethics of Ambiguity* (trans. Bernard Frechtman), New York: Citadel Press.

Beauvoir, Simone de (1997), *The Second Sex* (trans. H. M. Parshley), London: Vintage.

Beauvoir, Simone de (1999), *She Came to Stay*, New York: W. W. Norton & Company.

Ben-Ze'ev, Aaron (2004), *Love Online: Emotions on the Internet*, Cambridge: Cambridge University Press.

Bergoffen, Debra B. (1997), *The Philosophy of Simone de Beauvoir: Gendered Phenomenologies, Erotic Generosities*, New York: State University of New York Press.

Bernasconi, Robert (1991), 'Skepticism in the Face of Philosophy', in Robert Bernasconi and Simon Critchley (eds), *Re-Reading Levinas*, Bloomington: Indiana University Press.

Bernasconi, Robert (1999), 'The Third Party. Levinas on the Intersection of the Ethical and the Political', *Journal of the British Society of Phenomenology*, 30:1.

Bhabha, Homi (1994), *The Location of Culture*, London: Routledge.

Blade Runner, film, directed by Ridley Scott. USA: The Ladd Company/Sir Run Run Shaw, 1982.

Bloechl, Jeffrey D. (1996), 'How Best to Keep a Secret? On Love and Respect in Levinas's "Phenomenology of Eros"', *Man and World*, 29.

Brooks, Peter (1978), 'Godlike Science/Unhallowed Arts: Language and Monstrosity in *Frankenstein*', *New Literary History*, 9:3.

Brown, Wendy (1994), ' "Supposing Truth Were a Woman . . . ": Plato's Subversion of Masculine Discourse', in Nancy Tuana (ed.), *Feminist Interpretations of Plato*, University Park: Pennsylvania State University Press.

Burn, Ian, and Ann Stephen (1986), 'Traditional Painter: The Transfiguration of Albert Namatjira, *Age Monthly Review*, 6, 7 November.

Butler, Judith (2002), 'Is Kinship Always Already Heterosexual?', *differences*, 13:1.

Butterfield 8, film, directed by Daniel Mann. USA: MGM, 1960.

Carson, Anne (1986), *Eros: The Bittersweet: An Essay*, Princeton, NJ: Princeton University Press.

Cavarero, Adriana (1995), *In Spite of Plato: A Feminist Rewriting of Ancient Philosophy*, (trans. Serena Adnerlini-D'Onofrio and Aine O'Healy), Cambridge: Polity Press.

Chalier, Catherine (1991), 'Ethics and the Feminine', in Robert Bernasconi and Simon Critchley (eds), *Re-Reading Levinas*, Bloomington: Indiana University Press.

Chanter, Tina (1995), *Ethics of Eros: Irigaray's Rewriting of the Philosophers*, New York: Routledge.

Chow, Rey (1999), 'The Politics of Admittance: Female Sexual Agency, Miscegenation, and the Formation of Community in Frantz Fanon', in Anthony C. Alessandrini (ed.), *Frantz Fanon: Critical Perspectives*, London: Routledge.

Christensen, Jerome (2003), 'Critical Response II: Taking it to the Next Level: You've Got Mail, Havholm and Sandifer', *Critical Inquiry*, 30.

Conway, Mary T. (2004), 'A Becoming Queer Aesthetic', *Discourse*, 23:3.

Cox, Barbara (2004), 'A (Personal) Essay on Same-Sex Marriage', in Robert M. Baird and Stuart E. Rosenbaum, *Same-Sex Marriage: The Legal and Moral Debate*, Amherst, NY: Prometheus Books.

Critchley, Simon (1992), *The Ethics of Deconstruction: Derrida and Levinas*, Oxford: Blackwell.

Culler, Jonathan (1990), *Barthes*, London: Fontana Press.

Davis, Dawn Rae (2002), '(Love Is) The Ability of Not Knowing: Feminist Experience of the Impossible Ethical Singularity', *Hypatia*, 17:2.

Derrida, Jacques (1981), 'Plato's Pharmacy', in *Dissemination* (trans. Barbara Johnson), Chicago: The University of Chicago Press.

Derrida, Jacques (1987), *The Post Card: From Socrates to Freud and Beyond* (trans. Alan Bass), Chicago: The University of Chicago Press.

Derrida, Jacques (1988), *Limited Inc*, Evanston, IL: Northwestern University Press.

Derrida, Jacques (1991), 'At This Very Moment in This Work Here I Am', in Robert Bernasconi and Simon Critchley (eds), *Re-Reading Levinas*, Bloomington: Indiana University Press.

Derrida, Jacques (1993), 'Le toucher', *Paragraph*, 16:2.

Derrida, Jacques (1995), *The Gift of Death* (trans. David Wills), Chicago: University of Chicago Press.

Derrida, Jacques (1997a), *Politics of Friendship* (trans. George Collins), London: Verso.

Derrida, Jacques (1997b), 'Politics and Friendship: A Discussion with Jacques Derrida' www.sussex.ac.uk/Units/frenchthought/derrida.htm (accessed 8 July 2005).

Derrida, Jacques (1999a), *Adieu to Emmanuel Levinas* (trans. Pascale-Anne Brault and Michale Nass), Stanford, CA: Stanford University Press.

Derrida, Jacques (1999b), 'Hospitality, Justice and Responsibility: A Dialogue with Jacques Derrida', in Richard Kearney and Mark Dooley (eds), *Questioning Ethics: Contemporary Debates in Philosophy*, London: Routledge.

Derrida, Jacques (2000), *Of Hospitality: Anne Dufourmantelle Invites Jacques Derrida to Respond* (trans. Rachel Bowlby), Stanford, CA: Stanford University Press.

Desperate Housewives, Season 1, TV series, produced by Marc Cherry. USA: ABC, 2004.

Deutscher, Penelope (2002), *A Politics of Impossible Difference: The Later Work of Luce Irigaray*, Ithaca, NY: Cornell University Press.

Deutscher, Penelope (2006), 'Repetition Facility: Beauvoir on Woman's Time', *Australian Feminist Studies*, 21:51.

Diprose, Rosalyn (2002), *Corporeal Generosity: On Giving with Nietzsche, Merleau-Ponty, and Levinas*, Albany: State University of New York Press.

Dogville, film, directed by Lars von Trier. Denmark: Zentropa, 2003.

Dreyfus, Hubert L., and Paul Rabinow (1983), *Michel Foucault: Beyond Structuralism and Hermeneutics*, Chicago: University of Chicago Press.

DuBois, Page (1994), 'The Platonic Appropriation of Reproduction', in Nancy Tuana (ed.), *Feminist Interpretations of Plato*, University Park: Pennsylvania State University Press.

Duras, Marguerite (1961), *Hiroshima Mon Amour* (trans. Richard Seaver), New York: Grove Weidenfeld.

Düttmann, Alexander García (1993), ' "What Is Called Love in All the Languages and Silences of the World": Nietzsche, Genealogy, Contingency', *American Imago*, 50:3.

Düttmann, Alexander García (2000), *Between Cultures: Tensions in the Struggle for Recognition*, London: Verso.

Eco, Umberto (1995), ' "I Love You Madly," He Said Self-consciously', in Walter Truett Anderson (ed.), *The Fontana Postmodernism Reader*, London: Fontana Press.

Fanon, Frantz (1967), *Black Skin, White Masks* (trans. Charles Lam Markmann), New York: Grove Press.

Fassin, Eric (2001), 'Same Sex, Different Politics: "Gay Marriage" Debates in France and the United States', *Public Culture*, 13:2.

Ferrari, G. R. F. (1992), 'Platonic Love', in Richard Kraut (ed.), *The Cambridge Companion to Plato*, Cambridge: Cambridge University Press.

Ferrell, Robyn (1996), *Passion in Theory: Conceptions in Freud and Lacan*, London: Routledge.

Firestone, Shulamith (1971), *The Dialectic of Sex: The Case for Feminist Revolution*, New York: Bantam.

Foucault, Michel (1980), *The History of Sexuality*, vol. 1 (trans. Robert Hurley), New York: Vintage Books.

Foucault, Michel (2000), *Ethics: Subjectivity and Truth*, in Paul Rabinow (ed.), London: Penguin Books.

Fox, Katrina (2005), 'Love Warriors', *LOTL* [Lesbians on the Loose], November.

Frankenstein, film, directed by James Whale. USA: Universal, 1931.

Friedan, Betty (1973), *The Feminine Mystique*, Harmondsworth: Penguin.

Gatens, Moira (2003), 'Beauvoir and Biology: A Second Look', in Claudia Card (ed.), *The Cambridge Companion to Simone de Beauvoir*, Cambridge: Cambridge University Press.

Halperin, David M. (1986), 'Plato and Erotic Reciprocity', *Classical Antiquity*, vol. 5.

Hegel, G. W. F. (1977), *Phenomenology of Spirit* (trans. A. V. Miller), Oxford: Oxford University Press.

Heinämaa, Sara (2003), *Toward a Phenomenology of Sexual Difference: Husserl, Merleau-Ponty, Beauvoir*, Lanham, MD: Rowman & Littlefield.

Hiroshima Mon Amour, film, directed by Alain Resnais. France/Japan: Nouveaux Pictures, 1959.

Human Rights and Equal Opportunity Commission (1997), *Bringing Them Home: National Inquiry into the Separation of Aboriginal and Torres Strait Islander Children from Their Families*, Sydney: Sterling Press.

Irigaray, Luce (1984), 'Sorcerer Love: A Reading of Plato, *Symposium*, "Diotima's Speech" ', in *An Ethics of Sexual Difference* (trans. Carolyn Burke and Gillian C. Gill), Ithaca, NY: Cornell University Press.

Irigaray, Luce (1985a), 'This Sex Which Is Not One', in *This Sex Which Is Not One* (trans. Catherine Porter), Ithaca, NY: Cornell University Press.

Irigaray, Luce (1985b), *Speculum of the Other Woman* (trans. Gillian C. Gill), Ithaca, NY: Cornell University Press.

Irigaray, Luce (1991), 'Questions to Emmanuel Levinas: On the Divinity of Love', in Robert Bernasconi and Simon Critchley (eds), *Re-Reading Levinas*, Bloomington: Indiana University Press.

Irigaray, Luce (1993), *An Ethics of Sexual Difference* (trans. Carolyn Burke and Gillian C. Gill), Ithaca, NY: Cornell University Press.

Irigaray, Luce (1996), *I Love To You* (trans. Alison Martin), New York: Routledge.

It's a Wonderful Life, film, directed by Frank Capra. USA: Liberty, 1946.

Jacobus, Mary (1982), 'Is There a Woman in This Text?', *New Literary History*, 14.

Jayamanne, Larleen (1993), ' "Love Me Tender, Love Me True, Never Let Me Go . . .": A Sri Lankan Reading of Tracey Moffatt's *Night Cries – A Rural Tragedy*', in Sneja Gunew and Anna Yeatman (eds), *Feminism and the Politics of Difference*, Sydney: Allen & Unwin.

Jedda, film, directed by Charles Chauvel. Australia: Charles Chauvel Productions, 1955.

Johnston, Jill (1995), 'Wedding in Denmark', in Nayland Blake, Lawrence Rinder and Amy Scholder (eds), *In a Different Light: Visual Culture, Sexual Identity, Queer Practice*, San Francisco: City Lights.

Joy, Morny (2000), 'Love and the Labor of the Negative: Irigaray and Hegel', in Dorothea Olkowski (ed.), *Resistance, Flight, Creation: Feminist Enactments of French Philosophy*, Ithaca, NY: Cornell University Press.

Katz, Claire Elise (2001), ' "For Love is as Strong as Death": Taking Another Look at Levinas on Love', *Philosophy Today*, 45:5 (SPEP Supplement).

Kofman, Sarah (1988), 'Baubo: Theological Perversion and Fetishism' (trans. Tracy B. Strong), in Michael Allen Gillespie and Tracy B. Strong (eds), *Nietzsche's New Seas: Explorations in Philosophy, Aesthetics, and Politics*, Chicago: University of Chicago Press.

Kristeva, Julia (1987), *Tales of Love* (trans. Leon S. Roudiez), New York: Columbia University Press.

The L Word, Season 1, TV series, created by Ilene Chaiken, Kathy Greenberg and Michele Abbott. USA: Showtime, 2005.

Levinas, Emmanuel (1969), *Totality and Infinity: An Essay on Exteriority* (trans. Alphonso Lingis), Pittsburgh, PA: Duquesne University Press.

Levinas, Emmanuel (1987), *Time and the Other* (trans. Richard A. Cohen), Pittsburgh, PA: Duquesne University Press.

Levinas, Emmanuel (1998a), *Otherwise Than Being: Or Beyond Essence* (trans. Alphonso Lingis), Pittsburgh, PA: Duquesne University Press.

Levinas, Emmanuel (1998b), 'Philosophy, Justice, and Love', in *Entre Nous: On Thinking-of-the-Other* (trans. Michael B. Smith and Barbara Harshav), London: Athlone Press.

Love, video, directed by Tracey Moffatt and Gary Hillberg. USA: Women Make Movies, 2003.

Megaw, Vincent, and M. Ruth Megaw (2000), 'Namatjira', in Sylvia Kleinert and Margo Neale (eds), *The Oxford Companion to Aboriginal Art and Culture*, Melbourne: Oxford University Press.

Mellencamp, Patricia (1995), *A Fine Romance: Five Ages of Film Feminism*, Philadelphia, PA: Temple University Press.

Nancy, Jean-Luc (1991), *The Inoperative Community* (trans. Peter Connor et al.), Minneapolis: University of Minnesota Press.

Nancy, Jean-Luc (2003a), 'Shattered Love', in *A Finite Thinking*, Stanford, CA: Stanford University Press.

Nancy, Jean-Luc (2003b), 'In Praise of the Melee', in *A Finite Thinking*, Stanford, CA: Stanford University Press.

Nietzsche, Friedrich (1974), *The Gay Science* (trans. Walter Kaufmann), New York: Vintage Books.

Nietzsche, Friedrich (1982), *Daybreak: Thoughts on the Prejudices of Morality* (trans. R. J. Hollingdale), Cambridge: Cambridge University Press.

Nietzsche, Friedrich (1986), *Beyond Good and Evil* (trans. R. J. Hollingdale), Harmondsworth: Penguin.

Nietzsche, Friedrich (2003), *Thus Spoke Zarathustra* (trans. R. J. Hollingdale), London: Penguin Books.

Night Cries – A Rural Tragedy, film, directed by Tracey Moffatt. Australia: AFC, 1989.

Nussbaum, Martha C. (2001), *Upheavals of Thought: The Intelligence of Emotions*, Cambridge: Cambridge University Press.

Oliver, Kelly (2001a), *Witnessing: Beyond Recognition*, Minneapolis: University of Minnesota Press.

Oliver, Kelly (2001b), 'The Look of Love', *Hypatia*, 16:3.

Orlando, film, directed by Sally Potter. UK: Adventure Films, 1992.

Pateman, Carole (1995), *The Sexual Contract*, Cambridge: Polity Press.

Plato (1994), *Symposium* (trans. Robin Waterfield), Oxford: Oxford University Press.

Plato (2002), *Phaedrus* (trans. Robin Waterfield), Oxford: Oxford University Press.

Queer as Folk, Season 4, TV series, produced by Sheila Hockin with executive producers Ron Cowen, Daniel Lipman and Tony Jonas. USA: Showtime, 2005.

Raval, Shilpa (2001), ' "A Lover's Discourse": Byblis in Metamorphoses 9', *Arethusa*, 34.

The Rocky Horror Picture Show, film, directed by Jim Sharman. UK: Adler/White, 1975.

Rougemont, Denis de (1983), *Love in the Western World* (trans. Montgomery Belgion), Princeton, NJ: Princeton University Press.

Russo, Vito (1987), *The Celluloid Closet: Homosexuality in the Movies*, New York: Harper & Row.

Sandford, Stella (2000), *The Metaphysics of Love: Gender and Transcendence*, London: Athlone Press.

Sappho (2002), *If Not, Winter: Fragments of Sappho* (trans. Anne Carson), London: Virago.

Sartre, Jean-Paul (1995), *Being and Nothingness: An Essay on Phenomenological Ontology* (trans. Hazel E. Barnes), London: Routledge.

Schor, Naomi (1999), 'Blindness as Metaphor', *differences: A Journal of Feminist Cultural Studies*, 11.2.

Scott, Joan (1990), 'Deconstructing Equality-Versus-Difference: Or, the Uses of Poststructural Theory for Feminism', in Marianne Hirsch and Evelyn Fox Keller (eds), *Conflicts in Feminism*, New York: Routledge.

Sedgwick, Eve Kosofsky (1985), *Between Men: English Literature and Homosocial Desire*, New York: Columbia University Press.

Sharpley-Whiting, T. Denean (1996), 'Anti-black Femininity and Mixed-race Identity: Engaging Fanon to Reread Capécia', in Lewis Gordon, T. Denean Sharpley-Whiting and Renee T. White (eds), *Fanon: A Critical Reader*, Oxford: Blackwell.

Sharpley-Whiting, T. Denean (1999), 'Fanon and Capécia', in Anthony C. Alessandrini, (ed.), *Frantz Fanon: Critical Perspectives*, London: Routledge.

Shelley, Mary (2003), *Frankenstein: Or the Modern Prometheus*, London: Penguin.

The Shop Around the Corner, film, directed by Ernst Lubitsch. USA: MGM, 1940.

Singer, Irving (1984 and 1987), *The Nature of Love*, vols 1–3, Chicago: The University of Chicago Press.

Solomon, Robert C., and Kathleen M. Higgins (eds), (1991), *The Philosophy of (Erotic) Love*, Lawrence: University Press of Kansas.

Spivak, Gayatri Chakravorty (1999), *A Critique of Postcolonial Reason: Toward a History of the Vanishing Present*, Cambridge, MA: Harvard University Press.

Sprinkle, Annie, and Elizabeth Stephens, http://loveartlab.org, accessed 21 April 2006.

The Stepford Wives, film, directed by Bryan Forbes. USA: Palomar/Fadsin, 1975.

Sullivan, Andrew (2004), 'Virtually Normal', in Robert M. Baird and Stuart E. Rosenbaum (eds), *Same-Sex Marriage: The Moral and Legal Debate*, Amherst, NY: Prometheus Books.

Twin Peaks, TV series, written and directed by David Lynch. USA: ABC Television Network Group, 1990–1.

Vasseleu, Cathryn (1998), *Textures of Light: Vision and Touch in Irigaray, Levinas and Merleau-Ponty*, London: Routledge.

Vintges, Karen (1996), *Philosophy as Passion: The Thinking of Simone de Beauvoir*, Bloomington: Indiana University Press.

Warner, Michael (2000), *The Trouble with Normal: Sex, Politics, and the Ethics of Queer Life*, Cambridge, MA: Harvard University Press.

Weeks, Jeffrey (1997), 'The Delicate Webs of Subversion, Community, Friendship and Love', in Sue Golding (ed.), *The Eight Technologies of Otherness*, London: Routledge.

Wills, David (2005), *Matchbook: Essays in Deconstruction*, Stanford, CA: Stanford University Press.

Woolf, Virginia (2004), *Orlando: A Biography*, London: Vintage.

Young, Iris Marion (1990), *Throwing Like a Girl and Other Essays in Feminist Philosophy and Social Theory*, Bloomington: Indiana University Press.

You've Got Mail, film, directed by Nora Ephron. USA: Warner Bros, 1998.

Ziarek, Ewa Plonowska (1998), 'Toward a Radical Female Imaginary: Temporality and Embodiment in Irigaray's Ethics', *diacritics*, 28:1.

Ziarek, Krzysztof (2000), 'Proximities: Irigaray and Heidegger on Difference', *Continental Philosophy Review*, 33:2.

Index